JESUS IN THE JEWISH SCRIPTURES

How the Old Testament Bears Witness to Jesus

Nick Lunn

T0349778

FAITHBUILDERS

JESUS IN THE JEWISH SCRIPTURES: How the Old Testament Bears Witness to Jesus by Nick Lunn. © Copyright Nick Lunn 2020.

Bethany, 7 Park View,
Freeholdland Road,
Pontnewynydd, Pontypool NP4 8LP
www.faithbuilder.org.uk

British Library Cataloguing-in-Publication Data. A catalogue record for this book is available from the British Library

ISBN: 978-1-913181-18-5

Cover Design by Patrick Knowles © 2019

Scripture quotations, unless otherwise attributed, are the author's own translations.

Printed and bound in Great Britain.

CONTENTS

PREFACE

A considerable number of books already exist on the market that deal with a similar subject matter to this present volume. So why the need for yet another one? A few words of justification are warranted at the outset for the appearance of a further treatment.

Books that tackle the matter of Jesus in the Old Testament generally focus on a limited number of ways in which he, the coming Messiah, is referred to there. From my knowledge of such books I would say that prophecy is by far the principal concern of most authors. Others might approach the issue through the application of typology, which is to say, seeing Christ represented by various figures or images. Others still might deal with the promises that God made to certain characters and how Jesus came to fulfil them. In short, I would say that books dealing with Jesus in the Hebrew Scriptures typically take up two or three different ways in which he appears in those writings. There are, however, even some treatments available that present just one single way of finding Jesus there, and do so perhaps in rather more detail than the others. One recent book I read entitled *Christ in the Old Testament* (mentioned in chapter 9) focussed entirely on one specific way in which he appears there.

In view of the foregoing, what I have endeavoured to do in this volume is to cover all the bases. Here the reader will find a discussion of not just two or three, but of *all* the major ways in which the Old Testament bears witness to Jesus. And when I say '*all*' the various ways, I mean according to the manner in which the older Scriptures are handled in the New Testament, both by Jesus himself and his appointed apostles. To the best of my knowledge there is no single volume that attempts to deal with all these. In that respect the present work can be said to be unique.

Furthermore, there is a particular one of these several ways that, as far as I am aware, has never been presented before outside of academic publications. Here I am talking about what I later describe as 'personation'. As shall be demonstrated, this was an extremely common approach to the interpretation of certain passages in the Old Testament both in the New Testament and in the writings of the early church fathers. In more recent times, however, it has been to a large extent lost from view. A number of biblical scholars have sought to revive this in their scholarly publications, and a similar attempt at a less academic level is also required. So here is, I believe, a second unique element within this book.

Lastly, I have tried to blend together here solid biblical exegesis, based squarely upon the texts in the original languages, with what I hope is an accessible explanation accompanied by plenty of illustrations. My two principal aims are to investigate, through the explicit guidance of the New Testament, the various ways in which the Old Testament speaks of Jesus, and then to present these in a manner comprehendible to the reader. The book is commended to preachers, teachers, and students of theology, but I also believe that any serious Christian reader who wishes to understand the Bible more would benefit from this book.

All biblical citations are my own translations, but I follow the original very closely (in the general tradition of the NASB ESV NRSV).

1. THE CHRISTIAN USE OF THE OLD TESTAMENT

Without doubt, at least as far as the western half of the church is concerned, the Old Testament has fallen on hard times. The facts speak for themselves. This first portion of the Bible, as read by Protestants, accounts for approximately 75% of its overall length. Yet over against this, one conservative estimate claims that only about 10% of church sermons are based upon this first section of Holy Scripture. The proportion, of course, varies considerably from one denomination to another, but on average a preacher is nine times more likely to deliver a sermon based on the New Testament. What is more, even when an Old Testament text forms the basis for the sermon, the greater part are sermons of a topical nature. This is to say that the preacher uses an Old Testament text, perhaps a verse or few verses from a psalm or a proverb, to hang his or her topic on. Less than half of the 10%, therefore, are actual expository sermons that expound extended passages of the Old Testament in context and apply them to present-day Christian believers.

One response to this situation might be that it is only to be expected. Since followers of Jesus Christ are not members of Israel but of the church, it is only natural that they should be attracted more to those biblical books that are about Jesus or which treat matters relating to the church, namely the Gospels, Acts, and Epistles. Here we read teachings that directly concern us as Christians, while in the Old Testament a good deal seems to concern the people of Israel. To modern readers these earlier books of the Bible appear much more remote and far less accessible than the later ones. I am quite sympathetic to such a feeling, but I do not consider it to be valid excuse for not reading, teaching, or preaching the Old Testament.

The fact is, the New Testament itself directs its readers back to the Old. This is something which is patently obvious even from a cursory glance. Time and time again, hundreds of times in fact, the Old Testament is quoted in the New. Where it is not explicitly quoted, reference is made to its persons and events on numerous occasions, either openly and unmistakably or by way of more subtle allusion. For sure the New Testament is full of the Old, there is no denying it. And what makes this significant for ourselves is the fact that where the writers of the New Testament make mention of the Old it is in contexts that are addressing Christians or which are at least appealing to people of the truth of the

Christian faith. Jesus and the apostles preached and taught the Old Testament. This in itself is a good reason for us today to give our attention to what these older books of the Bible have to say.

Not only does the New Testament frequently quote and refer back to the Old, it positively encourages us to do likewise. We recall the well-known words of the apostle Paul to Timothy, 'All Scripture is inspired by God and is profitable for teaching, for reproof, for correction, for training in righteousness; so that the man of God may be complete, thoroughly equipped for every good work' (2 Timothy 3:16–17). Doubtless most of us would agree with these sentiments. Yes, Scripture is inspired and so helps us grow spiritually, morally, and doctrinally. Yet at the same time, it needs to be borne in mind that when Paul wrote 'All Scripture' he meant the Old Testament, since the New was still a long way from completion, and even further from being assembled into a unified collection of books. The profitability, then, of which Paul speaks is that of the older Scriptures, and he is commending them, 'all' of them, to Timothy, a Christian believer. And if they were to be read with profit by Timothy, then the same surely applies to us too. Earlier, in his letter to the Romans, Paul had similarly spoken of the usefulness of the older Testament to the Christian believers: 'For whatever was written in earlier times was written for our instruction, so that through endurance and by the encouragement of the Scriptures we might have hope' (Romans 15:4). Note the apostle says that these ancient writings were written 'for *our* instruction', meaning us Christians.

It is the aim of this book, therefore, to encourage ordinary Christians to engage more in the reading of the Old Testament books. Out of the many possible incentives for doing so, we here take up just one primary, yet hugely significant, reason—and this is that these older Hebrew Scriptures speak of Jesus, our Lord and Saviour. They speak of him not just now and again, but frequently. They do this not just in one way, but in many, as we shall see. Jesus is at the very heart of our faith, and reading of him not only in the New Testament books but in the Old also can greatly encourage that faith.

Before proceeding to consider the witness of the older Scriptures to Jesus, this introductory chapter will first give some consideration to the Christian use of the Old Testament in general. What is there in these books that is so important or so valuable that Christian believers today should devote time to reading their pages? I will hopefully go some way to answering this question, albeit briefly, by looking at several distinct reasons why it is good for us to acquaint ourselves with this first part of the Bible. These reasons are: theological, doctrinal, exemplary, prescriptive, hortatory, and devotional, as well as christological.

(1) Theological

I am here thinking of theology in the narrower sense of the word, meaning discourse about God. The Old Testament presents to us the supreme being of God. It tells us much about who he is, what he is like, and what he has done. This God is one, and there is none beside him (Deuteronomy 6:4; Isaiah 44:8), a fact which contrasts strongly with the belief in many gods on the part of much of the ancient world, and a good part of the modern world too. God cannot presently be seen in person by human eyes, and since his form remains invisible, no image or idol of him is to be made and worshipped (Exodus 20:4; Deuteronomy 4:15–16).

God is eternal (Psalm 90:2) and all-powerful (Jeremiah 32:17). He is everywhere present through his Spirit (Psalm 139:7), and knows all things, even the inner recesses of the human heart (Psalm 44:21) and future events before they happen (Isaiah 42:9). As God he is the Creator of all things, of the universe and all that fills it (Genesis 1:1; Psalm 148:5; Isaiah 40:26; 42:5). He has not left the world to run independently of himself, but he continues to be directly involved in sustaining and providing for what he has created, even down to our very lives (Job 34:14–15; Psalms 36:6; 104:29; 135:6–7; Isaiah 42:5).

In character God is frequently described as 'holy' (e.g. Leviticus 20:7; 21:8; Joshua 24:19; Psalm 98:18; Isaiah 5:16). He is also 'merciful and gracious, slow to anger, and abounding in steadfast love', a description which is repeated like a refrain throughout the Old Testament (e.g. Exodus 34:6; 2 Chronicles 30:9; Nehemiah 9:17; Psalm 103:8; Jonah 4:2). A similar refrain is that 'The LORD is good, his steadfast love endures for ever' (e.g. Ezra 3:11; Psalms 100:5; 118:1; 136:1; Jeremiah 33:11).

The Old Testament, then, gives us a picture of God in terms of love, grace, mercy, and goodness. Together with this, as the one who rules over all, it is to him that all men and women are accountable for their actions. So God is also depicted as a judge, though thankfully one who 'will judge the world in righteousness' (Psalm 9:8). He is not a harsh judge. Rather, being of such a merciful and gracious character, God can be seen to be a forgiving God (Psalm 103:3; 130:4; Jeremiah 31:34). The Old Testament explicitly declares that God would much rather see people turn to him in repentance than have to punish them (Ezekiel 18:32; 33:11; Hosea 11:8–9).

(2) Doctrinal

There are many important teachings, or doctrines, that God wants his people to know and understand. The Old Testament contains a good deal of such teaching, certain aspects of which, in fact, are unique to the Old and yet essential for a proper understanding of the New. First and foremost the Old Testament gives an explanation of how everything went wrong with the human race right at the very beginning. This event is what we commonly refer to as the 'fall', and is described for us in Genesis chapter 3. Here we read of the first man and woman's act of disobedience to the single command they had received from God. Not to eat the fruit of one particular tree in the midst of many was a simple test of their faithfulness to their Creator. Sadly they failed. This disobedience is what the Bible calls 'sin'. So this very first part of the Bible is important for our understanding of sin (a doctrine which theologians refer to more technically as 'hamartiology').

The consequence of sin, Genesis teaches, is separation from God, the experience of suffering, and ultimately death. From this we conclude that pain and death are not a natural part of human experience, but an interruption of God's original intentions for those he created to bear his image (Genesis 1:27). From Genesis we also learn that it is not just physically that human beings are affected by the fall. There are also spiritual consequences. Our hearts and minds have become corrupted as a result of sin, and have become strongly inclined towards further sin (Genesis 6:5; 8:21). In this way these opening chapters give us an understanding of how human beings were originally created and what their nature is now through the intervention of sin. We see, then, that the beginning of the Old Testament provides us with important teaching about the nature of humankind (an area of doctrine scholars call 'anthropology'). It is directly against this back-story that the gospel of the New Testament is to be appreciated.

In addition to the above, the older Scriptures define the way for us fallen, sinful creatures to become right with God. From the very start the only way was by putting our faith in God and his word. Here the Bible frequently uses the verb commonly translated in English as 'believe'. But we need to appreciate that this does not merely mean to believe a fact or believe in the existence of someone or something. Rather it means to place our faith, or trust if you prefer, in a person. It is such an attitude of faith that pleases God and makes us righteous in his sight. So we are told with regard to Abraham, the forefather of Israel, that 'he believed the LORD, and it was counted to him as righteousness' (Genesis 15:6). This is the sole way of having a right standing before God. Righteousness in the Old Testament was not to be obtained through a rigorous attempt at keeping the commandments given to Israel in the law at Sinai. This is evident from the fact that Abraham was already accounted righteous several centuries before the law was given. This way of becoming right with God on the basis of faith, or justification as it sometimes known, is a crucial teaching (which scholars like to call 'soteriology'), and it is first given clear expression in the life of Abraham in the Old Testament.

The Old Testament also makes it very plain that, although just one nation, Israel, is first chosen by God, this election is for a purpose that concerns the whole world. The divine appointment of Abraham was so that 'all families of the earth will be blessed' (Genesis 12:3). Israel did not exist simply for its own sake but to bring light to the nations (Isaiah 60:3). The older Scriptures, therefore, have a global focus. God is concerned with all peoples of the earth, and wishes them all to hear his message of salvation (a subject matter that theologians call 'missiology').

The Hebrew books further speak to us about the final judgment (Psalm 96:13), the resurrection of the dead (Daniel 12:2), and the creation of a new heaven and earth (Isaiah 65:17), events that all take place at the end of the age (a topic of theological study more technically known as 'eschatology'). And apart from what has been mentioned, we could continue with many other doctrines that are found described for us in the Old Testament.

(3) Exemplary

The Old Testament also furnishes numerous examples of people behaving in a good and bad way. Jesus and the apostles often referred back to characters in the Old Testament, either positively or negatively, depending on the manner of their conduct. These examples were used as an encouragement to do good or as a warning about doing evil. On the positive side, we think of Elijah, who is given as a model of one who prayed earnestly (James 5:17; cf. 1 Kings 18:42–45). We read too of Sarah, an example of a woman who submitted to the authority of her husband (1 Peter 3:5–6; cf. Genesis 18:12). Then there is Job, who stands as a prominent instance of patience in the face of suffering (James 5:11; cf. Job 1–2; 42:10–12). Good conduct such as this on the part of men and women in the Old Testament is noted in the New to inspire Christian believers to follow their lead.

Among the warnings of negative consequences to evil behaviour, we find the inhabitants of Sodom and Gomorrah who suffered divine judgment (Jude 7; cf. Genesis 19). Esau, son of Jacob, is given as an example of immorality and godlessness for Christians not to imitate (Hebrews 12:16; cf. Genesis 26:34–35; 27:1–46). There are the several cases of the Israelites' unfaithfulness during their wilderness journey, matters that Paul says 'were written down as warnings for us' (1 Corinthians 10:6–12; cf. Exodus 32:1–35; Numbers 21:4–9; 25:1–18). When it comes to learning from other people's mistakes the various books of the Old Testament in fact provide us with almost countless instances.

In this exemplary use of Old Testament characters, however, care sometimes needs to be taken that we do not misunderstand what kind of example is being given. Typically the nature of the action performed will be self-evidently good or evil, or else there will be an accompanying comment in the Old Testament text that expresses either approval (e.g. 1 Kings 3:10) or disapproval (e.g. 2 Samuel 11:27). Yet on other occasions the case is not so obvious. We have all heard of laying a fleece, like the Old Testament character Gideon. This is generally understood to be a biblically acceptable way of learning God's will. A careful reading of the passage, however, shows that it is not commending Gideon's action here as an example to follow. Firstly, there is the often overlooked fact that God had plainly already declared his will to Gideon, through his angel, before the fleece episode (Judges 6:14–16). God told Gideon that he was sending him to fight against the Midianite oppressors of Israel and promised to be with him and give him victory. It is only later that Gideon says to God, 'If you will save Israel by my hand, as you have spoken, I will place a woollen fleece on the threshing-floor …' (v. 36). Gideon here was not trying to determine God's will, for God had previously said that he would save Israel by the hand of Gideon. Gideon's request is expressly described as a 'test' of God (v. 39). His purpose with the fleece was not to find out what God wanted him to do, but to bolster his faith which, at this stage, was not as sure as it ought to have been. God's granting the request, then, was a concession to Gideon's spiritual lack. What we see in Gideon is very unlike the usual response of believing men and women in the Old Testament, as well as the New, in which God speaks and people believe and take action accordingly. So some caution must be used on the part of the reader when it comes to its exemplary use.

(4) Prescriptive

Here we are thinking of conduct that is explicitly prescribed by God, which is to say, his commandments, whether to do or not to do something. It is well known that the Old Testament, especially that part called the law of Moses, contains numerous such commands. There is perhaps the feeling among not a few contemporary Christians that these laws do not concern them, and therefore there is no real point in reading such passages. Some may lift the half-verse which states 'we are not under law but under grace' (Romans 6:14) out of its wider context and suppose that this adequately settles the matter. But if so, why is it that Jesus and the apostles, as recorded in the New Testament, so often quote or apply these ancient Hebrew laws? Sometimes there are direct quotations of Old Testament commandments with obvious approval. So Jesus describes the greatest command as: 'You shall love the Lord your God with all your heart and with all your soul and with all your mind' (Matthew 22:37 = Deuteronomy 6:5). Coming close second is the command: 'You shall love your neighbour as yourself' (Matthew 22:39 = Leviticus 19:18). Paul twice quotes this latter command (Romans 13:9; Galatians 5:14), while the apostle James says, 'If you really fulfil the royal law found in Scripture, "You shall love your neighbour as yourself", you do well' (James 2:8). Obviously James expected his Christian readers to carry this out. Other commandments of the law are quoted for Christians to observe, such as 'Honour your father and mother' (Ephesians 6:2 = Exodus 20:12), and 'You shall be holy, for I am holy' (1 Peter 1:14 = Leviticus 11:44). Even where there is no word-for-word quotation it is evident that a command given by an apostle is identical in content to one found in the law of Moses. This is the case with not worshipping idols (1 John 5:21; cf. Exodus 20:4–5), not committing adultery (Hebrews 13:4; cf. Exodus 20:14), not stealing (Ephesians 4:28; cf. Exodus 20:15), and the care of widows and orphans (James 1:27; cf. Deuteronomy 24:19–21).

What explanation can there be for the application of these Old Testament laws to Christians in the New? Well, all the examples given above, and all similar cases in the Gospels and Epistles, have one important feature in common. The crucial thing about these Mosaic laws that are positively cited or applied in the New Testament is that they are without exception all commandments of a moral nature. Many Old

Testament commands, as most readers will be aware, concern matters such as sacrifice, washing, and regulations regarding clean and unclean foods. Laws of this kind are evidently not moral or ethical but rather are ceremonial or ritual. Not a single such law is applied to Christians in the New Testament. Once the new covenant in Christ had been established, nowhere do we read that Christians ought to sacrifice sheep and goats, circumcise their male infants, or perform one of the many rituals prescribed in the law. (Before his death and resurrection, of course, Jesus expected those Jews he addressed in the Gospels to be observant of such laws, but this is an entirely different situation). On the contrary, we find with respect to the numerous ceremonial commands that they are no longer in operation. Peter (Acts 10:11–15) is now allowed to eat foods which Leviticus prohibited. Circumcision of the flesh is no more a matter of any importance (Romans 2:25–29; 1 Corinthians 7:18; Galatians 5:6; 6:15). Paul gives a whole list of various Mosaic ceremonial observances that Christians are not to concern themselves with (Colossians 2:16). Clearly, then, the range of commands appearing in the Old Testament law are of different kinds.

Historically, for many centuries, Christian interpreters, who have undertaken an in-depth study of the Bible, have found it helpful to group the diverse Hebrew laws into a number of distinct categories. To do so was not a Christian invention, for the Jewish rabbis did exactly the same thing even earlier. The numerous laws were grouped into three different kinds: 'moral' (otherwise known as 'ethical'), 'ceremonial' (or 'ritual'), and 'judicial' (or 'civil'). Moral commands obviously concern ethical conduct. Ceremonial laws relate to the sacrifices, the priests, the service of the tabernacle, the religious festivals, foods and items that are considered ritually clean or unclean, and similar matters. Judicial laws concern rulers and judges, court cases, and penalties.

In more recent times to make such a distinction has fallen out of favour with some biblical scholars. Yet it must be said that, although it is true that the Bible itself nowhere expressly speaks of such a classification, the foregoing fact that commands of one kind are found applied to Christians in the New Testament, while those of another are not, does seem to suggest that the laws are indeed to be distinguished. This is further supported by the use of a number of different Hebrew words in describing the various laws. Just to give an illustration of this, we find that the word 'commandment' (*miṣwâ*) has both the broad meaning of anything at all that God commands, and a narrower sense of a specifically moral command. The word 'statute' (*ḥōq* or *ḥuqqâ*), on the other hand, always seems to refer to non-moral matters. The fact that both words are sometimes listed in descriptions of the law, 'commandments *and* statutes' (e.g. Leviticus 26:3; Deuteronomy 27:10), makes me think they are not synonymous terms. This distinction in terminology may again be taken as pointing to different categories of law. So I for one find the traditional threefold division helpful in reading the law of Moses as a Christian.

If any doubt remains about the differences between the various categories of law, then we do well to consider the statements: 'Obedience is better than sacrifice' (1 Samuel 15:22), and 'I desire mercy and not sacrifice' (Hosea 6:6, or 'rather than sacrifice', as NASB). Sacrifice, the offering of animals to God, is in fact a divine command, but the practice functions only as a temporary measure under the old covenant until the new covenant ushers in the ultimate and perfect sacrifice (Jesus). Such kinds of ritual, therefore, do not rank alongside the showing of mercy, which fulfils the enduring obligations of the moral law. The second of the above two verses is quoted by Jesus in Matthew's Gospel (12:7), directed at those Jews who were more concerned about ceremonial matters than moral.

All the different things prescribed in the law of Moses are the terms of the covenant that God made with Israel at Sinai. Christians are not under that covenant, but under the new covenant in Christ. So the Mosaic law plays no part in our relationship with God or our salvation, which is only through faith on the basis of divine grace. This is what Paul means when he says 'we are not under law but under grace'. But having said that, God's standards of morality, that is to say, his views concerning what is good and right for his people to do and what they ought not to do, have not changed. This is why Paul emphatically declares that 'the law is holy, and the commandment is holy, righteous, and good' (Romans 7:12). What this means is that when Christians read the moral laws of the Old Testament, they are still reading of important aspects of God's will for their lives. And this is why, I believe, Jesus and his apostles in the New Testament often draw attention to these original old covenant laws and apply them to Christian believers under the new covenant. This is not to say that these Old Testament laws, of themselves, provide a complete moral code for Christian conduct. The New Testament adds to the older revelation, especially in holding up Jesus himself as the exemplary man who lived in total obedience to the will of God. When it comes to matters of moral behaviour he in fact is the ultimate standard. Nevertheless, Old

Testament forecasts concerning the new covenant tell us that even under this new dispensation God will write his law upon our hearts (Jeremiah 31:33), and that we will be given the Spirit to help us keep it (Ezekiel 36:27). It goes without saying, of course, that as we remain in our fallen human bodies we still fail to keep God's laws perfectly and so often need to seek forgiveness.

Now what has just been said clearly only applies to the moral commandments. The whole elaborate system of rules and regulations regarding sacrifices and other rituals is no longer to be practised by Christians since the death and resurrection of Jesus. That does not mean they have no relevance at all for us today. As we will discover later, these diverse rituals all serve in some way to point to the person and work of Christ. There is much, therefore, that Christians can learn from them. Likewise the civil laws, which were applicable to the governance and judicial procedures of Israel as a nation under God, are not binding upon the church. But again, this is not to say they have nothing to teach us. It is interesting to note that sometimes a certain principle involved in one of these laws is evoked in a Christian setting. Both Jesus (Matthew 18:16) and Paul (2 Corinthians 13:1; 1 Timothy 5:17) draw upon the law that requires 'two or three witnesses' (Deuteronomy 19:15) to sustain a charge against a fellow believer. When Paul is dealing with a case of incest in the church at Corinth, he actually quotes the law that says: 'Remove the wicked person from among you' (1 Corinthians 5:13 = Deuteronomy 17:7; 19:19). The community of God needs to be protected from the corrupting influence of sinful behaviour, so the offender has to be removed from among the people. There is a close similarity in principle between Israel and the church here, and yet the law is not enacted in the same way. In the former case, the person was actually put to death. With respect to the church, however, the offender is separated from the congregation, an act we call 'excommunication', and fellowship may be immediately resumed upon repentance. The principle is the same, but the penalties differ considerably.

Finally in this section, a brief word ought to be added about more specific commands of God in the Old Testament. Here I especially have in mind the divine order to exterminate the Canaanites. It cannot be doubted that this action, as harsh as it may seem to us, is in fact commanded by God for the people of Israel to carry out when they enter the promised land, which happens in the book of Joshua, the sixth book of the Old Testament. Prior to this, the command is repeated on several occasions (e.g. Exodus 23:31; Numbers 33:53; Deuteronomy 20:17). Yet it should be noted from such passages that God says if the Israelites were to 'drive out' the Canaanites from the land, this would be an equally acceptable alternative to their destruction. The important thing for our purposes, however, is to understand that this command is not an integral part of the Mosaic law and should not be confused with it. The law of Moses was given to regulate the life and worship of the people of Israel for generations to come. It was to be practised by them in all places and at all times. The divine injunction to destroy the Canaanites, however, concerned one particular race of people (the Canaanites in their various clans), who lived in one specific place (the land of Canaan, then promised to Israel), at one particular time (after the exodus and wilderness journey). Unlike the laws of the Sinaitic code given through Moses, this command is extremely specific and highly circumstantial. There is no justifiable way, therefore, that the existence of such a command can be taken as a basis for a similar course of action in another place, at another time, by another group of people, against another group of people. And this has, shocking as it may seem, actually been done. Certain of the early settlers from the British Isles who went to the 'New World' actually used the divine command to exterminate the Canaanites as a means of justifying their violence against the Native Americans. They saw themselves as the new people of God, and the new sub-continent as the promised land, and so its current occupants had to be eradicated as Israel had done to the inhabitants of Canaan. To come to such a conclusion on the basis of these Old Testament texts is an abuse of the Bible's teaching of the worst kind.

Nevertheless, as we have seen with other Old Testament laws no longer in force, we can say that this command of God to destroy the Canaanites still has some relevance to Christians. Does not the New Testament speak of the need to for Christians to kill? It certainly does, but not in a physical sense. When the Israelites entered the land of their inheritance, they were instructed to kill off, or at least drive out, all of its former inhabitants. So we too, when we are converted to Christ, and receive a new nature through a spiritual rebirth, we are then to make war against our former nature, the 'old man'. Paul tells his readers that they should 'Put to death whatever is earthly in you: fornication, impurity, lust, evil desire, and greed (which is idolatry)' (Colossians 3:5). Elsewhere he explains that this can only be done 'by the Spirit' (Romans 8:13), that is, with divine assistance. Israel's failure to strictly execute God's command meant that many Canaanites continued to live among them, and eventually became a snare and led the Israelites into a multitude of sins. From this we learn of the urgency for us to subdue the old nature that remains within us, lest it get the upper hand and become a snare to us.

(5) Hortatory

Here we have in mind the idea of 'exhortation', which in more ordinary English simply means 'encouragement'. This is the word that Paul used when he spoke to the Roman believers of 'the encouragement of the Scriptures' (Romans 15:4), as quoted earlier in the chapter. In what ways can these ancient Hebrew books encourage Christians? There are in fact several ways.

Firstly, from the Old Testament we can be greatly encouraged by the exercise of divine providence that is seen there. There are two basic ideas expressed by the term 'providence'. The first speaks of God's provision. In the history of Israel we see again and again instances where God provides for his people. We observe this in the case of Hagar, the maidservant of Sarah who was cast out into the wilderness with her child, but provided for by God (Genesis 21:14–20), the prophet Elijah who was alone in desolate places at the time of famine (1 Kings 17:1–6), and the foreign widow of Zarephath who was on the verge of starvation (1 Kings 17:7–16). We see that God provided for the whole multitude of the Israelites during their entire forty-year journey through the desert (Nehemiah 9:21), and so much more besides. Such cases where God provided earthly necessities for individuals and communities in the Old Testament give comfort to Christian believers that he will also provide for their needs, both physical and spiritual.

The second sense of providence concerns God overseeing, or overruling, if you like. It refers to God's overall control of creation and events that take place within it, such that he is able to direct them to bring about his own good purposes. He accomplishes this through his sovereign power, often in ways human minds are unable to comprehend. The history of Israel furnishes us with many examples of events which clearly show the hidden hand of God at work behind the scenes. The widowed and impoverished Ruth came to Bethlehem and, we are told, 'She came and gleaned', as poor folk were permitted, 'in the field behind the reapers. And as it happened, she found herself working in the plot of land belonging to Boaz, who was of the family of Elimelech' (Ruth 2:3). This Boaz was no less than a relative of Elimelech, Ruth's deceased father-in-law. So begins the wonderful story of how Boaz, as the kinsman-redeemer, married Ruth and brought her and Naomi, her mother-in-law, deliverance through the birth of a son. Not only this but in the same events we also trace the beginnings of the family of David, king of Israel; the one to save his people from the oppression of the Philistines. Even more remarkable are the happenings recorded in the book of Esther. Throughout the entire book God is never explicitly mentioned. Yet it is obvious to the eye of faith that he is involved from beginning to end, providentially guiding the train of events to a favourable outcome for his people. It is no coincidence, for example, that Mordecai the Jew was in the right place at the right time to overhear men conspiring against the king and so was able to make the plot known and save the king's life, a matter then written up in the royal chronicles (Esther 2:21–23). Nor was it merely coincidental that on one particular night the king could not sleep, and when he asked for the chronicles to be read to him, it was that very account of Mordecai's good deed, which happened to have gone unrewarded up to then (6:1–11). These turn out to be highly significant components in the flow of events that is going to lead to the Jews being delivered from the scheming of the wicked Haman, and to their victory over those that would destroy them. All these operations of God through a seemingly ordinary series of events encourage us to believe it is indeed true that 'in all things God works for the good of those who love him' (Romans 8:28 NIV).

Encouragement can also be received from the numerous illustrations of the divine character that are evident in the history of Israel. We think here of God's faithfulness in fulfilling his promises. He gave a son to Abraham, as promised; a land to Israel; a dynasty to David. And we think too of God's patience and longsuffering with his people. I never cease to be impressed by the passing of several centuries during which God sent prophet after prophet to his wayward people. Only after a considerable time, during which they failed to respond, did God finally give them over to punishment. Surely this aptly illustrates the description of God as 'slow to anger'.

(6) Devotional

This use of the Old Testament is applicable to our devotional times in the presence of God. Here we primarily have in mind what may generally be referred to as prayer and praise. The older Scriptures provide a wealth of material to aid Christians in their acts of devotion in that large collection known as the book of Psalms. This is the longest book in the whole Bible, and the one that is most quoted (some 70 to 80 times) in the New Testament.

The book of Psalms contains prayers and songs of many kinds, suitable for a variety of occasions. Some are to be used corporately, when the congregation is gathered for worship, others may be used by the individual, when the believer comes into God's presence in private.

Just like the Jews, in both synagogue and temple worship, so the early Christians would commonly sing psalms in their assemblies. In fact, the New Testament positively declares that this should be so: 'Let the word of Christ dwell within you richly, with all wisdom teaching and admonishing one another with psalms and hymns and spiritual songs, singing with thankfulness in your hearts to God' (Colossians 3:16; cf. Ephesians 5:19). The same practice has been continued in the church right down to the present day, remaining a central part of the service in the more liturgically inclined denominations, with a number of modern worship songs being contemporary settings of psalms for singing in less formal services.

Wonderful psalms of praise include 29, 33, 47, 67, 96, 103, 111, 113, 117, 135, 145, 148, and 150. Some psalms praise God for his creation, some for his glory and majesty, others for his provision, or deliverance. The words are usually general enough in meaning for the expression of praise to be useable by both Jews and Christians.

Many of the psalms take the form of prayers. As such they are extremely useful for the believer who comes into the presence of God unsure of how to express his or her feelings. Quite a number of psalms consist of the expression of lamentation over some trouble that has come upon the speaker. On occasion the particular nature of the distress is identified, such as illness or affliction by enemies. But on the whole the contents are again sufficiently general so as to lend themselves to be prayed in a whole range of difficult situations. Among such psalms we include 3, 5, 13, 22, 39, 52, 64, 77, 88, 102, 120, 139, and 142.

Other prayers among the psalms are 'penitential' in character, which means they contain expressions of repentance following some particular sin. If we lack the words to say to God in such circumstances to express our regret, then a number of psalms lend themselves to be used as suitable prayers. Within this category are psalms 6, 32, 38, 51, 102, 130, 143.

The ongoing popularity of the psalms among Christians is testified to by the fact that often when publishers decide to print the New Testament separate from the Old (not a practice, I must confess, that I greatly approve of), they nevertheless keep the book of Psalms appended at the end. The benefits for the Christian of reading the psalms is evident.

(7) Christological

Last, but certainly not least, we come to Christ. It is perhaps the case that a Christian reader's primary interest in the Old Testament is the witness it bears to Jesus Christ. But even apart from this, it has hopefully been demonstrated that there are many significant benefits that Christians today can gain from reading the Old Testament. It is this particular aspect of the Hebraic Scriptures, namely their testimony to Jesus, with which we will occupy ourselves in the remainder of this book, and so to introduce it will require a whole chapter of its own (Chapter 2).

Suggestions for Further Reading

Atkinson, Basil F. C. *The Christian's Use of the Old Testament* (London: Inter-Varsity Fellowship, 1952).

Clark, Stephen B. *The Old Testament in the Light of the New: The Stages of God's Plan* (Steubenville, Ohio: Emmaus Road, 2017).

Gooding, David. *The Riches of Divine Wisdom: The New Testament's Use of the Old Testament* (Coleraine, N. Ireland: Myrtlefield Trust, 2013).

Owens, Robert J. 'The Old Testament in the Christian Church,' *Leaven* 9.2 (2001). [Viewable at: https://digitalcommons.pepperdine.edu/cgi/viewcontent.cgi?article=1551&context=leaven].

2. THE CHRISTOLOGICAL USE OF THE OLD TESTAMENT

Christology is the study of Christ. We can be quite certain that the writings of the Old Testament are, at least to some degree, about Christ. This we know because Jesus himself said as much: 'Moses wrote about me' (John 5:46). And it was not just Moses, for elsewhere we are told that Jesus explained to two of his disciples what was said about himself 'in all the Scriptures' (Luke 24:27). By the 'Scriptures' he meant 'Moses and all the prophets', as the verse says. A christological approach, therefore, to the Old Testament is fully endorsed by Jesus himself.

This particular use of the Hebrew Scriptures is, in fact, Christ's very own practice on many occasions in the Gospels. Repeatedly he would quote from these Scriptures with reference to himself. At the beginning of his ministry, for example, in the synagogue at Nazareth he read from the scroll of Isaiah about the one anointed by the Spirit of the Lord to preach good news and proclaim freedom (Luke 4:18–19 = Isaiah 61:1–2). After reading this, Jesus then added, 'Today this Scripture is fulfilled in your hearing' (Luke 4:21). The words of the prophet, uttered several centuries earlier, Jesus said, were now fulfilled in him.

Other similar citations by Jesus from the Old Testament with application to himself include the passage concerning the 'stone' rejected by the builders that has become the cornerstone (Matthew 21:42; Mark 12:10; Luke 20:17 = Psalm 118:22), the psalm which speaks of the one David calls 'my Lord', who is given a place at God's right hand (Matthew 22:44; Mark 12:36; Luke 20:42 = Psalm 110:1), and the passage about the stricken shepherd whose flock is scattered (Matthew 26:31; Mark 14:27 = Zechariah 13:7), and many more besides.

As might be expected, this practice of Jesus was later followed by the apostles in their preaching of the gospel. We are told regarding the ministry of Paul among the Jews of Thessalonica that 'he reasoned with them from the Scriptures, explaining and proving that the Christ had to suffer and rise from the dead, and saying that "This Jesus I am proclaiming to you is the Christ"' (Acts 17:2–3). We ought to remind ourselves once again that here 'Scriptures' can only mean the books of the Old Testament, since at this time it was too early for the New Testament to have been written. The same practice as Paul is also seen in the preaching of Apollos when it says, 'he vigorously refuted the Jews in public, demonstrating by the Scriptures that Jesus was the Christ' (Acts 18:28). It is clear that this was not a mere academic exercise. This resort to the Old Testament Scriptures was a crucial part of the life-giving proclamation of the gospel. Elsewhere Paul described these ancient books as 'the Holy Scriptures, which are able to make you wise for salvation through faith in Christ Jesus' (2 Timothy 3:15). Even the Old Testament, of itself, is able to save people by bringing them to faith in Christ.

What specific passages from the Old Testament the apostles actually turned to may be ascertained, to some degree at least, from the record of their evangelistic speeches in the book of Acts and from the letters they wrote to the churches. It is noteworthy that some of these texts are identical to those referred to by Jesus in his earlier ministry. No doubt these passages were part of the core teaching that was passed on to those subsequently entrusted with the task of preaching. So the text from Psalm 118 about the rejected 'stone' also appears in Acts 4:11. Psalm 110, about David's 'Lord' invited to sit at God's right hand, is similarly quoted in Acts 2:34. In Peter's speech at Pentecost a christological interpretation of Psalm 16:8–11 played a major part (Acts 2:25–28). In his later speech before the Jews in the temple the same apostle cited Deuteronomy 18:15–16 with application to Jesus (Acts 3:22). Philip, the evangelist, preached Jesus to the Ethiopian eunuch from Isaiah 53:7–8 (Acts 8:32–33), as did Paul to the Jews of Pisidian Antioch from Psalm 2:7 (Acts 13:33).

When it comes to the New Testament epistles, there are further direct quotations of Old Testament texts given a christological interpretation, and numerous allusions as well. So Paul, for example, in Romans cites another 'stone' passage, this time concerning a stumbling stone laid in Zion, and applies it to Jesus (Romans 9:33 = Isaiah 28:16). He also sees the prophecy about 'the root of Jesse' as being fulfilled in him (Romans 15:12 = Isaiah 11:1). The writer of the Epistle to the Hebrews quoted the Old Testament on numerous occasions with reference to Jesus (e.g. Hebrews 1:5 = Psalm 2:7; Hebrews 1:5 = 2 Samuel 7:14; Hebrews 2:6–8 = Psalm 8:4–6; Hebrews 2:12 = Psalm 22:22; Hebrews 5:6 = Psalm 110:4; Hebrews 10:5–7 = Psalm 40:6–8). The apostle Peter likewise quotes the passage about the stone laid in Zion (1 Peter 2:6 = Isaiah 28:16), as well as the prophecy of the Suffering Servant (1 Peter 2:22 = Isaiah 53:9).

We need to also make mention of the work of the Gospel writers. As well as recording the words of Jesus, they composed a narrative of events about him, under the direction, we believe, of the Holy Spirit. And in so doing they frequently turned to Old Testament texts to demonstrate how what Jesus was doing, or what was happening to him, fulfilled them. From their inspired compositions, Matthew, Mark, Luke, and John, showed how the life of Jesus—his birth, his ministry, and his suffering—all fulfilled what was laid down centuries earlier in the law and the prophets. As instances of such, we take his birth in the town of Bethlehem (Matthew 2:6 = Micah 5:2), the coming of John the Baptist to prepare the way for him (Matthew 3:3; Mark 1:2–3; Luke 3:4–6 = Isaiah 40:3), the manner of his ministry (Matthew 12:18–21 = Isaiah 42:1–4), and the piercing of his body at his crucifixion (John 19:37 = Zechariah 12:10).

The foregoing suffices to show that at every level of the New Testament writings—in the recorded words of Jesus, in the Gospel writers' own narration, in the speeches of the apostles, and in the letters they wrote to the churches—we find Old Testament Scriptures that are understood christologically. Since this was a prominent way of interpreting the ancient Hebrew books employed by Jesus himself, the Gospel writers, and apostles, then in our own reading of the Bible today we ought to adhere to the same well-established practice.

Having proved the common practice of reading the Old Testament with reference to Christ on the part of Jesus and the early Christians, we might briefly consider to what extent the Old Testament is about him. Are we talking about occasional isolated texts, or is it more frequent than that? Above we quoted part of Luke 24:27 where Jesus spoke of the Old Testament witness to himself as given by 'Moses and *all* the prophets' and of matters concerning himself written 'in *all* the Scriptures'. The twofold use of 'all' suggests more than an infrequent occurrence. Later in the same chapter, we note, he adds 'the Psalms' to Moses and all the prophets (v. 44). As seen above, there are many psalms interpreted christologically in both the teaching of Jesus and of the apostles. The title 'Psalms' was a common way of referring to that section of the Hebrew Scriptures that contained the Psalms, Proverbs, Job, and the other poetic and wisdom books, since Psalms was the longest book in that section. From the words of Jesus in Luke 24, then, we understand that the Old Testament testifies to him across the board. It is not only the books of the prophets that do so. This means Christ is to be found in the law and in the historical books, and in the poetic books too. Examples from each will be examined later in this book.

It is not just that Jesus is spoken of in all the groupings of Old Testament literature and in all the prophets, there is also the fact that mention is made of him in a range of diverse ways. Many think of the Old Testament testimony to Jesus merely in terms of prophecy, but it bears witness to him in several other ways besides. He is, for example, very much the content of a number of divine promises that are made to different Old Testament characters. It is also of great significance that the witness to Jesus takes on not just the form of words, but also of figures. This is a major aspect of the way in which the older Scriptures point to Christ. To discuss each of these ways in turn is one of the main purposes of this present book.

When it comes to the question of the precise frequency of the Old Testament references to Jesus it is actually impossible to say. The only thing I would point out is that very clearly the New Testament does not indicate every single passage in the Old that speaks of Christ. This is evident from the fact that some obviously messianic prophecies are not quoted or alluded to there at all, such as the prediction in Isaiah 9:6 regarding the son to be born who would sit on the throne of his father David.

Clearly then, when the New Testament gives christological interpretations of Old Testament texts it is in no way being exhaustive. It quotes a significant number of such passages which, amongst other things, provide us with examples of how Christians should approach the older Scriptures, and then having guided us in this way, it is for us to make further discoveries in our reading. From my own study of the Bible over the years I get the distinct impression that Christ is to be found in Old Testament texts more frequently that might be supposed, especially in the form of figures (to be discussed in Chapter 7).

We do, furthermore, need to bring in, alongside the diverse manner and frequency of Old Testament references to Christ, the range of matters revealed concerning him that appear in these older Scriptures in different forms. The Hebrew writings do much more than simply speak of the fact of Christ's future coming into the world. There is, in actual fact, considerably more. The Old Testament witnesses to both his deity and his humanity, gives significant details about his birth, it testifies to his character, speaks of his life and ministry, the opposition of his own people, and eventual betrayal, death, and resurrection. It further bears witness to his subsequent ascension into heaven, his sitting down at the right hand of God the Father, and his sending of the Spirit upon his people. It speaks also of his church and the inclusion of the Gentiles, and judgment upon the nation of the Jews that rejected him. Besides these things, the Old Testament also gives a series of lesser details, such as his use of parables in his teaching, the manner of his triumphal entrance into

Jerusalem, the division of his garments at the cross, and quite a number of other details.

At this point we ought to make reference to a conception of Christ which was common among early interpreters of God's word, such as the famed Augustine (bishop of Hippo in the early fifth century). When reading the Old Testament from a christological perspective, this did not necessarily mean one looked strictly for indications of the person of Jesus alone. To understand that these ancient Scriptures were about Christ meant they bore witness to what Augustine called the 'whole Christ' (*totus Christus*). This of course included Jesus himself as an individual, but also Jesus as the corporate Christ. Considered in this way, 'Christ' would also include those in Christ, that is to say, the church. For the writers of the New Testament the church could not be separated from Christ himself, for it is, we are told, 'the body of Christ' (e.g. 1 Corinthians 12:27; Ephesians 4:12). So when we claim that the Old Testament is about Jesus, we are to apply this in a holistic way. Christ himself, his church, the teachings of Christ, the experiences of Christ, are all embraced within a christological approach to the Hebrew Scriptures.

One other important matter that needs to be mentioned in the context of such christological interpretation is that the reading of Scripture is essentially a spiritual exercise. The truths of God's word are 'spiritually discerned' (1 Corinthians 2:14), which in context means with the aid of the divine Spirit. It is the Spirit who leads us into all truth (John 16:13). This contrasts quite sharply with the idea that the meaning of the Bible is to be determined by a set of rationalistic principles. Not that I am against the use of reason in reading Scripture. Not at all. Rather I am saying that it is not human reason alone that will benefit the Christian reader. Prayer for and openness to the Spirit's leading are of greater importance in the interpretation of Scripture than the application of reason. Alongside this, there is the ancient Christian practice of interpreting Scripture by Scripture. What other texts of the Bible say on a particular matter should be our first port of call. As we proceed I hope that the reader will be aware that in order to understand specific Old Testament texts I resort, as far as I am able, to the words of Scripture expressed elsewhere. God, I believe, is their ultimate author, and so they form a unity and possess an inner consistency which can help us immensely in our interpretation of them.

Lastly, we would do well to remind ourselves of the obvious fact that the Old Testament was never intended to present anything like a full revelation of Christ. In a sense he is there in a veiled, almost hidden, form.

We find him to be present in the diverse parts of the Old Testament in varying degrees, that is to say, more so in one text than in another. In some places, such as in a direct verbal prophecy, the reference to Jesus will be unmistakable. In others, where he is present in a figure, it is less obvious. In others still, Christ is nowhere apparent in any form at all. Yet, when such is the case, this does not necessarily that he is entirely omitted from view. Where there may be no direct or indirect reference to him in a particular passage, it is often the case that the passage may nevertheless be used to eventually lead to him. Some Old Testament passages do indeed seem to relate events and persons that are radically different, or far removed, from Christ. This need not mean that they are utterly irrelevant to our understanding of him. Certain passages actually lead us to Christ by describing opposites or contrasts, or by presenting a negative (as in the photographic sense), which helps us all the more appreciate the positive. So while there is no mention of Jesus, in words or figures, the passage may yet have a christological contribution to make, in that it can lead us into a deeper understanding of Christ. In regard to this matter of no direct mention of Jesus I am reminded of the classic anecdote told by Charles Spurgeon, the nineteenth-century Baptist preacher:

> A young man had been preaching in the presence of a venerable divine, and after he had done he went to the old minister, and said, 'What do you think of my sermon?'
>
> 'A very poor sermon indeed', said he.
>
> 'A poor sermon?' said the young man, 'It took me a long time to study it'.
>
> 'Ay, no doubt of it'.
>
> 'Why, did you not think my explanation of the text a very good one?'
>
> 'Oh, yes', said the old preacher, 'very good indeed'.
>
> 'Well, then, why do you say it is a poor sermon? Didn't you think the metaphors were appropriate and the arguments conclusive?'
>
> 'Yes, they were very good as far as that goes, but still it was a very poor sermon'.
>
> 'Will you tell me why you think it a poor sermon?'
>
> 'Because', said he, 'there was no Christ in it'.

'Well', said the young man, 'Christ was not in the text; we are not to be preaching Christ always, we must preach what is in the text'.

So the old man said, 'Don't you know young man that from every town, and every village, and every little hamlet in England, wherever it may be, there is a road to London?'

'Yes', said the young man.

'Ah!' said the old divine, 'and so from every text in Scripture, there is a road to the metropolis of the Scriptures, that is Christ. And my dear brother, your business in when you get to a text, to say, "Now what is the road to Christ?" and then preach a sermon, running along the road towards the great metropolis—Christ. And', said he, 'I have never yet found a text that had not got a road to Christ in it, and if I ever do find one that has not a road to Christ in it, I will make one; I will go over hedge and ditch but I would get at my Master, for a sermon cannot do any good unless there is a savour of Christ in it'. (Charles H. Spurgeon, 'Christ Precious to Believers', Sermon No. 242, 1859)

Though the illustration is somewhat dated, in that it depicts an England of a by-gone age, I am nonetheless in wholehearted agreement with its sentiments.

So we come now to consider the diverse ways in which testimony is given to Jesus by the Old Testament writings. The headings of the following chapters all consist of a single word that names the principal idea involved. Some of these are words with fairly plain meanings, such as promise, prophecy, and presence. Others are of a slightly more technical nature, these being *protevangelium,* prefiguration and personation, which will all be explained in due course. I must hasten to add that I have not sought any deliberate alliteration here. In every instance the word beginning with the letter 'p' is in fact the most natural term to use to describe the idea involved. At the outset we will devote a short chapter to the notion of progression, meaning the way the biblical story develops. Here the christological idea is more suggestive than explicit, but how the story moves forward is an important concern when thinking of the Old Testament in connection with Jesus.

Suggestions for Further Reading

Greidanus, Sidney. *Preaching Christ from the Old Testament: A Contemporary Hermeneutical Method* (Grand Rapids, Michigan: Eerdmans, 1999).

Kaiser, Jr., Walter C. *The Messiah in the Old Testament* (Grand Rapids, Michigan: Zondervan, 1995).

Leathes, Stanley. *The Witness of the Old Testament to Christ* (London: Rivingtons, 1868).

Veras, Richard. *Jesus of Israel: Finding Christ in the Old Testament* (Cincinnati, Ohio: Servant Books, 2007).

3. PROGRESSION

One important characteristic of the Old Testament, at its broadest level, is that it tells a progressive story. Those who have read any significant amount of its writings will be well aware of this. To others it may be a new idea. And certainly, speaking from experience, I know that there are not a few preachers who present sermons from it as though it were just a series of disconnected texts. This presence of progression in the Hebrew Scriptures is, we ought to note, not something to be taken for granted. Such a thing is quite absent from the sacred books of other major religions. One theologian of a previous generation made the observation:

> The Koran, for instance, is a miscellany of disjointed pieces, out of which it is impossible to extract any order, progress, or arrangement. The 114 Suras or chapters of which it is composed are arranged chiefly according to their length—the longer in general preceding the shorter. It is not otherwise with Zoroastrian and Buddhist Scriptures. These are equally devoid of beginning, middle, or end. They are, for the most part, collections of heterogeneous materials, loosely placed together. How different everyone must acknowledge it to be with the Bible! … It is not a collection of fragments, but has, as we say, an organic character. It has one connected story to tell from beginning to end; we see something growing before our eyes: there is plan, purpose, progress … (James Orr, *The Problem of the Old Testament*. New York: Scribner, 1906, pp. 31–32)

The Old Testament, then, presents a story with a definite progression. But while this is the case, once the reader has come to the end of this Testament it is quite obvious that what he or she has finished reading is incomplete. The progression apparent within it does not lead to a satisfactory ending. In fact, in our English versions of the Bible the very last word of the Old Testament is the word 'curse' (Malachi 4:6)—not a very comforting place to stop!

This incompleteness of the Old Testament is evident in several different ways. Firstly, the problem of the fall remains conspicuously unresolved. In Genesis 3 the first human beings fell into sin, which resulted in the coming of suffering and death upon the whole human race. These effects of the fall have not been removed at the end. Sin and death still exercise dominion over humankind. So the Old Testament itself provides no remedy to humanity's basic problem. The divine image in human beings remains tarnished. Moreover, this is the case despite the fact that the Scriptures of Israel testify to a line of men and woman who were devoted to God in their life-times. Some were exceptionally noteworthy on account of their righteousness and godliness relative to their fellows. Here we may make mention of Noah, who was righteous before God in his generation (Genesis 7:1), Abraham, the 'friend' of God (Isaiah 41:8), Moses, who was more humble than anyone else on earth (Numbers 12:3), and David, a man after God's own heart (1 Samuel 13:14). There was Joseph, Joshua, Caleb, Boaz, Ruth, Asa, Hezekiah, Josiah, Daniel, Esther, Job and many others. Yet the fate of each of these was no different from that of any other. These too all died. What this means is that sin even had a hold in the lives of men and woman of this character. Although there was much goodness in them, they still fell short. None of them attained such a righteousness and holiness of life that they should deliver themselves from death because of it, let alone be able to free others. So it is, that with respect to many of these, their particular sins are specifically recorded for us, as with Noah's drunkenness (Genesis 9:20–23), Moses' lack of faith in the matter of striking the rock (Numbers 20:10–12), and David's adultery with Bathsheba (2 Samuel 11:1–4). Clearly then, if the human race was going to overcome sin, it would not be any ordinary man or woman that would achieve it. One thing the Old Testament does is present one person after another who goes some way further than most others in the direction of godliness, but who at the end of the day nonetheless remains a sinner subject to death. The expectation is created, therefore, that to resolve the human problem there needs to be some manner of drastic intervention, from somewhere other than ordinary members of the human race, who have constantly failed. Certainly it was a divine intervention that was required.

Associated with the fall of humankind is the curse upon the earth. Due to their disobedience God said to the man, 'Cursed is the ground because of you; in toil you will eat of it all the days of your life. It will produce thorns and thistles for you' (Genesis 3:17–18). Since this time human beings have had to labour hard to cultivate the ground, and it definitely has not ceased to give forth its unwanted growth, as anyone involved in farming or horticulture will tell you. But right from the earliest days, there was the expectation that someone would come who would bring relief from this curse. We see this in the birth of Noah. When his father, Lamech, named him, he said, 'This one will give us rest from our labour and from the toil of our hands caused by the ground which the LORD has cursed' (Genesis 5:27). Yet clearly this hopefulness with regard to Noah was disappointed. Neither Noah, nor any other person recorded in the Hebrew Scriptures, was able to do such a thing. It would only be much later, in the age to come, that this would be accomplished (Revelation 22:3).

Then there is the condition in which Israel is left as the Old Testament draws to a close. It was the purpose of God in these ancient times to choose one particular nation to be a light to the world and to be a blessing to all nations. As part of this divine election and purpose, God promised them numerous offspring, he gave them a dynasty of kings, and placed his own presence among them in that special building called the 'house of the LORD' or the 'temple'. This stood in Jerusalem as an ongoing symbol and token of the divine presence among his people. As we follow the storyline of the Hebrew Scriptures, each of these themes is developed and comes to some manner of fulfilment, but then, significantly it comes under threat. Towards the end it actually declines and, in some respects, ceases to be. Because of the prolonged disobedience to God's law, and despite the numerous prophetic warnings, the people of Israel were eventually taken off into exile by their enemies. This first happened to the northern kingdom, when the Assyrians deported many thousands in the late eighth century B.C. (2 Kings 17:1–41) Then Judah, the southern kingdom, experienced a similar fate at the hands of the Babylonians in the late seventh and early sixth centuries (2 Kings 24:10–25:26). Although there was a return several decades later, once the Persians came to power, it is clear from the lists given in the book of Ezra and from the book of Esther, that the number of those that actually returned was comparatively small. The people were evidently no longer the great multitude they had once been (cf. Exodus 1:7; 1 Kings 4:20). More than this, the Jews no longer had a king, nor any form of self-rule for that matter. The irony is that Zerubbabel, who was of the royal line of David (1 Chronicles 3:17, 19; cf. Matthew 1:12), rather than sit on the throne of his ancestors, was relegated to the role of a provincial governor (Haggai 1:1), under the greater authority of Persia. Significantly, Ezra described himself and his people as 'slaves' in their own land (Nehemiah 9:36). And then there was the matter of the temple. In the days of Solomon, when it was constructed, this had been a structure of great splendour (1 Kings 6:1–38), but the Babylonians destroyed it. After the return from exile, another temple was built, yet there was a significant difference. Whereas in the case of the earlier temple, as well as the tabernacle before it, once the construction had been completed the glory of God was visibly seen to come and occupy it as a token of his presence (Exodus 40:34; 1 Kings

8:10–11), when this later temple was built nothing of such a nature happened. This is an indication that, though they remained God's chosen people, he was not with them in the same way as he had been previously. From what we know, it would seem that the ark of the covenant, that symbolic throne of the Lord placed in the innermost chamber of the sanctuary, was absent from the second temple.

Clearly then, it was not simply that God's stated purposes through Israel had not been achieved, but that as we come to the close of the Old Testament the nation has moved further away from their accomplishment, not nearer. The notion that this people should be a light to those of other nations and bring them to a knowledge of God is something far from what the Jews actually did after the exile. The last books of the Hebrew Scriptures, these being Ezra, Nehemiah, and Esther, testify to ongoing hostile relationships. We do not read here of any Gentiles joining themselves to Israel to worship the one true God, as Isaiah had also predicted (e.g. Isaiah 60:3).

It must be agreed, therefore, that the storyline running through the Hebrew Scriptures plainly does not reach the goal that is expected, and indeed required. It leaves the reader looking to the future for more to come. Indeed, ever since the Old Testament era reached its end, the Jews did just this. They looked for a coming age in which God's people would have a new king who would reign in righteousness and deliver them from the oppression of their enemies, a time when there would be a new and glorious temple filled with the divine presence, and the Gentiles would be gathered in to join with them in the blessings and worship of the God of Israel.

The Old Testament leaves us looking for a unique and unprecedented act of intervention to save not only Jews but Gentiles also. And since the human race in general and Israel in particular had proved themselves over the course of many centuries that no mere human being could bring about such a salvation, it had to come from another quarter, from God himself. So in the fulness of time, God came into the world, taking upon himself the nature of a man, Jesus of Nazareth, the Christ.

It is Christ, the divine Son, who restores all that humanity lost, and brings to completion all that Israel failed to achieve, though on a scale and in a manner far exceeding all expectation, and perhaps even comprehension. He is the king who will reign in righteousness, he is the temple in whom God will dwell in all the fulness of his glory, and it is he who will bring people of all nations to trust and serve the Lord. He is, moreover, the definitive remedy to the human problem. It is he who will utterly and finally do away with all sin, suffering, and death. In sum, Jesus is the 'someone' that the Old Testament is working its way towards and Jesus who gives its ultimate meaning.

Suggestions for Further Reading

Goldsworthy, Graeme. *According to Plan: According to Plan* (Leicester: Inter-Varsity Press, 1991).

Hunter, Trent, and Stephen Wellum. *Christ from Beginning to End: How the Full Story of Scripture Reveals the Full Glory of Christ* (Grand Rapids, Michigan: Zondervan, 2018).

Kaiser, Jr., Walter C. *Recovering the Unity of the Bible: One Continuous Story, Plan, and Purpose* (Grand Rapids, Michigan: Zondervan, 2009).

Leithart, Peter. *A House For My Name: A Survey of the Old Testament* (Moscow, Idaho: Canon Press, 2000).

4. PROTEVANGELIUM

The very first indication that a Saviour would come is found immediately after the fall of humanity into sin, in the third chapter of Genesis. The utterance of God that is recorded there (v. 15) forms, in a very real sense, the foundation of all that follows in the redemptive plan of God. Concerning this verse Charles Spurgeon, the Baptist preacher, declared that 'There lie within it, as an oak lies within an acorn, all the great truths which make up the gospel of Christ' (*Metropolitan Tabernacle*, Volume 22, p. 662). It could be said, therefore, with a considerable degree of truth, that the rest of Scripture is simply the fleshing out of this one statement.

When the first man and woman eat of the forbidden fruit through the temptation of the serpent, so bringing sin into God's good creation, God then pronounces punishment against all three participants, the serpent, the woman, and the man, in that order. Verse 15 occurs among the words addressed to the serpent. There God speaks as follows:

> And I will put enmity between you and the woman, and between your offspring and her offspring; he will strike your head, and you will strike his heel.

Some call this a prophecy, others describe it as a promise. As it is spoken to the serpent, it should probably not be taken as a promise. The first part would seem to be a statement of divine intention, while the last line is a forecast, in brief, of the manner in which the sin that had just intruded God's creation will be removed from it. So it is in essence a prophetic utterance. Yet rather than conjoin it with other prophecies (to be dealt with later), since this is the very first of such, and because of its seminal nature, I felt it appropriate to give it a short chapter of its own.

On account of what God is saying here, which will presently be unpacked, the contents of the verse has long been known in the church as the *protevangelium* (or as the uncontracted *proto-evangelium*), meaning literally the 'first gospel' or the 'first good news'. Significantly, the saying is found on the lips of God rather than spoken by just a human prophet or an angel. God himself, therefore, is seen to be the first messenger of the gospel, right in the wake of the event that made such a message necessary.

To begin, as regards the language used, we note that 'enmity' (*'êbâ*) is a relatively rare word. Its other uses all describe animosity between humans, that is, rational beings. In the second line the noun 'offspring' is the Hebrew term *zera'*, literally meaning 'seed', which is still preserved in some of the older translations. This term, it is important to note, allows both a collective and an individual sense, many or one. The main verb in the last line, here twice rendered 'strike', is the Hebrew *šûp* (pronounced 'shooph'). This has traditionally been understood to mean 'crush, wound, deliver a blow', or similar. Some, however, have tried to dispute this sense and make it mean something completely different. Yet the fact is that this is the meaning given to the verb, not just by Christian scholars and translators, but even in some standard Jewish sources, such as in the ancient Aramaic paraphrase known as the Jerusalem Targum (*nᵉkâ*, 'strike, harm'), and in the classical commentary of the highly authoritative rabbinic scholar Rashi (*kâtat*, 'crush'). Moreover, the mutual character of the action within a context of hostility, together with the direct objects 'head' and 'heel' as the affected parts, seem to require such a sense. There is just one other clear use of the same verb elsewhere in the Old Testament: 'for he *crushes* me with a tempest, and multiplies my wounds without cause' (Job 9:17 NRSV). Here again 'crush' is a meaning particularly well suited to the context. We can be fairly confident, then, that in Genesis 3:15 God is foretelling violent actions to be performed against each other by the two antagonists mentioned.

The words immediately preceding these, in verse 14, appear on the surface to concern the literal serpent, or snake, to which God says, 'Because you have done this, cursed are you more than all cattle and more than every wild animal. On your belly you will go, and you will eat dust all the days of your life'. These words plainly identify the serpent as blameworthy. It is being cursed on account of its actions. Yet reptiles, like other non-human animate life-forms, are merely 'brute beasts' (Psalm 73:22), 'unthinking animals [*aloga zōa*], creatures of instinct' (2 Peter 2:12 NLT). A literal snake could not be accountable for its actions. Nor would such a creature feel any concern at being placed under a curse or being made to slither along in the dust. So perhaps there is more going on here than meets the eye.

The serpent was first introduced at the very beginning of the chapter (Genesis 3:1), where it is described as 'the most subtle of all the wild animals' (NJB). This places the serpent squarely among the other creatures of God's creation, and is therefore to be included amongst those brought into being with the words: 'Let the earth bring forth living creatures according to their kind, cattle and creeping things and wild animals according to their kind' (Genesis 1:24). What this means is that, like all the other creatures, this serpent was 'good' (1:25). So if we understand the temptation to have been caused by a literal snake, it poses something of a problem. At the heart of the temptation there is a lie, a deliberate falsehood, in order to incite the woman and the man into committing sin. The lie uttered by the serpent was: 'You will not surely die. For God knows that when you eat from it your eyes will be opened, and you will be like God, knowing good and evil' (3:5–6). How could a lie, with the intent to deceive, issue forth from the mouth of one of God's good creatures, especially from one that was a mere irrational reptile?

To resolve the apparent problem we need to resort to a practice, long-established within the church—that of interpreting Scripture by Scripture. What does the rest of the Bible have to say about the serpent in Genesis 3? We discover that other passages shed much light on the problem we have highlighted. Elsewhere Scripture tell us that in the words and actions of the literal physical serpent in Eden we are to detect the words and actions of a spirit-being that was far from good in his intentions. It is this spirit, otherwise known as 'Satan', who is the real source of temptation and evil. But we find that in biblical language the literal and the spiritual are closely identified. In the New Testament we read of 'that ancient serpent, who is called the devil and Satan, the deceiver of the whole world' (Revelation 12:9; cf. 20:2). So Satan is the actual deceiver of humankind. Referring to the devil, Jesus said, 'He was a murderer from the beginning, and does not stand in the truth because there is no truth in him. When he speaks a lie, he speaks from his own nature, for he is a liar and the father of lies' (John 8:44). Satan, then, is the originator of lies and the one who brought death upon humanity. It is 'the devil' who 'has been sinning from the beginning' (1 John 3:8). Such passages leave little room for doubt. At the physical level the serpent of Genesis 3 was just a snake, but from a spiritual and more important perspective, the snake moved under the direction of '*the* serpent', that spirit-being of evil responsible for enticing man and woman into sin through his falsehoods.

So when it comes to a proper interpretation of the serpent within the wider biblical context, I for one would agree with those commentators who make a basic distinction between the instrument of the temptation and its author. The former is clearly the reptilian creature, the snake, whereas the latter is a being of an altogether different nature, the real cause of the problem, and while his involvement is left implicit within our text of Genesis 3, it is explicitly and unambiguously expressed in other parts of Scripture.

In view of the foregoing, I confess I have little sympathy for those who see in Genesis 3 nothing more than an etiology (or aetiology). An etiology is a story, often mythical, that serves to explain the cause or origin of something. Here it is claimed that the account provides a mythical explanation for the natural aversion of human beings towards snakes. Stories of this kind fall into the same category as those explaining how the leopard got its spots, how the giraffe came to have a long neck, how the turtle got its shell, and so on. I find it remarkable that some should place the contents of Genesis 3 alongside such stories. Anyone reading Genesis 1 to 3 can see that we are in a totally different category of literature. Its primary concern is both the creation and fall, expressed in divine and moral terms. Man and woman's loathing for snakes (which as a matter of fact is not true for all humans, and why snakes anyway?—why not spiders?) is simply far too trite a subject matter for this context, miles away from the theological and anthropological themes of such great consequence for the human race that are dealt with in these passages.

All this being so, the fact is that Genesis 3:14, quoted above, clearly applies to the literal serpent. It is the snake that will go on its belly and 'eat dust' (taken as a figure of speech). Some, both Jews and Christians, are of the opinion that the snake originally possessed legs, which were then removed by God and the creature condemned to slither along in the dirt. This may or may not be the case. But the thing I want to note here is that some form of judgment actually does fall upon the literal snake. This is not in any way because it is morally reprehensible. We have seen that this is not possible for an irrational creature. Rather, divine punishment comes upon the physical serpent for an altogether different reason, which is in order that the literal creature may serve as an object lesson to those deceived through its instrumentality, namely the human race. Each time a man or woman sees a snake slithering in the dust of the ground, with its potentially venomous bite, we are reminded of the debased nature and harmful intentions of the one who used it to such foul purposes back in Eden. It is a living symbol that points to the events of the fall, and through its divine assignment to move in the dirt and to eat dust it is also a testimony to God's displeasure at what had occurred.

Coming now to consider the words that God spoke in this *protevangelium* of Genesis 3:15, as v. 14 had most relevance to the instrument of the temptation, it would seem from the language of v. 15 that it primarily concerns the author of the temptation, namely Satan. For one thing, the very word 'enmity' itself is hardly a feeling that can be experienced by anything other than a rational being. There are other indications pointing in the same direction that will come to light as we proceed.

First we note the general tenure of v. 15. It is couched in language that is almost poetic in style, as is often the case in prophecies and solemn declarations. There is also a measure of indefiniteness about certain aspects of the utterance. The reason for this may lie in the fact that this is the very first such prophetic forecast, which the following revelations of Scripture are going to expand upon—more of which shortly.

In the first two lines of v. 15 God says, 'I will put enmity between you and the woman, and between your offspring and her offspring'. One thing jumps out at us here. Why does it only say 'the woman'? Why not rather say 'the man and the woman', as both ate the prohibited fruit of the tree? Since the declaration limits the enmity to the serpent and the woman, this plainly cannot be speaking of hostility between snakes and human beings in general. Closely related to this is the fact of the continuation of the enmity between the serpent's offspring and the woman's. As we are now dealing with the 'ancient serpent' that is 'the devil and Satan', we are not thinking of physical offspring. Since the devil is a spirit-being he does not bear biological children. But he does have 'offspring' nevertheless. The Bible says as much. We hear of those who are identified as 'the son of the devil' (Acts 13:10), 'the children of the devil' (1 John 3:10), as well as 'the offspring of vipers' (Matthew 3:7; 12:34; Luke 3:7), and 'serpents, the offspring of vipers' (Matthew 23:33). In every instance these descriptions are, of course, applied to human beings, to those who are evil, who are hypocrites, and who oppose the gospel. So the words 'your offspring' in v. 15, then, refer to those people who share the devil's character and who act as he acts. This means, therefore, that 'her offspring', that is, the offspring of the woman, cannot simply indicate all human beings. There are a considerable number among humankind who are in fact the offspring of the serpent in the manner described. So when it says 'her offspring' it must, in the word's collective sense, be referring to another portion of the human race, those who have the opposite characteristics of the offspring of the serpent.

From the foregoing we conclude that in this passage of Genesis it is not only the 'serpent' that is to be interpreted in a specific way, according to other passages of Scripture, but now the 'woman' also. This is not the literal, individual female Eve, though Eve may serve as an emblem of her.

Rather it is the idealised woman that represents the mother-figure of the righteous and faithful or, if you prefer, the human community of God (already in the preceding narrative of her creation Eve is interpreted by the apostle Paul in a symbolic manner—Genesis 2:21–24; cf. Ephesians 5:31–32). She is the matrix within which all the godly are given birth. In the Old Testament she is variously termed 'the virgin Daughter of Zion' (e.g. Isaiah 37:22), 'the most beautiful among women' (e.g. Song of Solomon 1:8), and God's 'bride' (e.g. Isaiah 62:5). In the New Testament she is most notably depicted in that vision of Revelation 12 in which John saw 'a woman clothed with the sun, with the moon under her feet, and a crown of twelve stars on her head' (v. 1), in which also the woman is being opposed by the serpent called Satan. It is this 'woman' that stands over against the serpent in Genesis 3:15.

Both woman and serpent, therefore, stand for another reality. Both of them are symbolic, or as one writer puts it, 'figurehead' characters. Each, as we shall see directly, is the spiritual progenitor of a spiritual offspring.

The second line of the verse speaks of the offspring of this 'woman', who would experience constant enmity with the corresponding offspring of the serpent. Since the woman's offspring indicates a certain portion of humankind, the word 'offspring' does involve the literal biological issue born by woman. But more importantly, as the woman signifies the earthly community of God, her offspring are also to be understood in a spiritual sense, as with the offspring of the serpent, though this time with the contrary characteristics. Each individual born to this mother shares in the faith and righteousness that she embodies. So in the phrase 'between your offspring and her offspring' we are to see the ongoing enmity between the righteous and the wicked, or, as the apostle John puts it, between the 'the children of God and the children of the devil' (1 John 3:10).

From the time of the expulsion from Eden onwards, the two respective offspring have stood opposed to one another. This is one particular theme, among others, that the book of Genesis highlights. Immediately in Genesis 4 the enmity surfaces in Cain's murder of Abel. The apostle's comment on this is: 'Do not be like Cain, who was of the evil one and murdered his brother. And why did he murder him? Because his own deeds were evil and his brother's righteous' (1 John 3:12; see also Hebrews 11:4). Here Cain is unmistakably identified as being 'of the evil one'. The same contrast is well illustrated by the godless Lamech (Genesis 4:23–24) and the devout Enoch (5:21–24), both seventh in line of descent from Adam, the former through Cain, the latter through Seth.

It comes to the fore again in Pharaoh's seizure of Sarah (12:10–20), the woman divinely chosen to be the mother of the promised son of Abraham (see later). And so it continues. As we progress through the book the same enmity appears between Ishmael and Isaac, between Esau and Jacob, and then coming into Exodus between Pharaoh and Moses, and later between the Canaanites and Israelites, and later still, among others, between David and Goliath, and between the wicked Haman in the book of Esther and the Jews he sought to annihilate. Passing into the New Testament we find most prominent among the offspring of the serpent Herod the Great who sought the death of the infant Jesus, the Pharisees, those 'offspring of vipers' who so vehemently opposed the ministry of Jesus, and the chief priests and elders who conspired to have him killed. The history recorded in the Bible amply testifies to the truth of the divine forecast—the persistent enmity 'between your offspring and her offspring'.

The final line of the verse is without doubt the most significant. There, having just mentioned the opposition of the two offspring, God then declares in words still addressed to the serpent that 'he will strike your head, and you will strike his heel'. In the first two lines the order of participants has been the serpent then the woman, and the offspring of the serpent then the offspring of the woman. Here in the last part that order is reversed, as the initial pronoun 'he' refers to the offspring of the woman, while the serpent is indicated by the second pronoun 'you'. This change of order could be taken as a literary way of underlining the greater importance of the former of the two antagonists. Besides this different order, there is now also an imbalance between the parties mentioned. In the first line it was the serpent and the woman, that is to say, two parties then present when God is speaking. The second line is the respective offspring of these same two. The last line, however, confronts the offspring of the woman with the serpent, not the offspring of the serpent. This fact is crucial. In this last phase of the enmity the conflict is between the offspring of the woman and the serpent itself. (This, we notice, is another good reason for not taking the serpent literally, as the same being is still present at this future time, after a prolonged duration of offspring).

Furthermore, in this final line of the verse the term 'offspring' has become restricted to a single offspring of this woman. It is no longer intended in its collective sense. It is speaking of one specific offspring, not many in general. This is clear, to get slightly technical for a moment, both from the use of the singular Hebrew pronoun *hû'*, meaning 'he', and from the singular direct object suffix on the verb *tᵉšûpennû*, 'strike *him*' (where the original phrase is literally 'you will strike him [on] the heel'). The Hebrew does not here use plural forms, as is the case when the plurality of the offspring is being emphasized (as in Genesis 17:8, '*their* God'; Exodus 32:13, '*they* will inherit'; Jeremiah 30:10, '*their* captivity', etc.). So we are being presented with an individual male offspring of the woman in combat with the serpent itself.

Then there is the matter of the nature of the injuries caused. It is foretold that the human offspring, a particular man, will inflict a blow to the serpent's head. To crush the head of a snake is a completely decisive stroke, which will terminate its life. In so doing, however, the man who delivers the fatal blow will himself expose his foot, or heel, to the fangs of the snake. Here God announces that the woman's offspring will receive a strike to the heel from the serpent. Such a wound is not so final as the crushing of the head. It is indeterminate. A man may indeed die from such a bite, or he may recover, depending on the effect of the injected venom on his body. So the prophecy depicts the fate of the serpent with absolute certainty, but not so the ultimate fate of the man.

Standing back and considering these words as a whole, one may remark that there is a kind of vagueness about the prophecy. This is indeed so. We have previously noted the fact that in the Old Testament not all things relating to what is to come in the New are expressed with clarity. At the same time that there is revelation of future matters, there is also a manner of hiddenness. Events are not fully disclosed in advance, but are foretold in poetic predictions, in images and visions, and in figures. And since Genesis 3:15 is the first prophecy of all, what it reveals is far from providing a complete picture of things to come. It gives us no clue as to the timescale involved. There is no way to judge how many generations pass after Adam and Eve before the prediction comes true. There is also no identification of the particular individual male offspring involved. All we know is that he is human, a male, and belongs among the offspring of the woman, that is to say, is one of the righteous, as opposed to the offspring of the devil. Yet over against this lack of clarity the prediction does in fact tell us a good deal in just a few words. It speaks of a definite future relief from the event of the fall and offers some intimation of the means by which this would put into effect. There will first be an unspecified time of ongoing enmity between the woman and the serpent and their offspring, but this will eventually climax in the complete destruction of the serpent. In other words, here in Genesis 3, as soon as sin enters the world, there is a divine announcement proclaiming a conclusive victory over it. Those who heard this, namely Adam and Eve who were standing by as God spoke to the serpent, were being informed and assured that the evil which had just entered creation was not there to stay. They immediately received the good news that the intruder would be banished. They are not told when, or who would do it, but they did know that it would be accomplished by a man and that he would suffer a blow to the heel in doing so. By this means it was evident that the intervention of sin and death into God's good creation would not endure.

As the Old Testament story progresses many of the details left unrevealed in Genesis 3:15 are filled in. During the centuries from Adam to Abraham, this *protevangelium* was the only source of hope and object of faith for the many generations that lived at that time. But for them it was enough. It is when we come to Genesis 12 that there is a significant advance in what is revealed about the woman's offspring. He is going to be a descendent of Abraham. Then by the time we get to the end of Genesis we know he will be from the tribe of Judah. Further on still, we even come to discover the particular family of Judah into which he will be born and the precise place of his birth. So the picture, indistinctly portrayed at first, is gradually brought into sharper focus. John Calvin, the sixteenth-century French reformer, described it this way:

> In the beginning when the first promise of salvation was given to Adam, it glowed like a feeble spark. Then, as it was added to, the light grew in fulness, breaking forth increasingly and shedding its radiance more widely. At last—when all the clouds were dispersed—Christ, the Sun of Righteousness, fully illumined the whole earth. (*Institutes of the Christian Religion*, 2.10.20)

The Fulfilment

Ultimately, then, the singular offspring of the woman who is predicted to crush the head of the serpent is, according to the unfolding of the biblical account, Jesus Christ. He was 'born of woman' (Galatians 4:4), specifically from the virgin Mary, who then embodied the mother-figure of the prophecy. He came into the world precisely to conquer Satan, along with sin and death, as the apostle John tells us: 'The reason the Son of God appeared was to destroy the works of the devil' (1 John 3:8). More exactly, this was done through the destruction of the devil himself. The writer to the Hebrews states:

> Therefore, since the children share in flesh and blood, he [Jesus] himself likewise shared in the same, so that through death he might destroy him who had the power of death, that is, the devil, and free those who through fear of death were held in slavery all their lives. (Hebrews 2:14–15)

Notice that this passage says it is 'through death' that he would destroy the devil. This is a literal description of what the Genesis prophecy expressed more poetically as the fact that the serpent would 'strike his heel'. As it transpired, and as later revelations in the Old Testament were to foretell, this bite of the serpent would prove fatal, in the first instance at least. It was only by means of his death on the cross that Christ was able to accomplish the destruction of Satan. In his crucifixion Jesus not only underwent the penalty due to sin for the sake of all humankind who put their faith in him, but he also took to the cross the old human nature, stemming from Adam, which had been corrupted by the effects of sin. That fallen nature in which Satan had gained a foothold was put to death on the cross. And yet, because Jesus had not sinned in that nature, he was raised to life again. So at his resurrection, a new pure humanity, a new Adam so to speak, came into being, untarnished by the effects of the fall. It is through our union with Christ, by faith, that we share in the hope of new bodies like his at the general resurrection of the dead, and a restoration to the presence of God, to dwell with him for ever.

We should not go any further without pointing out a fact that will be apparent to most Bible readers, which is that in the wisdom of the divine plan the destruction of Satan takes place in two separate stages. At his first coming, Jesus went to the cross to free us from sin, and to create a new humanity, over which Satan no longer has any hold whatsoever. Through Christ's resurrection death is entirely overcome, so that Paul could exclaim, 'Where, O death, is your victory? Where, O death, is your sting?' (1 Corinthians 15:55). But although this new creation has already begun, the old creation remains for yet a little while, and there Satan still exercises a remnant of power. Then at Christ's second coming, as the book of Revelation informs us, Satan is finally utterly and totally eradicated (20:10).

While the New Testament clearly states that Jesus came to destroy the devil, in fulfilment of the foundational prophecy of Genesis 3:15, we find that this verse is not actually quoted. Direct quotation, however, is not the only way to refer back to an earlier text. This can also be done by allusion. Very definitely the *protevangelium* is alluded to at least twice in the apostolic writings. One of these we have already made reference to, which is the vision of Revelation 12. This is worth quoting at some length:

> A great sign appeared in heaven: a woman clothed with the sun, with the moon under her feet, and a crown of twelve stars on her head. And being with child she cried out, as she was in labour and in pain to give birth. Then another sign appeared in heaven: and behold, a great red dragon with seven heads and ten horns, and on his heads were seven diadems. And his tail swept away a third of the stars of heaven and threw them to the earth. And the dragon stood before the woman who was about to give birth, so that when she gave birth he might devour her child. And she gave birth to a son, a male child, who was to rule all the nations with an iron sceptre. But her child was caught up to God and to his throne. (Revelation 12:1–5)

There are three basic participants in this vision—the woman, her child, and the dragon, which is also described, as noted earlier, as 'that ancient serpent, who is called the devil and Satan' (v. 9). The significant thing to point out for our purposes is the fact that this dragon, or serpent, is expressly shown to be wanting to destroy the woman's child, that is, her offspring, rather than the woman herself. The dragon was standing there 'before the woman so that when she gave birth he might devour her child' (v. 4). So here we have much that corresponds with Genesis 3:15. There is the woman, who from her description is a clearly symbolic woman, and the serpent, again a symbol, which is Satan. There is also the woman's child, a male offspring, whom the serpent wants to destroy. This latter element agrees with the last line of the Genesis prophecy, where the conflict is between the woman's single male offspring ('he') and the serpent itself. The child set to 'rule all the nations with an iron sceptre' is plainly Christ, the messianic king (see Psalm 2:9; Revelation 19:15). So there is good reason to believe that this vision is structured upon the ancient prophecy.

Another New Testament passage where Genesis 3:15 is undoubtedly in mind is Romans 16:20, where Paul says, 'The God of peace will soon crush Satan under your feet'. In this verse the apostle speaks of Satan being crushed 'under your feet', that is, the feet of the Christians. Here it is necessary to recall what was mentioned in Chapter 2 about the idea of the 'whole Christ' (*totus Christus*). Believers are said to be 'in Christ', they form his 'body'. So what is true of him is likewise true of them. If he has crushed Satan underfoot, then in him they also have the same power. Such a defeat of Satan is here promised to the Roman believers, and so to us. This could be speaking of overcoming Satan in a particular situation the Romans were facing, known to Paul's readers but not to us. Much more likely, however, the apostle is reiterating the ultimate victory over the serpent according to the terms of the ancient prediction. Either way the apostle's words are undoubtedly reminiscent of the *protevangelium*.

In the post-apostolic church this christological reading of Genesis 3:15 was taken up by numerous ministers, theologians, and commentators. Irenaeus of Lyons (c. AD 180), for example, wrote that '[Christ] waged war against our enemy, and crushed him who had at the beginning led us away captives in Adam, and trampled upon his head' (*Against Heresies*, 5.21.1). Ambrose of Milan (c. AD 388) similarly declared that 'Christ came to the earth and trod upon that serpent the devil' (*The Prayer of Job and David*, 4.1.4). We find the same view to have been held by Martin Luther, John Calvin, and other leading figures of the Reformation, and in many of the classic Protestant commentaries during the subsequent centuries.

Last of all, it is noteworthy that the interpretation given here, which is a distinctly Christian interpretation of a particular Hebrew Scripture, is quite in agreement with old Jewish interpretations of the same passage. This confirms that the early Christians were not merely imagining things in Genesis 3:15. Evidence shows that even before Jesus was born, as well as after, the Jews understood elements of this text in a way similar to that just described. That the literal snake was an instrument of Satan was a view held by a number of early Jewish writers, as was the perpetual enmity between the two offspring, the wicked and the righteous. Interestingly two of the Aramaic versions of Genesis (Targum Jonathan and the Palestinian Targum) add the explanation to the verse that these things will be fulfilled 'in the days of King Messiah'.

We have seen, then, that right at the beginning, when humanity first succumbed to the wiles of the devil and fell into sin, a wonderful message of hope was given. Despite ongoing enmity for a certain duration between the wicked and the righteous, there would eventually come one offspring of the woman who, at the cost of his own suffering, would bring a fatal blow to the serpent, and so destroy evil at its root. The next chapters will show how this initial Edenic prophecy, this 'first good news', was developed in later Hebrew Scriptures, with more and more details gradually revealed.

Suggestions for Further Reading

Doukhan, Jacques, *On the Way to Emmaus: Five Major Messianic Prophecies Explained* (Clarksville, Maryland: Lederer Books, 2012), pp. 11–39.

Gordon, Robert. *Christ in the Old Testament, Volume 1* (Glasgow: Free Presbyterian Publications, 2002), pp. 35–45.

Hengstenberg, Ernst W. *Christology of the Old Testament, Volume 1* (Edinburgh: T&T Clark, 1854), pp. 4–20.

Sailhamer, John H. *The Pentateuch as Narrative: A Biblical Theological Commentary* (Grand Rapids, Michigan: Zondervan, 1992), pp. 106–109.

5. PROMISE

The idea of God making promises is very prominent in the Bible. While this is so, we begin by pointing out that the Hebrew language of the Old Testament in fact has no particular word for 'promise'. This does not mean, of course, that the Israelites had no notion of what a promise was. It is often the case that an idea can be present when a specific word to express that idea is not.

When we come across the verb 'promise' in our modern English versions of the Old Testament, the Hebrew word being translated is often simply 'speak' (*dibbēr*), or sometimes 'say' (*ʾāmar*). We see this, for example, in a comparison of older and more recent translations of Genesis 21:1, where KJV and ASV, speaking of God's promise for Sarah to bear a son, simply have 'as he had spoken', while the modern versions have 'had promised' (e.g. NIV NRSV NJB NLT). When the noun 'promise' occurs in English, it is usually just the noun for 'word' (*dābār*) in Hebrew. So in Psalm 105:42 KJV and ASV we read 'his holy word', and more recent translations say 'his holy promise' (NIV NRSV NJB NLT).

From this we conclude that in certain contexts an utterance by someone, especially when that someone is God, contains the added dimension of being a promise. For sure, this is how the New Testament writers understood the case, since in Greek a specific verb (*epangellō*) and noun (*epangelia*) exist with the meaning of 'promise', and these are used by the apostles in connection with certain aspects of the divine purpose revealed in the Old Testament. So Paul, for instance, in listing the spiritual benefits of Israel declares that 'to them belong the adoption, the glory, the covenants, the giving of the law, the temple ministry, and the promises' (Romans 9:4).

Before we look at what these Old Testament promises were about, it will be helpful to consider briefly what a promise is, and how promises made by God are different from prophecies given by God. Both promises and prophecies relate to the future, and so it is common to find future tense statements involved in both. Both equally involve an utterance that looks to some manner of fulfilment. In these two respects there is an overlap between them. A promise, however, contains an element of personal commitment on the part of the one making it, and so the use of the first person singular ('I') is more frequently found here than in prophecy. Moreover, there is usually the explicit intent that the person receiving the promise is to be benefited in some way by the other keeping it. To this end the making of a promise in particular is in order that the recipient may be given the assurance that it will be fulfilled. A prophecy, on the other hand, need not have any of these latter elements. Prophecy, as wonderful as it is, may simply be the plain prediction of a future fact, where the commitment of the speaker and the benefit or assurance of the receiver is not particularly in view, or at least not explicitly so. When God therefore says to Joshua, 'I will never leave you, nor forsake you' (Joshua 1:5), that is a promise. But when the birthplace of the coming Saviour is declared to be Bethlehem (Micah 5:2; cf. Matthew 2:6), that is a prophecy. That the Saviour would eventually be born is indeed a divine promise, but the place where he would be born is a matter of prophecy. Many other details about the ministry of Christ in the Gospels, such as his riding into Jerusalem on a donkey, the scattering of his followers upon his arrest, the dividing of his garments at the cross, all fall into the category of prophetic predictions, and are not therefore promises.

In light of the foregoing, we find it to be the case that when something having the nature of a promise is spoken by God, since it contains the desire to also impart assurance regarding its fulfilment, it can be accompanied by some solemn act of affirmation on God's part. Such an act would either be the swearing of an oath or the establishing of a covenant. Both of these form a significant part of the divine promises we are going to consider, as we shall see.

The Old Testament obviously contains numerous promises of God, made to both individuals and communities. Some have long-term fulfilments, others are more immediate. But when it comes to the larger purpose of God in Christ, there are two principal sets of promises that concern us. These are promises given by God to two Old Testament characters of considerable importance. Firstly, there are the promises made very early in the progression of the divine plan to Abraham, the forefather of the nation of Israel and the race of Jews. Secondly, there are the promises given some centuries later to David, the first of a dynasty of Hebrew kings who reigned in Jerusalem. The remainder of this chapter will examine each of these in turn.

The Promises to Abraham

Abraham lived approximately 2,000 years before Jesus, and enters the biblical record in the latter part of Genesis 11. He was an inhabitant of a place called Ur of the Chaldeans, probably a city in the region known as

Mesopotamia, in the vicinity of the rivers Tigris and Euphrates. It would seem that he and his family were caught up in the idol worship that was the common religious practice in that place at the time (see Joshua 24:14). But in God's wisdom, a significant new stage in his purpose to save humankind was to begin with this man Abraham (or 'Abram', as he was first named).

Following the fall of the first man and woman in Genesis 3, and the entrance of the curse into the world, the human race declined even further into wickedness until it was necessary for God to bring a great flood upon the earth. Only Noah and his family, together with selected animals, were preserved within the ark, the great wooden vessel that carried them safely over the waters (Genesis 6–8). When Noah emerged from the ark, God repeated to him the same instructions given earlier to Adam and Eve, to multiply and fill the earth (Genesis 9:1, 7). Noah was, then, in effect, a second Adam figure, the head of new humankind, delivered from the flood to start the race afresh upon the earth. Yet Noah too fell into sin, again in respect to the fruit of a tree like Adam (Genesis 9:20–27). Also, the new human race descended from Noah that repopulated the earth proved to be ungodly and rebellious. It is recorded how they tried to build a great tower to reach up to heaven, but God thwarted their purposes by dividing their languages (Genesis 11:1–9). Following this account Genesis introduces us to the descendants of Noah's son Shem (from whom come the peoples we describe as 'Semitic'), and it is in this line that we first encounter the person of Abraham and his wife Sarah. The couple are childless and Sarah is described as being unable to bear children (Genesis 11:26, 29–30).

This new development in the divine purpose begins with God calling Abraham and his closest family members out of Ur to go to a land that he would show him (Genesis 12:1), this being the land of Canaan, on the eastern seaboard of the Mediterranean Sea. Evidently such a call involved leaving behind their traditional gods, the idols of Ur, and since the Lord, the one true God Yahweh, not only spoke to Abraham but actually made an appearance to him (cf. Acts 7:2), this can only have resulted in Abraham forsaking his former gods to worship the Lord. The words of Abraham's call are as follows:

> Go from your country and from your relatives and from your father's house to the land that I will show you. I will make you a great nation, and I will bless you, and I will make your name great, and you will be a blessing. I will bless those who bless you, and

the one who curses you I will curse. And in you all the families of the earth will be blessed. (Genesis 12:1–3)

The next verse tells us that Abraham did just as God had commanded him, and gives us the additional fact that he was seventy-five years old at the time (v. 4).

There are four notable things to draw attention to in these words of God. Firstly, there is the fact that rather than make a new start with the whole race, as was the intention in the case of Noah, God is now focussing on a single man who he will make into a great nation. This marks the very beginnings of that people who came to be known as Israel. It is for this reason that they are often referred to as the 'chosen people'. From Abraham onwards, for many centuries to come, the divine purpose is going to work itself out through this particular nation. Secondly, we learn that God did not call Israel, and not even their forefather Abraham, by virtue of any particularly great godliness. Abraham, as we have seen, was an idolater who originally did not know the Lord, and at this time the nation of Israel simply did not exist, other than in the foreknowledge of God. It was his purpose to create a great nation, not deal with one that was already great in some way. In other words, the initiative is entirely God's. Thirdly, we note the repetition of the word 'bless' and 'blessing', five times in all. The call of Abraham cannot be rightly understood without appreciating that God's intention to bring about blessing, with all that this entails, lies at its very heart. Since the fall of the man and woman into sin, a recurring word in connection with the working of God in early human history has been that of 'curse', as appears in Genesis 3:14, 17; 4:11; 5:29; 8:21. But now, in a single divine utterance, those five expressions of cursing are countered by five promises of blessing. This is a clear indication of what it is exactly that God intends to do through Abraham. The curse that entered creation by means of sin is to be removed, and replaced by a state of blessing. God will in the first instance bless Abraham himself. He will make him into a great nation, and make his name great. So it is that the name of Abraham has gone down in history, and remains in use till this day, as being that of the man who was the forefather of the Jewish nation, Israel. The blessing, however, extended far beyond this. We observe, fourthly, the fact that the call of Abraham is ultimately global in its scope. What the promises speak of concerns not just Abraham, nor merely the nation that would descend from him, but he was told that 'in you all the families of the earth will be blessed' (12:3). While the literal sense of the opening Hebrew phrase here is 'in you', its meaning is actually closer to the sense of 'through you' (as NIV NLT). We see, then, that in the promises were both the fact that 'I will bless you' as well as 'you will be a blessing', namely to others. In calling Abraham, and in forming from him the nation of Israel, God's sights are very much upon the whole world. It is noteworthy that this particular aspect of blessing for all nations through the promise is described by the apostle Paul as 'the gospel', when he writes, 'And the Scripture, foreseeing that God would justify the Gentiles by faith, preached the gospel beforehand to Abraham, saying, "In you all the nations will be blessed"' (Galatians 3:8).

Following the arrival of Abraham and his family in Canaan, the Lord appeared to him again, and Abraham built an altar to worship him. On this occasion God declared to him that 'To your offspring I will give this land' (12:7). This shows the two central elements involved in the promise. To accomplish the wider purpose of bringing the divine blessing to all nations, God will give Abraham both 'offspring' and a 'land'. What the successive chapters of Genesis go on to describe, and the other Hebrew Scriptures afterwards, is the reiteration, expansion, and movement towards the fulfilment of the diverse aspects of the promise. Although in the divine purpose the ideas of offspring and land are of course inextricably linked, it is helpful if we now treat the promises under two distinct sub-headings. As the first of these more directly relates to the person of Christ we shall devote greater space to the offspring aspect of the promise.

The Offspring

The particular Hebrew term that we are dealing with is *zera*ʻ, which as observed in the previous chapter basically means 'seed'. This may also have the sense of 'offspring', and that is how we will commonly translate it in this chapter. One important feature of this noun, we recall, is that it can have both a singular and a corporate meaning. It may be applied to one particular offspring, or it may refer to offspring collectively. It is for this latter reason that many English Bibles sometimes render *zera*ʻ in the plural as 'descendants' (e.g. Genesis 15:12 NASB NRSV NIV NJB). This translation also alerts us to the fact that a man's 'offspring', according to the sense of *zera*ʻ, is not limited to his immediate children, but also includes all those descended from him for generations to come.

God's promise concerning Abraham's offspring is remarkable. At the time of this promise Abraham, it is to be remembered, had no children, nor was Sarah capable of bearing any. Therefore it was quite impossible, humanly speaking, for the contents of this promise to come about. Rather it uniquely lay within the divine sovereignty to grant what was promised. Only an express act of God, a supernatural intervention, could cause Abraham's wife to conceive.

Also remarkable is the fact that God did not set about fulfilling this promise with any sense of haste. In view of the fact that both Abraham and Sarah were quite advanced in years, one might have thought that God would have brought about the pregnancy sooner rather than later. But that was not to be the case. The time until the eventual birth of Abraham and Sarah's first son was actually quite prolonged, and would have seemed especially so for an ageing couple. Why the delay? We cannot of course completely fathom the divine mind, but we can make an educated guess at the reasons. In the first instance, to leave the birth for a number of years made it more apparent that it was doubly a divine act. It was not just a matter of removing the sterility of a barren woman, but of causing a woman in her nineties to bear a child! The former of itself would have been an amazing act of God, but the latter even more so. The apostolic comment about this, made by Paul in Romans, was that the miracle was rather like bringing life out of what was as good as dead (Romans 4:17–19, where Paul describes Abraham as believing in 'the God who lives life to the dead'), something similar to resurrection in fact.

Alongside the necessity of divine involvement, there is the rejection of human involvement. In the face of his childlessness, and the lack of an heir, there were a number of culturally acceptable expedients to which Abraham could have resorted. As it proceeds, the Genesis narrative speaks of three possible ways that the problem might be solved by merely human means, and each of these three is in turn discounted. Mention is firstly made of Lot, Abraham's nephew, who accompanied him on his journey to Canaan (Genesis 12:4–5). If a man were without an heir, then at that time and in that culture, as indeed is still the case in certain parts of the world today, it would be quite natural for a man to adopt his nephew, so that he would in effect become his son and receive his adoptive father's inheritance. Consequently, following the divine promises of Genesis 12, Lot is providentially taken out of the picture in Genesis 13. Both Abraham and Lot had their own herds and flocks and the part of Canaan in which they resided was not able to sustain them all, and so this situation resulted in a quarrel between their respective herdsmen. Abraham therefore gave his nephew the choice of where to live, and Lot chose to go and live among the cities of the plain, near

Sodom (Genesis 13:5–13). This separation and new independence for Lot means that he is no longer a potential son for Abraham. For sure, when Lot encounters trouble in Genesis 14, Abraham comes to his rescue, as any good uncle would, but basically as far as their households and livelihoods are concerned, each has gone his own way.

Another possibility for a childless man would be to adopt a trusted household servant as his son and heir. As Abraham advances even further in years, and God's promise remains unfulfilled, such an adoption looks to him to be what might end up happening. He complains to God, 'I remain childless and the heir of my estate is Eliezer of Damascus … You have given me no offspring, so a member of my household will be my heir' (Genesis 15:2–3). In his response, however, God plainly declares, 'This man will not be your heir, but one who will come from your own body will be your heir' (v. 4). So as Abraham was not to adopt Lot, neither was he to adopt Eliezer.

Yet a third course of action open to the childless couple was a practice which entailed Abraham fathering a child through a surrogate mother. Such a custom is known to us from ancient documents. The childless husband could take another woman for the express purpose of her conceiving his child and upon the birth she was to give the child over to the man and his barren wife as their own. In Genesis 16 we read how Sarah herself makes such a proposal to Abraham. She invites him to sleep with her maidservant Hagar who could produce a son for him. The short-term result was the birth of Ishmael, an actual son for Abraham when he was eighty-six years old (v. 16). But the long-term consequence was not at all favourable. It meant rivalry between Ishmael and the son of the promise later to be born. It also led to friction between Sarah and Hagar, with the eventual result that Hagar and her son were cast out of Abraham's household. In Genesis 17 God explains to Abraham that Ishmael was not to be his heir through whom the promise would work itself out. Rather it would be a son born to Abraham and his own wife Sarah, even though by now Abraham was a hundred and Sarah ninety (v. 17). It is in the next chapter (Genesis 18) that God gives the final notice regarding the approaching miraculous birth, then at along last Isaac is born (Genesis 21:1–7). It is then that God tells Abraham, 'It is in Isaac that your offspring will be called' (Genesis 21:12; Romans 9:7), following which Ishmael and his mother are sent away.

Such a delay and a stripping away of all potential human ways of solving the problem of Abraham's childlessness would have taught

Abraham much about the exercise of faith. In the face of the passage of time, the increasing physical debilitation of his own body and that of Sarah, and the removal of all hope in a natural solution, the only fitting response was to take God at his word and have faith in his promise. And indeed as the story unfolds this is what Abraham exactly does. Following the restatement of the promise, that not only would Abraham have offspring but offspring too numerous to count (Genesis 15:4–5), we are told that 'he believed the LORD, and he reckoned it to him as righteousness' (v. 6). Where we read 'believed' here the meaning of course is 'put his faith in'. This is the first statement in Genesis concerning Abraham's faith, and as we read the following chapters we find it is sorely tried and tested. But ultimately faith triumphs. It is for his 'faith' in particular that Abraham is later commended in the New Testament. Paul writes, 'Hoping against hope, he believed that he would become "the father of many nations", according to what was said, "So will your offspring be" … he did not waver at the promise of God in unbelief, but grew strong in his faith, giving glory to God' (Romans 4:18, 20).

Abraham's faith was in the fulfilment of God's promise according to his word. And for his part, God gave added assurance to Abraham. First of all, he established a 'covenant' with him. A covenant is a solemn undertaking, or agreement, on the part of one or more parties. It can be unilateral, in which one party places himself or herself under obligation to fulfil the terms of the agreement unconditionally. Or it may be bilateral, in which case both parties have obligations to fulfil. A covenant is often accompanied by some manner of ritual, such as the offering of sacrifices. The death of the animals seals the covenant by the shedding of blood, and also serves as a kind of warning of what the covenant-maker should be prepared to undergo in the event that he or she break the terms of the covenant. The covenant ritual takes place in Genesis 15:9–21. Animals are killed and their carcasses divided into two. Then Abraham witnesses what we call a 'theophany', a visible manifestation of the divine presence by means of a fiery vision, and amazingly it is this that passes between the separated halves of the dead animals. This symbolic act shows that it is God who takes upon himself the responsibility of upholding the terms of the covenant, even upon pain of death!

Some time later, God gives further confirmation regarding his promises by means of an oath. On this occasion God swears that he will keep his promise, affirming it by means of an oath formula. In taking an oath one usually swears by what is considered most sacred. Ironically, as there is nothing more sacred than God he has to swear by himself. This takes place in Genesis 22. By this time Abraham's son Isaac is a young man, but the promise regarding offspring extends far beyond a single immediate son, and it is this future, greater aspect of the promise that is here confirmed by God with an oath (v. 16; there is an enlightening comment on this event in the New Testament, see Hebrews 6:13–17). So by this means, the promise, even though already binding as God's express word, becomes even more so, and Abraham is stirred to demonstrate an even greater faith.

From what has been said above, it is clear that the birth of Isaac was not the complete fulfilment of what God had promised. His birth was an utterly astounding act of divine intervention in a situation that was humanly speaking impossible. Nevertheless, it was only the first stage in God's enactment of his promises. Greater things were yet to come. This is made apparent in the Genesis narrative itself. As mentioned above, the promises were reiterated and expanded with the passing of time, and also with the passing of the generations. Abraham had been told by God '*in you* all the families of the earth will be blessed' (12:3; 18:18). But later the same ultimate purpose of the promise becomes '*in your offspring* all the nations of the earth will be blessed' (22:18). Yet this promise of blessing the nations plainly did not come about within the lifetime of Abraham's son Isaac. Rather we find that after the death of his father the exact same promise was repeated to Isaac, in the self-same words, 'in your offspring all the nations of the earth will be blessed' (26:4), except that here 'your offspring' refers now to Isaac's own offspring. So the promise has been passed on to the succeeding generation, and is then again passed on to Isaac's son Jacob (28:14), and for this reason, the Abrahamic promises may also be called the 'patriarchal' promises. At the same time, the development of the initial promise brings out the fact that there is a corporate sense, already indicated to Abraham, as well as an individual sense to the 'offspring'. This is evident from the promised offspring being described as 'unable to be counted' because God will 'multiply' them (e.g. 13:16; 15:5; 22:17; 26:4; 32:12). This is also what was originally meant when, at the time of Abraham's call out of Ur, God had told him that he would make him 'a great nation' (12:2).

By the time we get to the end of the book of Genesis, Abraham's grandson Jacob, together with all his sons and daughters, and their children, amount to approximately seventy people (Genesis 46:27), obviously not yet a great nation. In the divine providence the multiplication of Abraham's descendants takes place when Jacob's family are obliged to go down to Egypt during a time of severe famine. Here they increase enormously (Exodus 1:7). It is because of this that Pharaoh, king of Egypt, feels threatened and they are eventually enslaved. After some time God delivered his people, with mighty signs and wonders, bringing them out of Egypt and eventually into the land of Canaan that he had promised them. There in the land, now called Israel, they later become a great nation under the rule of David and the successive kings that God granted his people (1 Kings 5:7). Indeed, we find the very words of the Abrahamic promise applied to the king—'in him all nations will be blessed' (Psalm 72:17), which shows how God's promises to Abraham and his promises to David are working towards the same essential goal. During this time, however, when Israel was a great nation under its kings, the blessings from which those of other nations benefited were somewhat limited. We do read of the amazement of the Queen of Sheba at the wisdom of King Solomon (1 Kings 10), the miracle for the widow of Zarephath through the prophet Elijah (1 Kings 17), and the healing of the Aramean general Naaman through the prophet Elisha (2 Kings 5), and a few similar such events, but Israel was hardly the light to the Gentiles that it ought to have been.

While it may be true that the promises and covenant with Abraham were unilateral, and that ultimately God would bring to a complete and utter fulfilment what was promised with regard to the offspring of Abraham, there was nevertheless the necessary response of faith—both faith in his word and faithfulness towards him. The Israelites did not manifest such faith, as noted in the previous chapter. This being so the promises were not fulfilled to their fullest extent in them. To be sure, there was some significant measure of fulfilment. A numerous people had wonderfully sprung forth from an aged man and a barren and elderly woman. They had, moreover, been given a land to live in that had previously belonged to a powerful and warlike nation. In these physical blessings, God was acting truly according to his word. Yet in its final manifestation the blessing that was the utmost expression of the promise had an essentially spiritual goal. The curse upon humankind was due to sin, and so the blessing necessarily had to provide the answer to that problem—the removal of sin from the human race, along with its attendant suffering and death. The Old Testament period saw none of this fulfilled. Clearly, therefore, the fulness of the promise regarding the 'offspring' of Abraham through whom all nations would be blessed still lay in the future.

Where this promise to Abraham was ultimately heading was to one particular offspring of Abraham, and this, as the New Testament emphasizes, is none other than the person we know as Jesus Christ. The opening chapter of that Testament in its very first verse presents Jesus as 'the son of Abraham' (Matthew 1:1), and the following verses trace the genealogical lineage of Jesus all the way from Abraham, the forefather of Israel. The connection between the advent of Christ and the Abrahamic promise is recognised right at the beginning of Luke's Gospel. During the time of her pregnancy Mary, the mother of Jesus, uttered that song we call the *Magnificat* (Luke 1:46–55), in which she declared of God that 'he has helped his servant Israel, in remembrance of his mercy—as he spoke to our fathers—to Abraham and his offspring [lit. 'seed'] for ever' (vv. 54–55). Similarly, Zechariah, father of John the Baptist, in his prophetic song known as the *Benedictus* (Luke 1:67–79), spoke of the salvation that God was now bringing to pass, 'to show mercy to our fathers, and to remember his holy covenant, the oath that he swore to Abraham our father' (vv. 72–73). Plainly Jesus was born in precise conformity with what God had uttered two thousand years earlier by way of a promise to Israel's great ancestor. He is *the* offspring of Abraham. Hence when Jesus came into the world the time for the blessing to be experienced, by both Jew and Gentile, had finally arrived.

So it is that, after Christ's ascension, when the apostles preached and taught the gospel the connection was frequently made with what God had promised to Abraham. In one of his early evangelistic speeches to the Jews of Jerusalem, Peter proclaimed to them that 'you are the children of the prophets and of the covenant that God made with your fathers, saying to Abraham, "And in your offspring all the families of the earth will be blessed". When God raised up his servant [Jesus], he sent him to you first, to bless you by turning each of you from your wicked ways' (Acts 3:25–26). Paul too presents Jesus in terms of the ancient promise, explaining that in its strict singular sense the promise regarding Abraham's offspring, or more literally his 'seed', was a promise relating to Jesus: 'Now the promises were spoken to Abraham and to his seed. It does not say, "and to seeds", as if it meant many, but rather one, "and to your seed", that is, Christ' (Galatians 3:16).

That Jesus was the final 'offspring' of Abraham who brings the divine blessing is amply demonstrated in each of the Gospels. Each account climaxes with Christ's death and resurrection. This is the means by which sin and death are overcome and the blessing instated. Jesus died for our sins, not his own, for he had none. And his rising from the tomb shows that he had once and for all conquered death. The extension of the blessing to all nations is shown by the book of Acts, which records how many thousands of Gentiles, all over the Mediterranean world, came to salvation from sin and death through Christ. As the apostle Paul said, the Gentiles (or 'nations') were now becoming 'sharers together in the promise in Christ Jesus through the gospel' (Ephesians 3:6). The same story has continued ever since, with thousands worldwide coming to experience the blessing of salvation each and every day.

Before we conclude our discussion of this particular promise, there is one last aspect of what it means to be the 'offspring' of Abraham that needs to be mentioned. Just as Isaac was the first individual offspring of the patriarch, but the fulfilment of the promise then expanded to include a numerous people, Abraham's corporate offspring of the nation of Israel, so it is with the ultimate spiritual fulfilment of the promise. Jesus, a literal descendant of Abraham, came as *the* individual offspring, through whom divine blessing would finally extend to the whole world. Now the New Testament explains to us that those who believe in Christ are also themselves counted as being Abraham's offspring. In its truest and most spiritual sense, to be a child of Abraham is not a mere matter of biological descent. This physical relationship with Abraham is what the Jews claimed to be of the utmost importance in the Gospels, and yet both John the Baptist and Jesus himself denied that this was so (Matthew 3:9; John 8:37–40). To be a genuine Jew, according to Paul, was something internal and spiritual (Romans 2:28–29). It is in fact those who believe in Jesus that display such a spiritual relationship to Abraham, for they demonstrate the same faith as he did, and trust in the same basic promises. Accordingly, believers are spiritual children, even if not physical, of Abraham, who, as the apostle Paul said, 'is the father of all who believe yet have not been circumcised' (Romans 4:11), that is to say, of Gentile believers in Christ. Again Paul declared, 'if you belong to Christ, then you are Abraham's offspring, and heirs according to the promise' (Galatians 3:29). So it is that when Zacchaeus, the formerly corrupt Jewish tax-collector, turned to faith in Christ, Jesus declares him to be a 'son of Abraham' (Luke 19:9). Previously he had been a son of Abraham, though only with respect to his physical descent, but now upon his conversion he becomes a true son of the patriarch in the deeper spiritual sense.

We have seen, then, that when the Scripture speaks of Abraham's 'offspring' it may indicate different descendants of the patriarch at different stages in God's plan. Each and every one of these is remarkable in its own way, especially when we consider that all go back to a childless and barren couple who were both way past the age of bearing children by natural means. But, of course, the most significant fact is that *the* son of Abraham is first (in order of importance) and foremost Jesus himself. It is ultimately him that the promise has in view, for it is only in him that 'all nations on earth will be blessed' according to the intention of the promise.

In order to summarize, and to help us more readily appreciate the development of the Abrahamic promise, it might be helpful to portray it diagrammatically as follows:

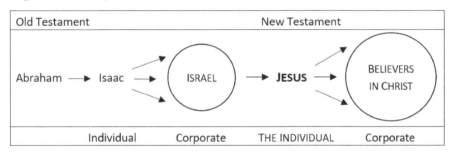

Here it can be seen how in the Old Testament the promise relates to Israel, while under the new covenant, inaugurated in the New Testament, it expands to include people of all nations who believe in Jesus. This, it is important to further note, harkens back to God's original instructions for the human race given to the first man and woman at the time of their creation. There we read that 'God blessed them, and God said to them, "Be fruitful and multiply, and fill the earth"' (Genesis 1:28). This blessing and multiplication that God intended for all the sons and daughters of Adam, he accomplished on a national scale first through Israel, and then on a global scale through the church of Christ. The book of Acts repeatedly tells us how the number of believers 'multiplied' in various lands (e.g. 5:14; 6:1; 9:31; 12:24; 16:5). In this way true humanity is being restored.

The Land

The promise that Abraham and his offspring would receive a 'land' concerns one of the blessings given through Christ and so may justifiably be treated as part and parcel of the gospel. However, since it touches upon the person of Jesus in a less direct way than the promise of offspring (though at a much deeper level there is a profound theological relationship—something we will have to save for another time), we will discuss this aspect of the promise more briefly.

The principal Hebrew word we are thinking about here is *'ereṣ*, meaning both 'land' and 'earth'. This shows that the term can sometimes cause a certain amount of ambiguity, as to whether a particular region of land is intended, or the whole earth. The same goes for the corresponding Greek word *gē*, occurring in the Greek translation of the Old Testament (the Septuagint) and the New Testament.

As noted in the previous section, the original call of Abraham involved him removing himself and his family from their home to a land that God would show them (Genesis 12:1), which proved to be Canaan. Once there God told him, 'To your offspring I will give this land' (12:7). Just like the promise of offspring, this promise of land is reiterated by God at regular intervals throughout the lives of Abraham, Isaac, and Jacob (Genesis 13:15, 17; 15:7, 18; 17:8; 24:7; 26:3; 28:4, 13; 35:12; 48:4; 50:24). In these repetitions the two aspects of offspring and land are frequently mentioned side by side, as in the original expression of the promise. This is quite logical. People need a place to live, and so the offspring that God promised to raise up to Abraham are also promised a territory of their own to inhabit, specially provided by God.

Now just as, at the time the promise was given, Abraham had no child, so too, since he had left Ur, he had no land. He was now in a foreign land hundreds of miles from home and, Genesis tells us, 'the Canaanites were then in the land' (12:6). This state of affairs is reiterated when it further says, 'the Canaanite and the Perizzite were then dwelling in the land' (13:7). This means the land was not available for the taking, but was rather already occupied. The Canaanites were, moreover, a particularly warlike people, organised into city states, and living for the most part in strongly fortified settlements. Later we learn that the descendants of Anak also lived among them, these being men of gigantic stature (Deuteronomy 1:28). In contrast to this Abraham was simply an elderly nomad with a relatively small number of servants at his disposal, who were mainly herdsmen and shepherds. It ought not be overlooked, then, that as with respect to the promise of offspring, it was quite impossible from a human perspective that Abraham could take possession of the land. As was the case with the birth of a child, so divine intervention would likewise be required in order to take the land.

In the outworking of the divine plan the promise to give the land saw a much longer delay before there was any manner of fulfilment than was the case with the giving of offspring. By the time we get to the end of the book of Genesis, none of the patriarchs had taken possession of the land, but it remained firmly in the hands of the various Canaanite tribes. When Abraham needed a plot of land to bury his deceased wife, he had to buy it from the local people (Genesis 23). Later Jacob too, it appears, had to purchase a similar plot for the burial of members of his household (Joshua 24:32). But God had promised that he would 'give' the land, not that they should buy it with silver, and that they would possess '*all* the land', not just a small plot here and there (Genesis 13:15). It was only several centuries later, long after the death of the patriarchs, when their offspring, the Israelites, had multiplied greatly, and were now enslaved in Egypt, that the first significant advance towards fulfilling the promise took place. In that situation God raised up Moses, some six or seven hundred years after the original promise, to deliver the people from slavery and lead them to the promised land. With a mighty hand God, through Moses, brought the Israelites out of Egypt and they started their journey through the wilderness towards Canaan. A journey that should have been made in a few weeks lasted for nearly forty years owing to the disbelief of the people. Finally, it was Moses' successor Joshua who led the people across the River Jordan into the land. With the help of God the original inhabitants were conquered and the people of Israel began to settle into the land promised to them long before.

The history of Israel in the land is a long and involved one, preserved for us in the narrative books of the Old Testament. In time the people were to grow into a unified nation under King David around 1000 BCE, and divine worship became centred upon a single great temple in Jerusalem, built by David's son Solomon. This could, and perhaps should, have been the political and religious basis upon which the nation might then have begun to be a light to the Gentiles. But that never happened. The history of the kings is essentially one of decline. The kingdom divided into two, north and south. The northern kingdom immediately fell into serious idolatry and later the worship of Baal, the Canaanite god. Despite the powerful ministries of the prophets Elijah and Elisha, and despite the divine revelations given through spokesmen such as Hosea and Amos, the northern Israelites refused to change their ways. Finally, in the late eighth century BCE God sent the Assyrian army against them, the land was invaded and overrun, and many thousands of people deported and resettled in other lands. Foreigners were then brought in and given land in northern Israel for them to live in (2 Kings 17). The southern kingdom, named Judah, followed their fellow Israelites in the same unfaithfulness and disobedience to God's law, and their kingdom too was eventually overthrown, this time by the Babylonians in the early sixth century. Thousands of inhabitants of Judah were taken into exile (2 Kings 25).

As was said in the previous chapter, although there was a return of some of the Jews from exile, the nation was never the same again. Apart from a brief period following the successful rebellion of the Maccabees, the land of Israel, or Judaea as it became known, was no longer the self-governed home of the descendants of Abraham. Rather it was ruled by a succession of pagan powers—the Persians, the Greeks, and the Romans—with garrisons of foreign troops stationed in the land, and the Jews placed under heavy taxation. After further revolts, this time unsuccessful, during the time of Roman rule, almost the entire Jewish population lost their lives, were enslaved, or deported.

Now the promise to Abraham and the other patriarchs was that the 'land' would be given to him and his offspring to enjoy as 'an everlasting possession' (Genesis 17:8; 48:4). Yet during the course of their history the Jews have not held it in their possession for long. Even to this day, although the state of Israel has been re-established, the Israelis only occupy a part of the original land. So if God's promise were true, as we believe it to be, then we are obliged to consider another manner of fulfilment. We are driven to the conclusion that ultimately the promise does not concern the mere physical land of Israel, but something much greater. In the case of the offspring we saw that the fulfilment of the promise clearly came in distinct stages, eventually leading to something considerably greater and more far-reaching—to Christ, the means of the blessing, and to the multitudinous church of all nations. There are both individual and corporate fulfilments of the promise, since the term 'offspring' allows these two senses. We find a similar application with the land promise. In its initial outworking the promise concerned the earthly land of Canaan, a small but then highly productive land ('flowing with milk and honey') in the near east. But it was not God's purpose that this small stretch of land should be the final dwelling-place of his people. Once we understand the offspring of Abraham to be Christ and those numerous believers in Christ, then we are obviously looking for a 'land' of far larger dimensions.

At this point we need to turn to the other sense of *'ereṣ*, which is 'earth'. It is highly significant that in his preaching Jesus declared that 'the meek will inherit the *earth*' (Matthew 5:5). Here the original promise is expanded. The apostle Paul does the same, specifically with respect to the Abrahamic promise, when he writes, 'the promise to Abraham and to his offspring that he would be heir of the *world* was not through the law, but through the righteousness of faith' (Romans 4:13). The Greek term *kosmos*, here translated 'world', may in fact mean the whole created order. It is nothing less than this which is the everlasting possession that God has in store for his people, the offspring of Abraham. We look forward to inhabiting a renewed creation, one that has been set free from the curse, that is, from the effects of the fall (Romans 8:21). And so the apostle Peter, speaking of our future expectation, says that 'in accordance with his promise, we wait for new heavens and a new earth, in which righteousness dwells' (2 Peter 3:13).

That small stretch of land initially occupied by Israel was merely the first step in the larger design of God to give, not just a single land, but the whole earth, and indeed the entire creation, as the possession of his people. The giving of the land to Israel was itself a wonderful gift of divine grace, and yet it was just a token of something much greater to come, which will only reach its complete fulfilment through the gospel of Christ, at the end of the present age when Jesus will return.

Finally, we again draw attention to the way in which the promise of 'land', or 'earth', relates to God's original mandate for humankind at creation, as we saw was the case with the promise of offspring. There God had directed the first man and woman to 'fill the earth [*'ereṣ*] and subdue it' (Genesis 1:28). Once humanity had fallen and the earth itself subjected to the curse, God then conceived of his redemptive plan firstly through the people of Israel and land of Canaan—that is, the 'offspring' and 'land' of the Abrahamic promise. We are expressly told that, in order to see an initial fulfilment of this promise, the Israelites had to 'subdue' the land promised them (e.g. Numbers 32:22; Joshua 18:1), which means to subjugate its occupants. And so it is that, in the fuller and final expression of the promise, the whole earth will be subdued by Christ and his people (cf. Psalms 2:8; 72:8), and the earth, and indeed the entire creation, redeemed and renewed.

The Promises to David

From the time of Abraham we are now transported a thousand years or so into the future to the youngest son of Jesse named David, who became the second king of Israel. Here there occurred another special revelation and another set of promises from God. Before this Israel had gone through a difficult period, that of the Judges. This was a time when there was gross unfaithfulness on the part of Israel, and the situation within the land became almost anarchic. Because of this God allowed his people to be overrun by foreign invaders. But when they cried out to him, he would save them by raising up a special deliverer, or 'judge', to free them from their enemies. Once delivered, however, they would soon fall back into their apostasy. The very last verse of the book of Judges tells us that: 'In those days there was no king in Israel; everyone did what was right in their own eyes' (21:25). Clearly it was perceived that if Israel should have a king, this would rectify the problem.

In this situation, through the mediation of the prophet Samuel, Israel appealed to God for a king. Unfortunately, what they requested was 'a king like all the other nations' (1 Samuel 8:5, 20), in other words, a strong military leader to overthrow the enemy invaders. Such was Saul, Israel's first king, from the tribe of Benjamin. Although showing much promise at first, and although a great warrior, Saul soon showed great weakness in spiritual matters, and proved to be disobedient to the commandments of God. He was eventually replaced by David of Bethlehem, originally a shepherd boy, much more spiritually sensitive than Saul, and described as a man after God's own heart (1 Samuel 13:14). Once David had become established as king over all Israel, and once he had chosen Jerusalem as his capital and brought the ark of God there, the Lord gave him an important message through the prophet Nathan. The special significance of this word from God is shown by the fact that it is the longest divine speech since the revelation of the law at Sinai several books, and several centuries, earlier.

As Genesis 12 is the foundational passage regarding the Abrahamic promises, so 2 Samuel 7 is the key chapter concerning the promises to David. Closely parallel to this, with minor additions and differences in wording, is the seventeenth chapter of 1 Chronicles, which together with 2 Chronicles covers much of the same material found in the books of Samuel and Kings. There is also Psalm 89, which deals again with the self-same subject matter but in a particularly poetic fashion, and to a lesser extent Psalm 132 covers similar ground. At this point the reader would be helped in following the discussion by reading 2 Samuel 7:1–17.

The particular circumstance that led to God making these promises was the desire of David, now that he himself was settled in a palace in Jerusalem, to build a 'house' for God within the capital (2 Samuel 7:1–2). By this he means a 'temple', where the ark of the covenant could be given permanent residence. It is in response to this intention on David's part that God sent the prophet Nathan to deliver the message to David, with the wonderful and far-reaching promises that it contains.

Before taking a closer look at the specific elements involved in the promises, we need to consider two significant matters. The first of these is that although the words 'covenant' and 'oath' do not appear in 2 Samuel 7, it is evident that both of these actually were included in what took place. We know this from elsewhere. Later in the same book, towards the end of his life, David recounted that 'he [God] has made with me an everlasting covenant' (23:5). Also Psalm 89, mentioned above, records that God himself had stated, 'I have made a covenant with my chosen one, I have sworn an oath to my servant David' (v. 3). Psalm 132 similarly says, 'The LORD has sworn in truth to David; he will not turn back from it' (v. 11). So while there is no covenant ritual or oath formula to be seen in 2 Samuel 7, we can be sure that, just as was the case with Abraham, God did in fact give David this extra affirmation of his word.

The second thing we need to understand is that God's promises made to King David are not entirely independent of those matters promised to Abraham a thousand years before. In fact, it could be said that the later promises arise out of the earlier. Already in the development of the divine promises found throughout Genesis mention is made of kings being included among the future offspring of Abraham. God had declared to him that 'kings will come forth from you' (17:6, 16; cf. 35:11). At the close of Genesis it is foretold that, out of the twelve tribes of Israel, the kingship would arise specifically from within the tribe of Judah (49:10). And so when we come to the law of Moses, as revealed in the remaining books of the Pentateuch (the first five books of the Old Testament), we find regulations given that would apply to the future rule of Israelite kings (Deuteronomy 17:14–20). From this we understand that the rule of a king from Judah is an integral element of the divine purpose, and was in mind right from the promises given to Abraham. As we proceed through some of the details of the Davidic promises we will note how certain aspects and also certain words and phrases echo the earlier words of God to

Abraham and the other patriarchs back in Genesis.

The promises made to David, as described in 2 Samuel 7, basically revolve around one particular word, and that is the Hebrew word *bayit*. This is the ordinary word for 'house', or perhaps 'home'. But its meaning may be extended to include those who live in the house, and so it can bear the sense of 'household' or 'family'. When applied to a king this would have the sense of 'dynasty'. So in Britain we speak of the royal family as the 'house of Windsor'. While many English Bibles prefer to keep the translation of *bayit* in this context as 'house', some modern versions, we note, actually render it as 'dynasty' in our chapter (e.g. 2 Samuel 7:16, NJB NLT). Now the first major element of what God announces to David concerns this latter sense, that of 'dynasty'. The second element relates to *bayit* in its more usual sense of 'house', although it applies to God's house rather than David's, as we shall see. The thing to bear in mind is that in each case we are looking at the same Hebrew word.

Besides the two principal aspects of the divine promise just mentioned, there are other ancillary promises which are given first. God tells David, 'I will make your name great' (v. 9). This is in fact the very first promissory statement in the passage. We recall that this is exactly what God had promised to Abraham (Genesis 12:2). As Abraham's name has gone down in history as being the forefather of the Jewish nation, so David's name is remembered for its similar greatness. The royal household reigning in Jerusalem was known for generations to come as 'the house of David' (e.g. 1 Kings 12:19; Isaiah 7:2; Zechariah 12:7), and the city itself was called 'the city of David' (e.g. 2 Samuel 5:7; 1 Kings 2:10; Isaiah 22:9). Still to this day the name of David is evoked by the very appearance of the Israeli flag. This bears the symbol that the Jews refer to as *māgēn dāwîd*, or 'shield of David' (described in English as the 'star of David'). So the name of the king who ruled over Israel three thousand years ago continues to be known and used today. God promises, therefore, that both the name of Abraham and the name of David would be made great, as indeed they are, and it is noteworthy that in the whole of the Old Testament the only other character besides these two whose name is said to be 'great' is that of the Lord God himself (e.g. Psalm 76:1).

God further says to David, 'I will give you rest from all your enemies' (2 Samuel 7:11). Here again there is a connection, albeit indirect, with the Abrahamic promises. Several centuries before David, on the border of the promised land, God had spoken to the now numerous offspring of Abraham of the time when 'the LORD your God gives you rest from all the enemies around you in the land he is giving you to possess as an inheritance' (Deuteronomy 25:19). They were granted some measure of rest towards the end of Joshua's lifetime (cf. Joshua 21:44). However, as the reigns of Saul and David both show, there was the continuous threat of invasion by nearby nations that these kings had to contend with. In fact the very next chapter in 2 Samuel (chapter 8) deals with the military victories of David over certain of these foreign enemies. A complete state of rest from enemies had evidently not been achieved at the time the promises were made to David, but it is this that the Lord promises him, and which shortly comes to pass. We also note in this context how this promise of rest from enemies made to David actually affects the whole nation of Israel. In these verses of 2 Samuel 7 the fates of the people and their king are in fact inseparably linked (vv. 10–11), something we will return to in due course.

We will now look at the two distinct aspects of the divine promises concerning the *bayit*. The first, as we said, relates to David's house or dynasty, and the second to the house of God, so we will treat these under two separate sub-headings.

The House of David

King Saul, who ruled over Israel immediately before David, had not been granted a dynasty to succeed him. This was no doubt due to his extreme disregard for the will of God. To David, however, God made this promise: 'The LORD declares to you that the LORD will make a house for you. When your days are fulfilled and you lie down with your fathers, I will raise up your offspring after you, who will come forth from your body ["loins"], and I will establish his kingdom' (2 Samuel 7:11b–12). We again observe connections with the Abrahamic promises. The phrase 'your offspring after you' (*zarăkā 'aḥărêkā*) is the same as that which occurs repeatedly in the earlier promises (e.g. Genesis 17:7; 35:12; 48:4). Here is that same word *zera'*, literally meaning 'seed', or 'offspring', in both an individual and collective sense. Also, the particular description of this offspring as one 'who will come forth your body' (*'ăšer yēṣē' mimmē 'eykā*) is found elsewhere uniquely of the offspring to be born to Abraham in accordance with the divine promise (Genesis 15:4). Concerning this 'house' of David God further declares to him: 'Your house and your kingdom will stand firm for ever before me; your throne will be established for ever' (2 Samuel 7:16). From these words we understand that God did not simply mean that David's immediate offspring would reign after him, but the promise applied to a whole dynasty, in fact the everlasting rule of the house of David (cf. v. 29). This was an amazing promise and wonderful privilege for the former shepherd boy.

It would appear, moreover, that the promise is ultimately unconditional. With respect to David's future offspring God told him, 'when he commits iniquity, I will chastise him with the rod of men and the blows of the sons of men, but my steadfast love will not depart from him, as I took it away from Saul, whom I removed from before you' (2 Samuel 7:14–15). What this means is that although individual kings in the line of David may commit sin, as all those Davidic kings recorded in the Old Testament in fact did to some degree or other, or even fall into total apostasy, as several of them did, there would nevertheless be a continuance of the basic promise. So one particular king might be punished for his particular misdeeds, but the faithfulness of God would remain with the dynasty in general. There is considerable assurance here of the ongoing maintenance of the promise.

Two further elements within the promise have yet to be mentioned. One of these is that the king has a special relationship with God. The Lord said to David regarding the offspring that 'I will be his father, and he will be my son' (2 Samuel 7:14). These are extremely significant words. In the first place, it should be understood that the relationship spoken of here is metaphorical. God, of course, is not the father of the king in any biological sense. What it is speaking of is a special intimacy, like that of a loving father with a devoted son. God will treat the king as a father does a child. One could say that God 'adopts' the human king as his son. This is most probably the originally intended sense of Psalm 2:7 (where God says to the king he has installed on Zion: 'You are my son; today I have begotten you'). The significance of all this lies in the fact that before these words spoken to David God already had a human son. Back at the time of the exodus from Egypt God had previously proclaimed the whole people descended from Abraham to be his son: 'Israel is my son', he said, 'my firstborn' (Exodus 4:22). The Israelite nation, out of all the nations of the earth, was especially chosen, or adopted, to be that closest to God, his 'firstborn' (*beḵôr*) through which he would ultimately bring about his purpose of redemption. Now at the time of David that special place is being granted to the king in David's line. It is as though the promise to Abraham regarding his offspring, which over time increased to become a great nation, was now being completely focussed into the one person of the Davidic king. Each successive king descended from David was henceforth God's especially adopted 'son'. Concerning this royal son God declared:

> He will cry out to me, 'You are my Father, my God, and the rock of my salvation'. I will also make him the firstborn [*bᵉkôr*], the highest of the kings of the earth. My steadfast love I will keep for him forever, and my covenant with him will stand firm. I will establish his offspring for ever, and his throne as the days of heaven. (Psalm 89:26–29)

So here we see a clear and notable development in the original Abrahamic promise. It is not that the original promise is being set aside in any way. The Davidic king, being of the tribe of Judah, was every bit also a descendent of Abraham, and so included within the terms of the patriarchal promises. It is just that now, in the divine wisdom, the final goal of those earlier promises—for all nations of the earth to be blessed through the offspring of Abraham—was to be fulfilled specifically through the royal house of David. It is for this reason that in another psalm, one that concerns the king, the precise words of the Abrahamic blessing are ascribed to this royal person: 'All nations will be blessed through him' (Psalm 72:17). The king, then, embodies the entire Abrahamic offspring and God's purpose with them, and it is for this reason that it was said above that their destinies are intimately intertwined.

There is one extremely important consequence of the king being God's adopted 'son'. If a father-son relationship exists between the two, as there is also a father-son relationship between David and his promised successor, then the dominion that the son receives will be that of his father. He does not need to create a kingdom of his own. With regard to David as father, God speaks to him of his future offspring's kingdom both as '*his* kingdom' (v. 12), that of his son, and as '*your* kingdom' (v. 16), that is, the kingdom of David. So when it comes to this relationship between the divine father and the human son, they too share in one and the same kingdom and rule. This is expressly spelled out in the 1 Chronicles 17 parallel passage, where in one moment God describes the kingdom of the Davidic son as '*his* kingdom' (v. 11), and then as '*my* kingdom' (v. 14). It is a fact then that the kingdom of Israel is in a real sense the kingdom of God, and the throne of its king is God's throne. This is clearly stated for us in verses such as 1 Chronicles 28:5, where David says, 'the LORD … has chosen my son Solomon to sit on the throne of the kingdom of the LORD over Israel'; and 1 Chronicles 29:23, where the chronicler writes, 'Solomon sat on the throne of the LORD as king in place of his father David'. What we see in this emerging Davidic kingdom of Israel therefore is nothing other than the beginnings of the kingdom of God on earth, with a human king on its throne through whom all nations will be blessed.

The last detail we note concerning the royal offspring and the kingdom is that this dynasty and rule would be 'for ever'. This is emphasised a number of times (2 Samuel 7:13, 16, 25, 29; Psalm 89:4, 28, 29, 36, 37). The divine promise speaks of an eternal kingdom, governed by an equally everlasting house of David. When it comes to the question of fulfilment, as we now do, this eternal perspective of the promise is important to bear in mind.

So in what way does God's promise to David come to be fulfilled? At this point we need to recall the manner in which the Abrahamic promises found fulfilment. In the first instance there was Isaac. He was, as the Genesis narrative makes clear, the offspring that Abraham anticipated according to the terms of the promise. But the fulfilment did not end there. The single offspring of Abraham grew in time to become a multitudinous offspring. Similarly with regard to this Davidic promise, it is David's son Solomon who initially occupies his father's throne, as verses cited above from 1 Chronicles 28:5 and 29:23 plainly state. But Solomon dies and his throne is passed on to his son Rehoboam (1 Kings 11:43), then to his son Abijam (14:31), and so on throughout the history of the Judaean monarchy. While this was so, the fact is that the blessing promised to come through this royal household, namely the salvation of people from all nations, never became a reality. It certainly did not come about through Solomon, David's immediate offspring. Although his reign was famous for its wealth and splendour, and although foreigners came from afar to listen to his great wisdom, Solomon later sinned against the Lord by worshipping the idols of his many foreign wives (1 Kings 11:1–6). While some were better than others, in actual fact none of the Davidic kings whose reigns are related in the books of Kings were able to govern Israel strictly according to God's law, nor usher in the divine blessing for the Gentiles. So, as with the offspring of Abraham, of which neither Isaac nor the nation descended from him were the ultimate fulfilment of the promise, that is to say, were not *the* offspring of Abraham, we find a similar situation with respect to the promised son of David. On account of their failings and the spiritual condition of the people they ruled, and whom the king embodied, the reign of the line of Davidic kings was eventually suspended. This, as we have previously said, happened at the time of the Babylonian exile. The people did return, and the descendant of David was among them, in the person of Zerubbabel (cf. 1 Chronicles 3:19), but he was no longer a king. The biological line of descent continued, but the authority to reign was gone, being replaced by the domination of foreign rulers.

Yet God had plainly said that the promised reign of the Davidic offspring would last for ever. His steadfast love towards the house of David, God had declared, would never completely fail. And so there had to be a future fulfilment beyond the time of the Old Testament. The Hebrew prophets themselves looked forward to such a thing. Through their revelations they proclaimed the coming of a future king in David's line (e.g. Isaiah 9:7; Jeremiah 33:17; Amos 9:11). Yet unlike his predecessors this particular king would reign in righteousness (Isaiah 32:1; Jeremiah 23:5), being endowed with the fulness of the Spirit of the Lord (Isaiah 11:1–5).

As a brief but relevant aside, we note that since it was the common practice for a king to be anointed with olive oil before taking up his reign (cf. 1 Samuel 16:13), the royal figure became known in Hebrew as the 'Messiah' (*māšîaḥ*, 'anointed one'). In Greek the equivalent term was *christos*, from which of course the word 'Christ' is derived. This title was used of David during his own lifetime (e.g. 2 Samuel 22:15; Psalm 132:17), and became one of the titles given to the anticipated future king descended from him (e.g. Daniel 9:25).

As we trace the biological lineage of David over the centuries following the close of the Old Testament period, it brings us to one particular individual, one who clearly fulfils the promises to his great royal forefather and the prophetic expectation. This person is Jesus. After there being no Davidic king to rule Israel for nearly six centuries, we read of the birth of the one who in the very first verse of the New Testament is not only the 'son of Abraham', but also the 'son of David' (Matthew 1:1). In the birth of this person the fulfilments of the Abrahamic and Davidic promises converge. And in that same verse this Jesus is given the royal title, 'the Messiah/Christ' (cf. NASB NRSV NLT, 'Jesus the Messiah'). The genealogical lineage of Jesus that immediately follows (vv. 2–17) gives prominence to both Abraham and David. It commences with the former. It is then grouped by the Gospel writer into three sections, the central one of which begins with David and ends with the last of the

Davidic kings before the exile. The Gospel writer Luke provides us with a second genealogy of Jesus, which also gives his Davidic descent, although differing from that found in Matthew. If, as many biblical scholars understand, the two New Testament genealogies of Christ, appearing in the Gospels of Matthew and Luke, represent those of both Joseph and Mary, then the former (Matthew 1:2–17) would be that of legal succession. Joseph was not Jesus' biological father, but Jesus was, to all practical purposes, regarded as his son when it came to the legal matter of heirship. So the royal lineage from David, through his immediate son Solomon (v. 6), passed to Jesus via Joseph. The other genealogy (Luke 3:23–38), being that of Mary, would present the actual biological line of descent, through another of David's immediate sons Nathan (v. 31).

The conception and birth of Jesus was announced in advance to Mary, his mother, by an angel sent from God. The words of this heavenly messenger, named Gabriel, are remarkable. Luke records them for us:

> 'Do not be afraid, Mary, for you have found favour with God. And behold, you will conceive in your womb and give birth to a son, and you shall call his name Jesus. He will be great and will be called the Son of the Most High. The Lord God will give him the throne of his father David, and he will reign over the house of Jacob forever, and his kingdom will have no end'. (Luke 1:30–33)

To anyone who has read the promises of 2 Samuel 7 the connections are obvious. The angel alludes to at least three elements of God's promises to David—the child would be God's 'Son', who would receive the throne of his great forefather David, and there would be no end to his kingdom. A crucial distinction, however, lies in the fact that while the original promise to David spoke of his dynasty, or 'house', as continuing for ever in the form of a succession of different kings, the angel here says '*he* will reign … for ever'. The offspring of David has now plainly become individualised, which is to say, the eternal promised rule will be exercised by a single one of David's sons. And to do this, by implication, this son himself must be one that lives for ever, and that is only true of Jesus, who at this resurrection once and for all conquered death.

Some months later, since both Mary and Joseph were of David's line, as we saw above, the two of them were required to travel to Bethlehem, the town of David (1 Samuel 17:12), to register for the census commanded by the Roman authorities. At this time the ancestral records of the Jews were stored in the temple in Jerusalem, so it would be known who was descended from which family and where they needed to go for the purposes of the census. It was shortly after their arrival in the place of David's own origin that Christ himself was born into this world (Matthew 2:1).

So Jesus came to the Jews as their long-awaited Messiah, the ultimate fulfilment of the promise given to David a thousand years earlier. Many, though far from all, recognised this. The diseased and afflicted appealed to him as the 'Son of David' (e.g. Matthew 15:22; Mark 10:48). The crowds who welcomed his entry into Jerusalem cried out 'Hosanna to the Son of David' (Matthew 21:15), and 'Blessed is the coming kingdom of our father David' (Mark 11:10). The apostles later preached Jesus as the one who would restore David's suspended dynasty (Acts 15:16; cf. 2:30). Paul wrote of him as such in his letters (e.g. Romans 1:3; 2 Timothy 2:8), and in John's apocalyptic visions Jesus also described himself as 'the Root and Offspring of David' (Revelation 22:16; cf. 5:5).

But when would Christ actually sit upon this throne? When would his kingdom come in all its fulness? Evidently, in the divine wisdom, God has purposed that the kingly rule of the Messiah would come in stages. In brief, we see that having completed his ministry on earth, having suffered and died for sin, and been raised to everlasting life, Jesus ascended into heaven where he sat down on his Father's throne, at his right hand (Hebrews 12:2; Revelation 3:21; 7:17; 12:5). So since that time, and still now, he reigns as king, seated upon an eternal heavenly throne (cf. Hebrews 1:8), ruling over a spiritual kingdom, which includes his church. Yet we continue to pray for the kingdom to come, to come fully that is, and for his will to be done here in all the earth (Matthew 6:10). It is at Christ's second advent, at some unspecified future date, known only to God, that this final stage of his rule will commence—not only over heaven but over the entire created order (*kosmos*), now restored from the effects of sin and death, and from the spiritual forces of evil that have dominated it for so long. At that time, according to John's apocalypse, a New Jerusalem will appear upon earth (Revelation 21:2), in which is situated the 'throne of God and the Lamb' (22:1, 3), that is, a single throne of Father and Son.

Moreover, just as there was a corporate aspect to the ultimate fulfilment to the Abrahamic promises, so too with the Davidic. Jesus, we said, is *the* offspring of Abraham, but all who believe in him are counted as his 'body', are included in him, and are equally counted as the offspring of Abraham. Above we noted that the destinies of the king and his people are inextricably intertwined, and in the final outworking of the promises to David that even extends to the authority to rule. The New Testament tells us that in that future age the royal dominion exercised by Christ, the eternal Davidic king, will be shared by his people. Paul plainly says, 'we will also reign with him' (2 Timothy 2:12), and the apostle John heard the words of a new song declaring that the redeemed 'will reign on earth' (Revelation 5:10). Jesus too gave this remarkable promise to his followers: 'He who overcomes, I will allow him to sit with me on my throne, just as I myself overcame and sat down with my Father on his throne' (Revelation 3:21). How amazing is that! God the Father, the Son, and believers will all share one and the same throne.

Last of all in this section, and again we saw something similar with respect to the earlier promises to Abraham, there is a connection with the words of God to the first human beings at the time of their creation. There God said to them, 'fill the earth, and subdue it; and *rule* over the fish of the sea and over the birds of the sky and over every living thing that moves on the earth' (Genesis 1:28). Humanity was created to exercise God's 'rule' over all creation, but their ability to do so was significantly diminished at the fall. Now this dominion is fully restored, with Christ and his people reigning over all things visible and invisible in the new heavens and earth.

The House of God

The second aspect of the divine promise to David concerns the fact that the promised offspring would also build a 'house' for God. It had been David's original intention, we recall, that he himself should construct a temple in Jerusalem. But God told him, 'I will raise up your offspring after you, who will come forth from your body ... he is the one who will build a house for my name' (2 Samuel 7:12–13). So David's offspring, according to the promise, would also be the temple-builder.

Like the previous promise this also concerned a *bayit*. Here, however, the 'house' was to be a dwelling-place for God upon earth, much more permanent than that of the tent, or tabernacle, in which the ark of the covenant had previously resided. Any reader familiar with the Old Testament history will know that it was David's immediate son and successor Solomon who built the great temple in Jerusalem as a sanctuary for the God of Israel. His father David found a suitable location, and gathered much of the material that would be used, but it was Solomon who put into effect the actual construction. This is recorded for us in 1 Kings 6 and 7. This temple, or 'house of the LORD', as it was called (1 Kings 6:1), was indeed built on a very grand scale, with various courts and chambers, pillars and panelling. Gold and bronze ornamentation was in evidence everywhere. It was adorned with such splendour as the edifice was seen as God's dwelling upon earth. Once it was completed the cloud of the glory of the Lord came and entered it (1 Kings 8:10–11) as a visible token of the divine presence, as had happened with respect to the tabernacle, that earlier portable, tent-like sanctuary (Exodus 40:34–35). This cloud is commonly referred to by biblical scholars (following the ancient Jewish rabbis) as the 'Shekinah glory'. Although not in itself a term that appears in the Bible, this is in fact a very suitable descriptive phrase. The word 'Shekinah' is derived from the Hebrew word *šākan* (*š* is pronounced 'sh'), which simply means 'dwell', especially, though not exclusively, in a tent. So 'Shekinah glory' could be taken as meaning something like the 'in-dwelling glory'. In seeing this glory fill the newly raised temple, Solomon and the people of Israel would understand that God had now taken up residence in this 'house' in the midst of his people.

It cannot, however, be the case that this temple in Jerusalem was the ultimate fulfilment of what was promised to David and his offspring. Certainly both the succession of Solomon and the Jerusalem temple were initial realisations of the divine promises, but just as Solomon was not *the* son of David in the fullest sense, as we have seen, in the same way this 'house' he had built was not what God had in mind as his final dwelling among his people. I believe Solomon himself was aware of this fact. 1 Kings chapter 8 contains Solomon's lengthy prayer at the dedication of the temple, during the course of which he exclaims to God: 'The heavens, even the highest heavens, cannot contain you. How much less this house that I have built!' (v. 27). The king clearly recognised that a building made of stones and cedar wood, although ornately decorated with gold and bronze, was by a long stretch no adequate place for the divine being to inhabit. How could a merely physical, man-made construction claim to contain the divine presence? Surely it did not. That Solomon's temple was not *the* dwelling-place of the promise is further shown by the impermanence of this house. Some four centuries after it was built God allowed the enemies of his people to destroy it (2 Kings 25:8–17). As the Davidic kings recorded in the Old Testament failed to meet the requirements for the manner of king God had purposed, so too the Jerusalem temple fell short of being a proper dwelling for God. Just as there was a greater king to come, there would also be a greater temple.

It was Jesus, the later and greater son of David, who would eventually come to establish a house for God. And Jesus, according to the teaching of the New Testament, fulfilled this in two ways. The Gospel of John especially presents the very body of Jesus as a sanctuary in which God dwells. When the divine Son of God entered the world he assumed our human nature, from the moment of his conception. This meant that within that body of flesh there was located in a very real manner the Deity of the Second Person of the Trinity. Hard as it is for us to understand such a thing, this is what we are led to believe. John first hints at this in the prologue to his Gospel. Having introduced us (1:1) to the divine Being who was to come into the world under the title of the 'Word' (*Logos*), the apostle tells us that 'the Word became flesh', that is, took upon himself our humanity, 'and he dwelt among us' (v. 14). The Greek verb 'dwell' here is *skēnoō*, which is derived from the noun *skēnē*, meaning 'tent' or 'dwelling'. This itself is closely related (via the Semitic language Phoenician) to the Hebrew term *šākan*, described above, from which we get 'Shekinah'. So when John penned those words 'he *dwelt* among us', those readers sensitive to the Old Testament would appreciate that he was making an allusion to the idea of God coming to dwell in a temple. This is confirmed by John's immediately following words in the same verse: 'and we saw his *glory*'. We recall that in the Old Testament it was through the visible appearance of the divine glory that it became known to onlookers that God had now taken up residence in his newly built sanctuary. This is what John is claiming for the man born as Jesus, the Word made flesh.

What is introduced in quite a subtle way in John's prologue is in fact spelled out in plain terms a short while later in the same Gospel. In chapter 2, when Jesus was in Jerusalem, he drove the money-changers, sellers of doves, and cattle out of the temple (vv. 15–16). When asked by the Jews for a 'sign' (that is, a miracle) to demonstrate his authority for doing such things (v. 18), Jesus said, 'Destroy this temple, and in three days I will raise it up' (v. 19). The Jews were no doubt puzzled at this and further asked, 'It has taken forty-six years to build this temple, and will you raise it up in three days?' (v. 20). They naturally thought he was talking about the physical temple made of stones, but John then adds the all-important explanation: 'But he was speaking of *the temple of his body*' (v. 21). This body, his human nature in which divinity resided, was the temple Christ meant. This would indeed be destroyed, at his crucifixion, but in three days, Jesus would raise it up again, at his resurrection. Jesus, we note, as well as describing his body as the temple, also presents himself as the builder. We must not overlook this fact—'*I will raise it* [the temple of his body] up in three days', he says (cf. John 10:17–18). He is the true temple-builder, who establishes a fit and proper dwelling-place for God upon earth.

The apostle Paul, too, had a similar view of the human body of Jesus. In a remarkable verse in Colossians he wrote that 'in him [Jesus] all the fulness of Deity dwells in bodily form' (2:9). I find these words absolutely astounding. Paul describes a truth that, let's face it, surpasses all human comprehension, and he does so in a most emphatic way. He is not just saying that the 'Deity' dwells in a body, but the '*fulness* of Deity', and it is not just the 'fulness of Deity', but '*all* the fulness of Deity' (see also Colossians 1:19). How much more could the apostle possibly stress that the divine Person residing within Christ was God in the fullest sense of the word?

But how can Paul's statement be true? If, as Solomon declared, even the highest heavens could not contain God, how could it be possible for a human body to do so? Of course no one can give a complete answer to this question. I do believe, however, that at least part of the answer lies in the composition of human nature. To be truly human, as Jesus himself became, means to possess a nature with elements that are both physical and non-physical. Human beings are endowed with something we call a 'spirit', and also with spiritual faculties (like rationality). The physical and the spiritual are quite different components of human nature, yet they are perfectly compatible, since they both obviously pertain to a single human individual. God's own nature is described in Scripture as being 'spirit' (John 4:24). God too has a whole range of spiritual faculties and qualities, though none that are physical. I believe that if God is spirit, and we too each possess a spiritual dimension to our nature, there is a point of commonality between the divine and the human. This is something which is not the case with a temple made of stones and wood, which is purely physical. Nor is it the case with the highest heavens, in the sense of the stars and galaxies, which likewise consist solely of physical substance. But when we come to a human being there is something existing within that nature which allows a uniting to the divine. It is this, I believe, that makes it possible for Jesus to be, in a very real sense, a temple of God. As his human nature consisted of both the physical and the spiritual, God could be perfectly joined to that nature in the latter of these two. And this being so, just as our own bodies accommodate our spiritual beings, so the body of Jesus houses the spiritual being who is God. 'In him', Paul says, 'all the fulness of Deity dwells in bodily form'. Oh, the depth of the riches of the wisdom God! How unfathomable are his ways!

Finally, Jesus builds a house for God in a second way. Like the other promises there is also a corporate aspect. Jesus makes his own literal, physical body a temple for God, but he also builds a temple from his extended body, the community of those who are 'in him' through faith, by which I mean the church. This, of course, is the church as a body of people who believe, not a building or institution. 'I will build my church', said Jesus (Matthew 16:18), and it is clear from the New Testament that this church presently serves as Christ's earthly 'body' and is therefore related to what has just been stated about his own body. Believers are expressly said to be 'the body of Christ' (1 Corinthians 12:27a; Ephesians 4:12), or 'his body' (Ephesians 1:23; Colossians 1:24), and each believer is individually a member of that body (1 Corinthians 12:27b; Ephesians 5:30). So the words 'he was speaking of the temple of his body', discussed above, by way of extension, apply to the church also.

In other places in the New Testament the church is actually described as the dwelling of God or in temple-like language. The apostle Paul's classic passage for this is found in the Epistle to the Ephesians. Addressing Gentile Christians he declares:

> So then you are no longer strangers and foreigners, but you are fellow-citizens with the saints and members of the household of God, having been built on the foundation of the apostles and prophets, Christ Jesus himself being the cornerstone. In him the whole building, being fitted together, is growing into a holy temple in the Lord, in whom you also are being built together into a dwelling-place of God in the Spirit'. (2:19–22)

The language here is unmistakable. The church is plainly a something that is being 'built'. In real terms of course the sense of this is organic, since the church, as the community of believers, is an entity consisting of living beings and so is 'growing'. It is being built as a 'holy temple', to be God's 'dwelling-place'. We note that this latter word *katoikētērion* ('dwelling-place') is used several times (in the Septuagint, the Greek version of the Old Testament) in Solomon's dedicatory prayer for the temple he built (1 Kings 8:39, 43, 49). Paul further adds the important fact that the means by which God will abide in this temple will be through the Spirit.

The foregoing passage from Ephesians relates to other verses in Paul's letters which speak of God's Spirit living in his church. Addressing believers collectively, Paul states, 'Do you not know that you are the temple of God and that God's Spirit lives in you? If anyone destroys the temple of God, God will destroy him. For the temple of God is holy, and you are that temple' (1 Corinthians 3:16–17). In a similar verse, the apostle seems to be saying that even the body of each individual Christian is a temple: 'Do you not know that your body is a temple of the Holy Spirit within you?' (1 Corinthians 6:19).

In this context we remember the important events that happened at Pentecost (Acts 2), when the Holy Spirit came upon the early believers. Many would describe this as the birth of the church, which it is. But I also see it as the inauguration of that church as the divine temple in which God dwells through his Spirit. We remember that in the case of the earlier sanctuaries, the tabernacle built by Moses and the stone temple built by Solomon, when they were completed the glory of the Lord came and settled upon them. At these events the divine glory is basically described as a 'cloud' (Exodus 40:34–35; 1 Kings 8:10–12), yet we know that this was no ordinary cloud but one tinged with a 'fire' that radiated light (see Exodus 24:16–17; Ezekiel 10:40), and most probably took on the basic form of a pillar (cf. Exodus 14:24). As there was this manifestation at the inauguration of the Old Testament sanctuaries, so too when the Spirit came upon the church there was an outward visible manifestation. We are told that 'There appeared to them what looked like tongues of fire that separated and came to rest upon each of them' (Acts 2:3). What is of significance here is that the tongues of fire, first appearing together, divided and settled on each person present. In other words, what was true for the Old Testament sanctuary, that it was a dwelling for God, is now true for every individual Christian. Both collectively and singly believers are the temple of God.

On this occasion at Pentecost, the new church's chief spokesman was the apostle Peter (Acts 2:14, 37). Interestingly, in the first of his letters the same apostle wrote to believers that 'you also, like living stones, are being built into a spiritual house' (1 Peter 3:5). Here again, in the words 'spiritual house', we clearly recognise temple language. This is how Peter sees the church. It is a spiritual house, or dwelling, because God is living in it through his Spirit. Yet unlike the old temple in Jerusalem, which was made of inanimate stones, each stone in this new house is 'living', that is, a human being, and by implication, since these 'stones' make up the house in its entirety, God must be dwelling in these living stones themselves. This is an incredible thought—that God would wish to make men, women, and young people, to be his dwelling! Besides being a great wonder and privilege, it also reminds us that a temple is a *holy* place, and our bodies therefore ought to be reserved for holy purposes.

At this point we bring this discussion to a close. There is a fascinating vision right at the end of the Bible of the New Jerusalem (Revelation 21–22), which also has much to teach us about God's temple, specifically within the context of the new heaven and earth. However, since it would take a great deal of space to examine the quite complex imagery involved in this vision, we must conclude our study of God's house here.

In this chapter it has hopefully been shown how the two promissory passages, Genesis 12 and 2 Samuel 7, are absolutely foundational for understanding the overall biblical message, a message that reaches its climax in the person and work of Jesus Christ, son of David, son of Abraham. The New Testament gospel we find to be deeply rooted in Old Testament promises and cannot be fully comprehended without them. Moreover, since the Gospels demonstrate that Christ came as the one who would fulfil those ancient promises, we can be confident of his promised future return from heaven to bring about their final and absolute fulfilment in a wonderfully renewed creation.

Suggestions for Further Reading

Dumbrell, William J. *Covenant and Creation: A Theology of the Old Testament Covenants* (Carlisle: Paternoster, 1984).

Goldsworthy, Graeme. *According to Plan: The Unfolding Revelation of God in the Bible* (Leicester: Inter-Varsity Press, 1991).

Kaiser, Jr., Walter C. *The Promise-Plan of God: A Biblical Theology of the Old and New Testaments* (Grand Rapids, Michigan: Zondervan, 2008).

Robinson, O. Palmer. *The Christ of the Covenants* (Phillipsburg, New Jersey: Presbyterian and Reformed, 1980).

6. PROPHECY

When we hear the word 'prophecy' in English, we think primarily of foretelling the future. This is also an aspect of what is meant by prophecy in the Bible, but its broader sense is 'the speaking of a divine revelation', regardless of whether it concerns present or future happenings. A prophet, therefore, may be one who passes on a message from God to his people in their current situation, or who tells them of things to come in the near or distant future. This being so, it should come as no surprise that, for the Jews, those books we often refer to as the 'historical' books of the Old Testament, such as Joshua, Judges, Samuel, and so forth, are included by them among the prophetic books. The narrative books from Joshua to 2 Kings as well as Isaiah, Jeremiah, Ezekiel, and the twelve Minor Prophets, are all grouped together as 'the Prophets'. If they wish to make a distinction they describe the first portion as 'the former prophets', and the second as 'the latter prophets', but all are among the prophets. It is probable that even Jesus and his disciples, being Jews, viewed the Hebrew Scriptures in this way. In Luke 24:44 Jesus refers to the sacred writings as 'the Law of Moses, the Prophets, and the Psalms'.

Seeing that our subject is that of the Old Testament witness to Christ, who came several centuries after these books were written, we will be restricting our discussion of prophecy to its predictive function, that is to say, the way in which the prophets foretold the future. We begin by drawing attention to the obvious fact that human beings, of themselves, are quite unable to see into the future in such a manner. For sure it might be possible, using the facts and figures available, for someone with the necessary expertise to predict something like a stock-market crash or the outbreak of war some time before it actually happens. But this is not prophecy. This is simply examining the present data and trends and following them through to their logical conclusion. When we speak of the Hebrew prophets, however, we are talking about people endowed with a gift that far transcends ordinary human insight or foresight. These were men, and in some cases women, who foresaw not only what was going to take place later in their own lifetimes, but also many years and even several centuries in the future. Their prophecies were, moreover, quite specific, as we shall see. The Bible itself attributes this ability to the Spirit of God at work in the prophet (e.g. Numbers 11:25; Nehemiah 9:30; Joel 2:28; Zechariah 7:12; Luke 1:67; Acts 11:28; 2 Peter 1:21).

If the Bible is indeed the word of God, then supernatural knowledge, such as prophecy, is something that we would expect to find within it. So theologians have traditionally seen the presence of prophecy in the pages of Scripture as one of the 'motives of credibility', as they would call it, for the Christian faith. This phrase simply means 'reasons to believe'. If prophetic predictions actually exist within the Bible, then it serves to demonstrate that this is not a book of mere human origin and, along with other similar 'motives', such as miracles, it lends credence to the things that Christians believe. Interestingly, God himself uses a similar form of argument in the prophecies of Isaiah. He himself is able to declare the end from the beginning (Isaiah 41:26; 42:9; 45:21; 46:10; 48:3), while there are no such predictions to be found among the unbelieving nations (43:9). Israel, therefore, should put their trust in him, and not in the false gods of the Gentiles.

Before we come to prophecy concerning Christ, we first draw attention to the fact that numerous prophecies exist in the Old Testament whose fulfilment also occurs within that Testament. Prophecy is not only a movement from the Old Testament to the New or beyond, but a prediction and its fulfilment may each appear in the Old. Such is the case, for example, with the divine revelation to Abraham that his offspring, the people of Israel, would become slaves in a foreign land (Genesis 15:13–14). The prediction becomes fact several hundred years later (Exodus 1:8–11). Sceptics, of course, respond to this by claiming that the passage containing the prediction, here in Genesis, must have been written after the event foretold had occurred. So rather than the account in Genesis being something that precedes Exodus, which is the order found in the Bible, they argue that the exodus took place before the Genesis passage was written, and that is how there can be a foretelling of a future event in the latter. Since supernatural prophecy is denied on their part, to resort to such a re-ordering of the texts is an absolute necessity, and this method of explaining away prophecy is unfortunately rife, not just among sceptics and atheists, but also within modern biblical scholarship that tends to be predominantly rationalistic in nature.

The fact is, however, that not all Old Testament prophecies allow this kind of juggling with the dates. While it might be relatively easy to resort to this with matters described in Genesis and Exodus, as these are two consecutive books, at other times it is stretching things too far. In the early part of the book of Isaiah there is an extended prophecy of the overthrow of Babylon (13:1–14:23). Isaiah was a prophet who was active in the latter part of the eighth century BCE, while the event he was foretelling took place in 539 BCE. Again some of a more sceptical mind-set might claim that these prophecies were added later to the book of Isaiah after the fall of Babylon had actually occurred. But what evidence is there for that? None whatsoever. This is not a conclusion that is demanded by, or supported by, the text of Isaiah itself. Instead it merely shows an *a priori* commitment (that is, reasoning derived from a preceding assumption rather than from observable evidence) to the denial of supernatural knowledge. This position demands that its adherents then take measures as they do in assigning late dates to the writing of the prophecies. They have no other option.

The Isaiah prophecy about Babylon is not the least of the problems the sceptics have to face. The Old Testament also foretells events that occurred after the close of the Old Testament age. Such is the case, for example, with the prophecies of Daniel. In both chapter 2 and chapter 7 of the book that bears his name Daniel described visions of great earthly kingdoms, beginning with Babylon and extending into the future. The kingdom that is greatest of all is the one that comes fourth in the visions. In chapter 2 we read that 'there will be a fourth kingdom, strong as iron; inasmuch as iron crushes and shatters everything, it will shatter and break all the other [kingdoms]' (v. 40). Later in the corresponding vision of chapter 7 Daniel writes, 'there before me was a fourth beast—dreadful and terrifying and extremely strong. It had large iron teeth; it devoured and shattered its victims and trampled what remained with its feet' (v. 7). Here we evidently have two varying prophetic portrayals of the same kingdom. In both visions it is specifically the 'fourth' in the sequence, it is 'strong', each has the element of 'iron', and in both cases it is said to 'shatter' its enemies. It is evidently an entity of exceptional power. Which worldly kingdom fits this description? Since Daniel saw these visions during the time of the Babylonian empire, we may take Babylon as the first kingdom. In fact Daniel 2:38 explicitly says that this is the case. Following the overthrow of this empire, the Medo-Persian empire held sway, and that in turn was succeeded by that of the Greeks. There can be little serious doubt that the fourth kingdom, which is represented as the mightiest of them all, is that of Rome. The influence of Rome did not begin to reach the eastern Mediterranean until the first century BCE. And the usual date given for the founding of the actual Roman empire is 27 BCE (when the senate and people of Rome instated Octavian, also known as Augustus, as its first emperor). Now it stands as an indisputable fact that the book of Daniel was in existence long before the establishment of Rome as a world empire. This is proved by the fact that portions of this prophetic book were found among the Dead Sea Scrolls dating from the second century BCE.

When it comes to the matter of Old Testament prophecies relating to Jesus Christ, we are of course looking far beyond the era in which these Hebrew books were written to a time which lay several hundred years in the future. In such a case, to assign the composition of the prophecies to a time after the events they predict is patently not an option. Yet the prophecies are there, not just a few but many (some would say over 200), and they are not mere generalisations but are frequently quite specific. The prophets did not just speak of a golden age to come in vague terms. Rather they foretold the coming of a Saviour and what he would accomplish in some detail. Some of these details are major, but some are of less importance. It is this wide range of various aspects of Christ's life and ministry that the prophets foresaw which further corroborates the supernatural nature of their foresight.

Here it is appropriate to comment upon an important development regarding the books of the Hebrew Scriptures that occurred during the interval between the two Testaments. During this period there took place what we refer to as the Jewish 'diaspora'. This simply means the spreading of Jewish communities among the lands of the Gentiles. In many major cities throughout the Mediterranean world, and further east into Asia, there were now Jews. Where there was a Jewish community there would also be a synagogue, a place where they would gather for worship and for the reading and study of their Scriptures. At this time, the language of wider communication was Greek, and those Jews who traded with their Gentile neighbours would most certainly have learned this language, and in time even to have used it as much as their own mother tongue or more so. Significantly, two centuries or thereabouts before Christ the writings of the Old Testament began to be translated into Greek, a version we commonly call the Septuagint (which means 'seventy', since according to tradition the first translation of the law of Moses from Hebrew into Greek was carried out by seventy translators). So we eventually arrive at the situation where the Jewish Scriptures, rather than being recited in Hebrew, were now being read in Greek during the course of the synagogue services among the Jews of the diaspora. What this meant was that Gentiles were now able to hear and understand the message of the Old Testament, including the prophecies. What was happening, in effect, was part of the divine preparation for the coming of the Christ. Unlike other ancient writings which were claimed to contain prophetic mysteries, such as the Sibylline Oracles, the books of the Hebrew prophets were now published abroad. They were not held as the possession of a specially initiated elite, but were read publically for the instruction of both Jew and Gentile. By this means we find that many of the latter become 'proselytes', or converts to Judaism, and underwent circumcision if they were male. Also there were many other Gentiles who did not take the whole step but remained 'proselytes of the gate', or 'God-fearers', that is, people who had reverence for the teachings of the Jewish Scriptures and attended synagogue without fully converting. So it was that the expectation for the arrival of the Saviour was being spread far beyond the actual borders of the Jewish homeland.

As we come to consider predictions relating to Jesus, we note that these may be viewed as 'motives of credibility' of a more particular kind. More than simply being demonstrations that the prophetic oracles are words of supernatural revelation, they also serve as a way of verifying Christ's messianic credentials. How may the people he came to, or how may we today, be sure that he was who he claimed to be? His fulfilment of numerous Old Testament prophecies, with respect to both major details and minor, serves as divine confirmation that he was, and still is, the one sent by God to save humanity. It ought not to go unremarked in this context that such a phenomenon, that is, such a prophetic fore-witness, is virtually entirely lacking with respect to founding figures of other world religions.

Furthermore, once we see that a good deal of Old Testament prophecy concerns Jesus, as he himself testified, we necessarily move away from a purely historical view of the writings of the prophets. It has been the common practice since the mid-nineteenth century, especially in theological colleges and faculties of divinity, for the words of the prophets to be interpreted from a purely historical perspective, adopting almost the same position as the sceptics. The primary, if not the only, question that is asked of the text is—what was the prophet saying to his own generation? This is not a bad question to ask, and it should indeed be the starting point for interpreting any Old Testament text. However, it should not end there, since on numerous occasions, through the gift of the Spirit given to them, the prophets spoke of matters way beyond their own time. There is a key passage in one of the New Testament letters that explains the role of the Hebrew prophets:

Concerning this salvation, the prophets who prophesied of the grace that would come to you made careful search and inquiry, seeking to know what person or time the Spirit of Christ within them was indicating as he predicted the sufferings of Christ and the glories to follow. It was revealed to them that they were not serving themselves but you, in these things which now have been announced to you through those who preached the gospel to you by the Holy Spirit sent from heaven. (1 Peter 1:10–12)

Several highly significant things are to be observed in these words. Firstly, we note that the divine Spirit at work within them is specifically identified as the 'Spirit of *Christ*'. If this is so, then it would be expected that Christ should be a major part, if not the main focus, of their utterances, which is in fact what the very next words say—the Spirit within them 'predicted the sufferings of Christ and the glories to follow'.

Secondly, it makes it clear that their prophecies concerned matters that would be of primary benefit, not to themselves, nor to their initial audience, but to 'you', meaning in context 'you Christian readers of this letter'. The prophets foretold 'the grace that would come to *you*', and 'they were not serving themselves but *you*'. These prophecies are relevant, then, to us Christians.

A third point is that the prophets themselves actually had some awareness, though evidently not complete, of what it was they were foretelling. They knew their messages concerned the one who would bring salvation at some future time, and that this would come about through suffering and subsequent glory. What this means is that both they and their hearers could have faith, albeit based on partial knowledge, in this future saving work of God. This important passage, then, plainly advocates a thoroughly christological, and not merely historical, approach to Old Testament prophecy. We may further add that this christological aspect of the prophetic witness was extensive, as the same apostle Peter declared elsewhere: 'the things which God announced beforehand by the mouth of *all* his prophets, that the Christ would suffer, he has thus fulfilled' (Acts 3:18; cf. also 3:24; 10:43, '*all* the prophets').

What we have seen in the preceding paragraph obviously does not mean that every single prophecy directly concerns Jesus. This is patently not the case. While many do expressly present different aspects of the person and ministry of the future Saviour, others do not. But even in a good many of these latter cases, though they do not speak explicitly of him, I would say that they nevertheless take on their fullest meaning only in the light of the complete revelation that was to come in Christ.

The prophetic oracle against Assyria in Isaiah chapter 10 may serve as an illustration of the foregoing. Here we need to remind ourselves that chapter divisions were not part of the original text and were only added much later by copyists and editors. The oracle actually begins in 10:5, with the words 'Woe to the Assyrian, the rod of my anger'. God's people of Judah had not been living according to God's will. They had strayed to such an extent that he called them 'a godless nation' and 'a people who provoke me to anger' (v. 6). As a result God had sent the Assyrian invader against his own people, in order to chastise them and bring them to their senses. This the Assyrian army did, but in a somewhat extreme manner. For them this was an opportunity to use excessive violence, to seize plunder, to enlarge their territories, and for them to boast of their achievements. All their successes they attributed to themselves (v. 10), rather than to God who summoned them for his own purposes. Consequently, once the Assyrians' work was done with respect to his people, God would then proceed to punish the Assyrians themselves (v. 12). The oracle continues to foretell the coming destruction of Assyria up to the end of verse 19. Following this there is a short oracle which looks to the Hebrew 'remnant' that will emerge from the other side of the Assyrian invasion. These will then 'truly rely on the LORD' (v. 20). The remainder of the chapter (vv. 21–34) contains a further oracle encouraging the people of Zion not to fear the Assyrians, who are soon to be judged.

At first sight there seems to be nothing here that relates to Christ. Yet reading the whole against the background of the wider literary context we cannot but notice quite a number of references to the coming Messiah. Just before our chapter we find christological passages in Isaiah 7:14; 9:1–2, 6–7, and then after Isaiah 10, chapter 11 (again there is no actual chapter break) immediately begins with a reference to the Messiah (11:1) and really focuses upon him and his work throughout the remainder of that chapter. In other words the Assyrian oracle we have considered, which seems to make no express mention of Christ, is sandwiched between other oracles that do. It is hard to conclude, therefore, that Christ has no bearing at all upon 10:5–34. In fact a closer examination of this text reveals that in 10:21, 'A remnant will return, a remnant of Jacob, to the Mighty God', the title 'Mighty God' (*'ēl gibbôr*) is identical to that occurring in 9:6 of the messianic king (uniquely in these two verses). Not only this, the very next verse (v. 22) is one that is quoted in the New Testament (Romans 9:27) with application to the Jewish remnant that would come to believe in Jesus. So while not at the forefront of the Assyrian oracle, Jesus is nevertheless there in the background. The flow of thought, then, would appear to be as follows: The Jews of Isaiah's days are being judged by God for their ungodliness, and he is using the Assyrian invader as his instrument of punishment. Since the Assyrians themselves act in such an excessive and prideful way, God will next punish them, and the Jews, or at least a significant 'remnant' of them, will be delivered from their hands. But this deliverance from the Assyrian, wonderful and real as it is, is only one that is temporal. Ultimately God has in store a much greater and more far-reaching deliverance for his people (moving now into chapter 11), one that will take place when the 'root of Jesse' will appear on the earth, an earth that will be gloriously transformed, and one that will embrace not only the Jews but those of the nations also. So, taken together, chapters 10 and 11 offer the people Isaiah was addressing a marvellous message of hope, immediate hope in the face of the threat of Assyria, and the long-term hope of a final and lasting deliverance at the coming of Messiah. Hence we see how the presentation of Jesus in the prophets is integrated with more immediate prophecies that do not speak of him, not directly at least. I am sure that this is how it works for the bulk of oracles recorded for us in the prophetic books. Even where Christ is not explicitly mentioned, the coming of Christ still has some significant bearing on the matter in hand.

As the reader will by now be aware, prophecy that foretells the person and work of the Messiah is just one branch of biblical prophecy, and no doubt the most important. Yet the subject matter of divine prophecy is broad in its scope and, besides foretelling matters relating to Christ, there are also remarkable predictions concerning the people of Israel, and also about a good many other nations and events. These also contribute significantly to the Bible's motives of credibility, but as they are not directly related to the Old Testament witness to Jesus we will not touch upon them here.

Characteristics of Old Testament Prophecy

Before coming to consider the messianic prophecies themselves, a few words are in order about the character of Hebrew prophecy in general.

(a) Distribution. In the first five books of Moses and in the historical books that follow there is not a great deal of direct verbal prophecy. Where this does occur it is usually in those sections of these books that are poetic in style, such as in the death-bed prophecy of Jacob (Genesis 49) and in the oracles of Balaam (Numbers 22–24). This of course does not at all mean that these books containing mostly law and narrative are without christological significance. Far from it. As we have seen, Christ is very much the concern of the patriarchal and Davidic promises, and the narrative sections largely relate the outworking of these. Also, we shall see (in the following chapter) that even where there are no verbal prophecies as such, there can be still be other indicators of Jesus and the gospel. These are what we will refer to as 'prefigurations'. In numerous ways Christ is prefigured in the persons and events recorded in historical narratives and in the various rituals of the Mosaic law. So the lack of a direct verbal prophecy relating to Christ in a particular Old Testament text does not mean that he is not to be found there. The direct prophecies, which form the subject of the present chapter, are primarily to be found in the writings of the (latter) prophets, as perhaps one might expect, and also in the Psalms. It is noteworthy that Isaiah, the first and longest of the major prophetic books, together with the Psalms, are the most frequently quoted Old Testament books in the New Testament.

(b) Poetic style. Verbal prophecy is generally expressed in a distinctive form of language. This for the most part is what could be described as poetry, or at least as a more elevated and ornate manner of expression. The reason for this may lie in the nature of the contents of the utterances. Perhaps it was fitting that words declaring direct divine communication should be spoken in a more exalted diction. Whatever the reason, the reader ought to be aware that in this manner of language a range of poetic conventions are employed which need to be taken into account when interpreting such passages. In poetry metaphors, similes, and other figures of speech are common. What this means is that a prophecy should not only be taken as christological when it explicitly speaks of the coming one as king, or anointed one (Messiah), or descendant of David. Christ can also be the subject of the prophecy when described through one of a whole range of metaphorical terms. He may variously be referred to as a 'stone' (Isaiah 28:16), 'horn' (Psalm 132:17), 'branch' (Jeremiah 33:15), 'shoot' (Isaiah 11:1), 'shepherd' (Ezekiel 34:23), 'the sun of righteousness' (Malachi 4:2), and more besides. The number of prophecies, therefore, that are messianic in nature is actually more that would appear on the surface.

(c) Visions. Mention should also be made of the fact that on occasion the Hebrew prophets saw their prophecies in the first instance and then described what they saw in the second. These were Spirit-inspired visions or, in some cases, dreams. Chronologically speaking, these become more common towards the latter part of the Old Testament period. Here we are thinking of the books of Ezekiel, Daniel, and Zechariah. A glance at these writings quickly reveals that many of their prophecies were first communicated to them visually. Just as we saw that prophetic poetry has its own style, it is similarly true that biblical visions have their own manner of imagery. Scripture uses particular images to express particular realities. A careful and repeated reading of such visionary prophecy, especially in conjunction with the book of Revelation in the New Testament, is the best and perhaps the only way to familiarise oneself with the significance of the many diverse images. We should pay especially close attention to those passages where the prophet is accompanied by an angelic figure who offers some explanation of the meaning of what is being seen (e.g. Daniel 7:15–16). One soon comes to realise that the beasts represent kingdoms of the world, and that horns on the head may symbolise the rulers of these kingdoms. Failure to correctly understand the images could lead to an overly literal interpretation of the visions with bizarre consequences, such as beasts with multiple heads, and stars literally falling from the sky.

Categories of Christological Prophecy

When we consider the way in which a prophecy foretells something about Jesus, we come to see that not all prophecies that relate to him do so in the same manner. There are different possible aspects to the content of a prediction and the way it is fulfilled. It might concern something specific that Jesus did or experienced, or it could be a more general truth about his role or character. It might be a prediction that applies to his first coming into the world, now past, or to his second that is still future. It could even be a prophecy that actually has more than a single fulfilment. These different considerations allow us to divide Old Testament prophecies into five distinct groups. As we believe the phenomenon of Hebrew prophecy to be ultimately of divine origin, perhaps we should expect such diversity. Here follow descriptions of each category with an illustrative text. To help the reader grasp what is involved in each the distinct features are also depicted in diagrammatic form.

(1) Prophecies of a specific event that is fulfilled at Christ's first advent. An example of such a prophecy would be Micah 5:2, which foretells that the coming king would be born in the town of Bethlehem. This may be represented as follows:

Prophecy [OT]	First Advent [NT]	Second Advent [End time]
1. ●——————➤ ●		

(2) Prophecies of a specific event that is to be fulfilled at Christ's second coming, and not during the New Testament age. A particular instance of a second-advent prophecy would be Psalm 2:9, which foretells Messiah's future rule over the nations with an iron sceptre (cf. Revelation 2:27; 19:15). This can be shown as:

Prophecy [OT]	First Advent [NT]	Second Advent [End time]
2. ●————————————————➤ ●		

(3) Prophecies of a specific event which has a dual fulfilment, one during the Old Testament period itself, and then another at the time of Christ's first advent. This is to say that at one and the same time it is both a short-term and a long-term prediction. I would take Isaiah 7:14 about the birth of Immanuel as an example. I understand this prophecy to have an immediate fulfilment within the life-time of the prophet, and then a later one at the birth of Christ, as will be explained in more detail below. In such instances of dual fulfilment the later of the two fulfilments is always the more significant, while the earlier, although a fulfilment of a sort, serves as a kind of precursor to the latter. This category can be tabulated as:

Prophecy [OT]	First Advent [NT]	Second Advent [End time]
3. ●➤ ● ——➤●		

(4) Prophecies of a specific event which have a dual fulfilment, one during the New Testament period, and then another at the time of Christ's

second advent. This manner of prophecy therefore involves a single prediction with two long-term fulfilments. We will shortly examine Zechariah 12:10, looking upon the one who was pierced, as an instance of such. We can display this type in the following way:

Prophecy [OT]	First Advent [NT]	Second Advent [End time]
4. ● ———————→ ●	———————→ ●	

(5) Prophecies which foretell some more general truth concerning Jesus, which is therefore applicable to the entire Christian age, and not just to the time of his first advent or to the second alone. As an example of this last category we may take the prediction of Deuteronomy 18:15–16 about a future prophet like Moses. Such a claim was not made for any of the interim prophets, great as many of them were, but it is Jesus in whom the prophecy finds fulfilment (cf. Acts 3:22). Once instated as this unique prophet, Jesus naturally continues to possess that particular prophetic status for the duration. This can be represented as:

Prophecy [OT]	First Advent [NT]	Second Advent [End time]
5. ● ———————→		

The above five categories do not, of course, exhaust the whole range of christological prophecy. Together with these Old Testament prophecies there are also those contained within the New Testament itself. Some of these are quite short-term in scope, involving a prediction to be fulfilled in the near future. Others are much more distant in scope and concern events to take place at the end of time when Christ returns. As an example of the former we may take Christ's prediction of his own resurrection (e.g. Mark 9:31). With regard to the latter we need only think of the book of Revelation, which plainly relates, among other things, what Jesus will do at the time of his second advent. Since our aim is to deal specifically with the Old Testament witness to Jesus, such New Testament prophecies do not form part of the present discussion.

New Testament Citation of Christological Prophecies

As many readers will be aware, when a prophecy about Jesus is fulfilled during the time of his first advent, attention is often drawn to this fact, either by Jesus himself or by the Gospel writers who recorded the events of his ministry. This is typically done through a quotation of the Old Testament prophecy in question which is accompanied in the majority of cases by some statement indicating its fulfilment. So it is, for example, that the birth narratives in Matthew's Gospel include the quotation of several prophetic passages along with the words: 'This was to fulfil what the Lord spoke through the prophet …' (e.g. 2:15), or similar. At the commencement of his ministry, during the synagogue service in Nazareth, Jesus read the passage from Isaiah concerning the one anointed by the Spirit of the Lord who had come to preach good news (61:1–2). He then said to the congregation, 'Today this Scripture is fulfilled in your hearing' (Luke 4:21).

However, it is not always the case that a prophecy is quoted and stated to have been fulfilled. Sometimes it is left for readers to recognise this through their knowledge of Scripture. Indeed it would surely prove to be somewhat laborious if absolutely every Old Testament prophecy fulfilled by Jesus were quoted in the New Testament and said to have now found its fulfilment. This would leave little room for investigation on the part of the reader and exclude the possible benefit and instruction that such a process would provide.

In some cases where there is no explicit quotation we can nevertheless be completely certain that a fulfilment has occurred. Note the following passages from the crucifixion scene as portrayed in the first three Gospels:

> And when they had crucified him, they divided up his clothes among themselves by casting lots. And sitting down, they kept watch over him there. (Matthew 27:35–36)

> And they crucified him, and divided up his clothes among themselves, casting lots for them to decide what each should take. (Mark 15:24)

> And they divided up his clothes by casting lots. (Luke 23:34)

These all record the same event in which the soldiers who crucified Jesus divided his clothing among them by means of casting lots (something like throwing dice). Any reader familiar with the Old Testament would recall that such a thing was in fact foretold centuries earlier in the Psalms. There in Psalm 22 we find on the lips of one who is rejected and suffering the words: 'They divide my clothes among them, and for my clothing they cast lots' (v. 18). Both the Psalm and the three Gospels speak of an event in very similar terms. There is the dividing of the victim's clothes on the part of some third person plural party ('they'), and the means whereby this is done is through the casting of lots. Even on these connections alone, we ought to be able to see the fact of the fulfilment. But here we are not left in any doubt. The fourth Gospel, that written by the apostle John, also makes reference to the same event at the crucifixion. But there John records the incident in somewhat greater detail:

> Then the soldiers, when they had crucified Jesus, took his clothes and made four parts, one for each soldier, and also the tunic. Now the tunic was seamless, woven in one piece. So they said to one another, 'Let's not tear it, but cast lots for it to decide who will get it'. This was to fulfil the Scripture: 'They divided my clothes among them, and for my clothing they cast lots'. (John 19:23–24)

The apostle John here goes one step further than the other Gospel writers and speaks explicitly of the fulfilment. He cites the actual words of the prophecy in the Psalm, introducing them with 'This was to fulfil the Scripture'. So with respect to this particular prophecy Matthew, Mark, and Luke leave the connection implicit, while John makes the fulfilment explicit.

A similar case is that of Jesus entering Jerusalem on a donkey at the beginning of Passion Week. This again is recorded in all four Gospels (Matthew 21:1–7; Mark 11:1–7; Luke 19:28–35; John 12:14–16), but the fact that this takes place in fulfilment of Zechariah 9:9 is only included in the accounts of Matthew and John.

In these foregoing two instances certainty about the presence of a prophetic fulfilment comes from comparison with the parallel passages in other Gospels. Sometimes, however, none of the four Gospel writers explicitly draws attention to the occurrence of a fulfilment. One feature of the trial narratives in the Gospels is the silence of Jesus in the face of accusations presented against him (e.g. Matthew 27:14; Mark 15:5; Luke 23:9). Although none of these expressly makes reference to any Old Testament prophecy, there can be little doubt that the minds of those readers familiar with the prophets would go to a verse in Isaiah 53: 'He was oppressed and afflicted, yet he did not open his mouth; he was led like a lamb to the slaughter, and like a sheep that is silent before its shearers, so he did not open his mouth' (v. 7). What lends credence to this being a fulfilled prophecy is the fact that this particular chapter of Isaiah, the whole of which concerns a Suffering Servant figure, is cited a number of times in the New Testament with application to Jesus (e.g. Matthew 8:17; Luke 22:37; 1 Peter 2:22). Significantly, later in the New Testament the very same verse about the silence of the sufferer actually forms part of a longer quotation from Isaiah 53 which is indeed applied to Christ in the Acts of the Apostles (8:32). So there would appear to be good biblical warrant for interpreting this prophecy in connection with the silence of Jesus before his death.

Then there are undoubtedly a good many Old Testament prophecies that are fulfilled with respect to Christ in the New where no citation or comment is made at all. It is simply for the reader to detect where this is so. Such a case would be the healings foretold in Isaiah 35. Here it is foretold that 'The eyes of the blind will be opened and the ears of the deaf unstopped. Then the lame will leap like a deer, and the tongue of the dumb shout for joy' (vv. 5–6). The Gospels describe Jesus healing various people suffering from these same four disabilities—the blind, the deaf, the lame, and the dumb—but without flagging up the fact that this was a fulfilment of the ancient prophecy, which it evidently was (cf. Matthew 15:31).

The foregoing alerts us, then, to the fact that not every instance of a fulfilled prophecy is labelled as such in the New Testament. An acquaintance, therefore, with the contents of the Old Testament is a great help in identifying prophecies that are fulfilled in the person and work of Jesus.

Prophecies Fulfilled at Christ's First Advent

The matter of prophecy about the coming Jesus is an immense subject and could easily fill a whole volume, and indeed has done so many times over. A few of these books will be recommended at the close of the chapter. So the treatment here will be necessarily selective. In the remainder of this chapter I will first give a survey of instances covered by one of the above categories; this being those in group (1), specific prophecies that Jesus fulfilled during his first advent. These are, of course, easier to examine than category (2), since they have already occurred and so we know the way in which they were fulfilled. While prophecies concerning matters yet future will, I believe, be fulfilled with the same definiteness, it is naturally not so easy to speak of the manner in which this is to take place before they have happened. Also with regard to category (1), I shall only list those prophecies for which the fulfilment is explicitly stated in the New Testament. Following this survey I will undertake a closer examination of two prophecies of a more complex nature, where there would seem to be a dual fulfilment. Then lastly, I shall mention a very special category of prophecy, which is applied to Jesus, and yet is not messianic as such.

With regard to the overview of the explicitly identified prophecies in category (1), readers should bear in mind that this of itself constitutes only a small portion of the whole of biblical prophecy. I do wish to stress this fact. Remember we are here considering only christological prophecies. Numerous other prophetic predications are recorded which concern nations, kings, and various divine judgments. These are not the topic of this chapter since they do not expressly relate to Jesus. Also we are not including the New Testament prophecies about Christ, as stated above, that remain to be fulfilled during the last times, the time of his return. The prophecies we are looking at are all contained in the Old Testament. Further still we are only dealing with prophecies that have a specific, rather than general, fulfilment. And even within this particular range I have decided to include only those prophecies that are actually quoted by the New Testament authors, so that there is no room for doubt from a biblical point of view that these are prophecies actually fulfilled in Jesus. Hopefully then, the reader can see that when it comes to the prophetic testimony of the Bible as a whole, there is considerably more than a single category to be discussed.

Here follows a list of the principal prophecies as just described. Each points to a particular event or circumstance that forms a part of Christ's life and ministry during his first advent, and which are expressly quoted in the Gospels, Acts, and Epistles, and in nearly all cases are explicitly identified as fulfilments. The list contains most of the more readily identifiable instances, but does not claim to be exhaustive.

Born from a virgin: Isaiah 7:14 → Matthew 1:23

Born in town of Bethlehem: Micah 5:2 → Matthew 2:6

Called out of Egypt: Hosea 11:1 → Matthew 2:15

Lamentation over loss of children: Jeremiah 31:15 → Matthew 2:18

Preceded by a forerunner to prepare the way: Isaiah 40:3 → Matthew 3:3; Mark 1:3; Luke 3:4–6

Anointed by the Spirit of the Lord to preach good news: Isaiah 61:1–2 → Luke 4:18–19

Ministry in Galilee: Isaiah 9:1–2 → Matthew 4:15–16

Zeal for God's house: Psalm 69:9 → John 2:17

Healed the sick: Isaiah 53:4 → Matthew 8:17

Character of early ministry: Isaiah 42:1–4 → Matthew 12:17–21

Taught in parables: Psalm 78:2 → Matthew 13:35

Entered Jerusalem on a donkey: Zechariah 9:9 → Matthew 21:5; John 12:15

The 'stone' rejected by the builders: Psalm 118:22 → Matthew 21:42; Mark 12:10; Luke 20:17; Acts 4:11; 1 Peter 2:7

Established a new covenant: Jeremiah 31:31 → Hebrews 8:8; cf. Matthew 26:28; Mark 14:24; Luke 22:20

Betrayed by a close friend: Psalm 41:9 → John 13:18

His followers scattered: Zechariah 13:7 → Matthew 26:31; Mark 14:27

Conspired against by Gentile rulers: Psalm 2:1–2 → Acts 4:25–26

Punished along with criminals: Isaiah 53:12 → Mark 15:28; Luke 22:37

His clothes divided by casting of lots: Psalm 22:18 → John 19:24

No bones broken at his execution: Exodus 12:46; Numbers 9:12 → John 19:36

His body pierced: Zechariah 12:10 → John 19:37

His dead body did not decay: Psalm 16:10 → Acts 2:27; 13:35

Ascended into heaven: Psalm 68:10 → Ephesians 4:8

Sat at God's right hand: Psalm 110:1 → Acts 2:35; Hebrews 1:13

Readers will notice that the majority of the prophecies concern the beginning and end of Christ's life and ministry. Perhaps this is because these are in some ways more prominent. The manner and circumstances of his birth and the commencement of his ministry is accompanied by a fair number of prophetic fulfilments. The central part of his ministry consisted largely of teaching and miracles. Old Testament prophecies exist that do point to these matters, but as there is less variety in what Jesus is doing here there are fewer prophecies. Then another series of prophecies relate to the climactic events of his death, resurrection, and ascension.

Seeing that this list is only one particularly defined strand of messianic prophecy, which itself is only one element within the wider range of biblical prophecy, when the phenomenon of prophecy is taken as a whole its overall effect, as far as the matter of motives of credibility is concerned, is seen to be very impressive. As mentioned earlier, the total number of Old Testament prophecies that find fulfilment in the New numbers in excess of 200, and some would put it nearer 300. In this context, one of the classic works on prophecy (listed at the end of the chapter) makes the following apposite remark:

> Now, the evidence of prophecy is essentially of a connected and cumulative nature. It does not consist so much in the verifications given to a few remarkable predictions, as in the establishment of an entire series, closely related to each other, and forming a united and comprehensive whole. This is peculiarly the case in respect to the prophecies which relate to the person and kingdom of Messiah, which more than any others form a prolonged and connected series. (Patrick Fairbairn, *The Interpretation of Prophecy*, p. 203)

Our primary interest here, as stated earlier, is not with evidence for the divine nature of the biblical revelation in general, but with the testimony of the Old Testament to Jesus Christ. And the fact is that the prophecies found in these ancient writings, along with their other forms of witness to him, discussed in the other chapters of this book, provide those with eyes to see good cause to accept Jesus as the long-awaited Messiah, and so to put their faith in him.

Zechariah 12:10

As some readers might not be familiar with the idea of a prophecy having two fulfilments, I will include a discussion of two Old Testament passages of this kind. Both of these are quoted as being fulfilled in the Gospels, but also have, I believe, another application at a different point in time. I will begin with the easier of the two texts. This is the prediction found in the latter part of the book of Zechariah, a prophet who lived and ministered some five centuries before Christ. The particular prophecy concerns looking upon one who was pierced and runs as follows:

> And I will pour out on the house of David and the inhabitants of Jerusalem a spirit of grace and supplication. They will look on me, the one whom they have pierced, and they will mourn for him as one mourns for an only child, and weep bitterly for him as one weeps for a firstborn son. (Zechariah 12:10)

This is a remarkable text. In the first sentence the first person subject 'I' is plainly God himself. This means that the first person object 'me' in the second sentence must also refer to God. This is the unambiguous reading of the Hebrew. From the verb tenses we understand that the prophecy concerns a future occasion, from the point of view of the prophet, in which this divine person will be pierced. In his Gospel the apostle John takes up this ancient prophecy and applies it to Jesus:

> Then the Jews, because it was the day of preparation, so that the bodies would not remain on the cross on the Sabbath (for that Sabbath was a high day), asked Pilate that their legs might be broken, and that they might be removed. So the soldiers came, and broke the legs of the first man and of the other man who was crucified with him. But when they came to Jesus, seeing that he was already dead, they did not break his legs. Instead, one of the soldiers pierced his side with a spear, and immediately blood and water came out. And he who saw this has testified, and his testimony is true; and he knows that he is telling the truth, so that you too may believe. For these things happened to fulfil the Scripture, 'Not a bone of him shall be broken'. And again another Scripture says, 'They shall look on the one whom they pierced'. (John 19:31–37)

Here the Gospel writer describes how, rather than break Christ's bones to precipitate his death, the soldiers at the cross complete his execution with a spear thrust to his side. This was out of the ordinary, as the usual practice for finishing off victims of crucifixion was to break their legs. But since there was another prediction about Jesus that none of his bones would be broken, the regular manner of bringing about death could not be carried out. Therefore, in the providence of God, it happened that Jesus, the divine Son of God, was pierced in accordance with the prophecy. This of course occurred during Christ's first advent, in the first century of the present era.

However, when we read Zechariah's prophecy in context this piercing of Christ's body at the cross cannot be the full meaning of the ancient oracle. If we look at what comes before and after 12:10 we may without much difficulty recognise that the other events the prophet predicted in this chapter did not take place at the time of the crucifixion, nor indeed at any other time during the first advent. Zechariah 12:1–9 deal with nations coming up and attacking Jerusalem, and God's deliverance of his people from these nations. After the prediction, 'They will look on me, the one whom they have pierced', the prophet then goes on to speak of the mourning that will take place, a great mourning which will result from looking upon the pierced one. At this time Jerusalem would experience a 'spirit of grace and supplication'. Evidently, this situation is very different from what happened before and after Christ's crucifixion. On that occasion there had been no prior invasion and deliverance, and following it there was no mourning over the pierced one on the part of Jerusalem. Rather the vast majority of its inhabitants remained unmoved in their unbelief and hostility to Christ and to his disciples who proclaimed him. We are led, therefore, to look for another situation in which this prophecy fits. And in this we are given an unmistakable clue in the last book of the New Testament, Revelation, that pictures the time of the end, that is, events before and after the second coming of Christ. In the opening chapter we read:

> Behold, he is coming with the clouds, and every eye will see him, even those who pierced him; and all the tribes of the earth will mourn because of him. So it is to be. Amen. (Revelation 1:7)

The words 'every eye will see him, even those who pierced him' point us unmistakably to Zechariah 12:10, as the marginal references in our Bibles tell us. Remember that the prophecy was not about the act of piercing itself, but rather about others looking upon the one that was pierced. Here the people who look upon him are 'those who pierced him'. From the terms of the original prophecy we understand these to be the Jews themselves. The subsequent phrase 'all the tribes [*phulai*] of the earth [*gēs*]' fits in with this. Translations which here have 'peoples' or 'nations' are strictly incorrect, as the word is plainly 'tribes', as in the twelve tribes of Israel. Also, as stated elsewhere, the word for 'earth' could also legitimately be translated as 'land'. We may compare this sense with the twelve 'tribes of Israel' listed later in chapter 7 of the same book (Revelation 7:4–8). It is these tribes, 1:7 says, that 'will mourn because of him', which is precisely how Zechariah 12:10 continues, with the mourning of the Jews at seeing the pierced one. I would argue, therefore, that the ultimate fulfilment of Zechariah's prophecy is to take place when Jesus returns, as Revelation 1:7 also says, 'Behold, he is coming with the clouds'. From a comparison with other prophecies (e.g. Ezekiel 37–38) we find his second advent to be at a time when Israel is being downtrodden by enemies, from which the returning Messiah will save the Jews. All this fits well with the context of Zechariah 12, where the Jewish nation is invaded and overrun, but are shortly delivered, and when they then look upon the one they pierced, the divine Christ, and mourn as a result. This mourning speaks of the repentance of the Jews once they come to realise that they crucified their Messiah the first time he came to them. At this future time God will pour out a spirit of grace and supplication upon his former chosen people. The prediction therefore relates that long-awaited and wonderful event of the conversion of the Jews at the time of Christ's second coming.

So we find that it is Revelation 1:7 that concerns the fuller working out of Zechariah's prophecy. John 19:37 is indeed speaking of the same piercing, but it is not at that point of time that the prophecy reaches its final fulfilment. John is describing a fulfilment of sorts, as he himself declares, yet it is one that is initial or partial. Revelation, written most likely by the same John, speaks of the same prophecy's future ultimate and complete fulfilment. In Zechariah 12:10, then, we have an example of a prophecy of category (4) above, one in which there is a dual fulfilment, one during the first advent, recorded in the New Testament, and the other at the time of the end when Christ returns.

Isaiah 7:14

This is one of the most famous, and perhaps most controversial, of all Old Testament prophecies. It occurs within the context of two enemy kings, Rezin of Damascus in Aram and Pekah of Samaria, coming up to fight against Jerusalem, ruled by King Ahaz of Judah. This is an event that can be dated about 730 years before the birth of Christ. In this situation God sent the prophet Isaiah to address Ahaz, and to give him the encouragement that these two kings would not succeed in capturing Jerusalem, but rather their own lands would be ravaged by an even more powerful enemy, the Assyrians. In order to demonstrate the truth of these words God permits Ahaz to ask for a sign (Isaiah 7:10–11). But Ahaz, in a display of mock piety, declines the offer, saying, 'I will not ask, nor will I put the LORD to the test' (v. 12). To this the prophet responds with the following words:

> Hear now, O house of David! Is it too small a thing for you to try the patience of men, that you will try the patience of my God also? Therefore the Lord himself will give you a sign: Behold, the virgin [*hā 'almâ*] will conceive and bear a son, and she will call his name Immanuel. He will eat curds and honey at the time he knows enough to refuse evil and choose good. For before the boy will know enough to refuse evil and choose good, the land whose two kings you dread will be forsaken. (Isaiah 7:13–16)

The familiar part of this prophecy is the prediction concerning the virgin who will give birth to a son, a son who will be Immanuel, meaning 'God with us' (v. 14). This statement is, broadly speaking, clear in what its words are saying, though there is some discussion about the Hebrew term that indicates the mother of this child. The original text here reads *hā 'almâ*, the first syllable *hā-* being the definite article 'the' (ignored in many English translations), leaving the feminine noun *'almâ*. Regarding this word there is one school of thought which claims that its basic sense is 'young woman', rather than 'virgin'. It is argued that if 'virgin' were the meaning intended the noun *bᵉtûlâ* would be used instead. There are, however, serious objections to this view. First and foremost, there is the fact that Joel 1:8 unambiguously uses this latter word of a married woman: 'Mourn like a *bᵉtûlâ* girded with sackcloth for the bridegroom of her youth'. Secondly, when the Hebrew Old Testament was translated into Greek long before the time of the New Testament, the translators, who were Jews, decided that in Isaiah 7:14 they would use the Greek term *parthenos* for the Hebrew *'almâ*, and *parthenos* means 'virgin'. But the final decider on the meaning of the word has to come, for Bible-believers, from the inspired Gospel writer Matthew who in his quotation of this verse also put *parthenos*, 'virgin'. From this it would seem, then, that on one hand *'almâ* may indeed include the idea of virginity, while on the other *bᵉtûlâ* need not. So the common objection is actually without foundation. The fact is that both these words have a considerable overlap of meaning. They both basically refer to a young woman, and if that young woman is unmarried it can safely be assumed, considering the culture, that she was a virgin. We note that in Genesis 24 the young Rebekah, of whom it said, 'no man had ever slept with her' (v. 16), is described as both *bᵉtûlâ* (v. 16) and *'almâ* (v. 43).

Now the New Testament makes it clear that this prophecy finds its fulfilment in the birth of Jesus from Mary. It also stresses the fact that this was a birth of a miraculous nature, as Mary was a virgin in the true sense of the word (Matthew 1:18, 25; Luke 1:27, 34). In his Gospel Matthew records the following:

> An angel of the Lord appeared to him in a dream and said, 'Joseph, son of David, do not be afraid to take Mary as your wife, because the child conceived in her is from the Holy Spirit. She will bear a son, and you will call his name Jesus, for he will save his people from their sins'. Now all this took place to fulfil what was spoken by the Lord through the prophet: 'Behold, the virgin will conceive and bear a son, and they will call his name Immanuel', which is translated, 'God with us'. (Matthew 1:20–23)

Here we find both the verbal citation of the prophecy in question, and the statement of its fulfilment. So as far as Matthew was concerned there was no doubt about the matter—Isaiah was foretelling an event that was to occur over 700 years after the prophet's own time, this event being the supernatural birth of Jesus the Messiah from a mother, Mary, who was a virgin.

There is, however, some difficulty in a simple acceptance of the foregoing application of the prophecy. This is the fact that such a view seems to ignore the historical context in which the prediction was originally given. The background to Isaiah's words regarding the birth of this child was given above, as was the continuation of his prophecy: 'For before the boy will know enough to refuse evil and choose good, the land whose two kings you dread will be forsaken' (v. 16). The 'two kings' are of course the kings of Aram and Samaria who were coming to attack Jerusalem, while 'the boy' is the son to be born from the *'almâ*. So what the prophecy is saying is that before this child to be born reaches the age at which he becomes mature enough to discern between good and evil, the lands of the two kings in question will be overrun. We know from history that this is indeed what happened within a few years of the prophecy. The Assyrians came and invaded both lands, and so Judah was entirely free of the threat they presented. What this strongly suggests, therefore, is that the 'sign' given to King Ahab, that is, the sign regarding the birth of a son, would appear to have direct relevance to Ahab's own historical situation, this being the invasion of his land by the two kings.

So we have Matthew applying the prophecy to Jesus several centuries after the time of Isaiah, and we have the context in which the prediction was spoken demanding a fulfilment in the near future. The best way to resolve this apparent problem is, I believe, to suppose that, like Zechariah 12:10 discussed above, the prophecy possesses not one but two fulfilments.

While Matthew 1:23 makes it certain that the prophecy concerned Jesus, we need to give some thought as to who it may have concerned in its initial setting. Here is where the article 'the' on *hā ʿalmâ* becomes significant, as also does the fact that the word, as noted above, need not contain the idea of virginity when speaking of a married woman. The article points to a known woman. Since in the delivery of the prophecy Isaiah was speaking to the king, it is most likely that the woman was known to one or both of these.

Some, especially Jewish commentators, have thought the woman to be Ahaz's wife, so making the child to be Hezekiah, the son of Ahaz the king. However, this cannot be possibly be the case. We are informed elsewhere that Ahaz reigned as king for sixteen years (2 Kings 16:2). We are further told that following the death of his father, Hezekiah became king himself at the age of twenty-five (2 Kings 18:2). This means that when Ahaz became king his son Hezekiah had already been born nine years previously. Consequently, at the meeting between the prophet and Ahaz in Isaiah 7 Hezekiah had to have been nine or more years old. So that possibility is ruled out.

The other possible woman intended by the prophecy is Isaiah's own wife. I personally find it convincing that she was in fact the initial *ʿalmâ* that the prediction of 7:14 concerned. Because she was married to the prophet, in this original setting there is no supernatural birth involved. Rather the manner of the 'sign' involved the timing of the birth and the maturing of the child. Shortly after the events of Isaiah 7 a son would be born to her and before he could even make a choice between good and evil the two invading kings would be no more. To me it seems that the passage that points us in this direction is the following, which comes just a few paragraphs after the prophecy:

> So I approached the prophetess, and she conceived and bore a son. Then the LORD said to me, 'Call his name Maher-shalal-hash-baz; for before the boy knows how to cry out "My father" or "My mother", the wealth of Damascus and the spoil of Samaria will be carried away before the king of Assyria' (Isaiah 8:3–4)

The 'I' here is Isaiah himself, who sleeps with his wife resulting in the birth of a son. The fact that 'she conceived and bore a son' echoes the exact wording of the prophecy ('will conceive and bear a son') is a strong indication that this is the birth that the prediction is about, at least in its first instance. And perhaps more importantly there is the expressly stated fact here (v. 4) that before this infant reaches a certain age, one that is not too far distant, Damascus and Samaria will be ruined. This corresponds closely to what was said with respect to the prophetic child in the previous chapter, that is, 'For before the boy will know enough to refuse evil and choose good, the land whose two kings you dread will be forsaken' (v. 16). The connections between the two sons are unmistakably close.

Against the foregoing interpretation it may be objected that the names of the two sons differ. One is 'Immanuel', meaning 'God with us', while the other is 'Maher-shalal-hash-baz', meaning 'The plunder quickens, the spoil hastens'. This latter is a twofold reference to the ruin of the two threatening kingdoms, which were soon to be plundered by the Assyrians. This objection may be satisfactorily answered by reference to other passages in which Messiah is named. A couple of chapters later in Isaiah we come across the following prophetic verse: 'For to us a child is born, to us a son is given ... and his name will be called Wonderful, Counsellor, Mighty God, Everlasting Father, Prince of Peace' (9:6). In the book of the prophet Jeremiah we further read: 'Behold, the days are coming when I will raise up for David a righteous Branch ... and this is his name by which he will be called, "The LORD our righteousness"' (23:5–6).

Now the plain fact is none of these names are the actual personal name of Messiah, which is 'Jesus'. Never in the Gospels is he called 'Prince of Peace', 'The LORD our righteousness', or any of the others mentioned here. Rather we are to understand these as appellations, or titles, and not names as such. They serve as fitting designations that are applicable to the figure in question, and which aptly describe his person and role, but none of them are real names by which he was addressed. So in the case of Isaiah 7:14 we are not to suppose that this child's name was 'Immanuel'. Even Jesus is not called such in the Gospels. Instead we are to see the name as bringing out the significance of what was taking place. In its original context the son may indeed have had the real name Maher-shalal-hash-baz, but the significance of the Immanuel aspect of the prophecy was brought out in the deliverance of Judah from the two invading kings. Their destruction was a sign, in that day and age, that God was with Judah. Later regarding Christ, of course, his father was instructed to give him the actual name 'Jesus' (Matthew 1:21), itself signifying his saving work (Jesus meaning 'The Lord saves'). But this is immediately followed by the giving of the name 'Immanuel' (v. 23), which relates to God being with humankind in a more literal manner than the first fulfilment, since he came in the form of the incarnate Son, God made flesh. So the twofold giving of a name in Isaiah is also reflected in the opening chapter of Matthew.

Another detail in the text of Isaiah that supports the foregoing interpretation is the fact that a short while after 7:14 Isaiah expressly refers to his children as 'signs', the same word used in the prophecy. He says, 'Behold, I and the children the LORD has given me are for signs and wonders in Israel from the LORD of hosts' (8:18). His son Maher-shalal-hash-baz is specifically a sign of the overthrow of the two kings presently threatening Judah. His other son, Shear-Jashub, is also a sign since his name means 'A remnant will return'. The idea of a 'remnant' is quite prominent in Isaiah (e.g. 1:9, 10:20, 21, 22; 11:11, 16). This name served to give confidence that the nation would not be entirely destroyed in the current tribulation.

So in this section we have explained the well-known prophecy of Isaiah 7:14 in terms of a dual fulfilment. We recall from what was said earlier in the chapter that the second fulfilment is the greater of the two, the one that provides the coming to pass of the terms of the prophecy in its fullest sense. In the first instance, the birth of the child is a natural biological act, in the second it is a supernatural act of God. This corresponds to the two possible senses of the term *'almâ*, not a virgin if married (the prophet's wife) but a virgin if unmarried (Mary). Furthermore, in the initial fulfilment the sign is that two earthly kings and their kingdoms are going to be destroyed, while in the ultimate fulfilment it is sin and the dominion of Satan that will be overcome. And, as just stated, it is only in the latter fulfilment that 'Immanuel' indicates the actual presence of God embodied in human nature. The second application of the prophecy can be seen, therefore, to far exceed the first in its scope and importance.

Finally, the reader should be aware that this way of understanding Isaiah 7:14, with two distinct fulfilments, is widely attested in the history of biblical interpretation. The German reformer Martin Luther adopted this approach in his commentary on Isaiah back in the sixteenth century. Over the centuries since then this view has been that advocated by such distinguished expositors as William Louth, John Pye Smith, and Albert Barnes, and was given a very sympathetic airing in the classic treatment of Isaiah by J. A. Alexander. In more recent times the dual fulfilment has been the view put forward by biblical scholars such as J. A. Motyer (1970), Geoffrey Grogan (1986), John Oswalt (1986), Gerard Van Groningen (1990), Robert Chisholm (2002), and James Hamilton (2005), among others.

Prophecies of the Divine Person

This very last section of the chapter is an important supplement to what precedes. Our primary concern has been to look at prophecies of a messianic nature, which reached their fulfilment in Jesus. Alongside this, however, we need to make mention of other prophecies which are not strictly messianic in character, and yet are still fulfilled in the person of Christ. What do I mean? Jesus Christ, according to the orthodox confession of the church, is one person in two natures. He possesses both a divine nature and a human nature. He is God become man. This astounding truth is only definitively revealed in the New Testament, but it also makes its impact upon the Old Testament prophecies. The prophet Isaiah, as mentioned previously, foretold the birth of the Messiah in the following terms:

> For to us a child is born, to us a son is given ... and his name will be called Wonderful, Counsellor, Mighty God, Everlasting Father, Prince of Peace. Of the increase of his government and peace there will be no end. He will reign on the throne of David and over his kingdom, to establish it and uphold it with justice and righteousness from that time on and for ever. (9:6–7)

The prophecy contains elements that are obviously messianic. It is evidently speaking of a king in David's line who will rule over his kingdom. This fits squarely into the context of the Davidic promises that were examined in the previous chapter. Alongside this, however, we note that to this king there is applied the adjective 'Everlasting', and his rule, it would seem, is one that will have 'no end' but continue 'for ever'. This can be so because the person in question is indeed 'Mighty God'. So here the prophet is bringing together both the divine and human aspects of Christ's nature.

On a number of occasions a prophecy appears only to concern the divine. That is to say, there are Old Testament prophecies which explicitly relate to 'God' or to the 'LORD' (*Yahweh*), where there are no explicit mentions of Messiah, and which in the New Testament are nevertheless quoted with application to Jesus. The most notable example of this is that passage which is cited near the beginning of all four Gospels (Matthew 3:3; Mark 1:3; Luke 3:4–6; John 1:23), the prophecy recorded in the book of Isaiah that heralds the commencement of Christ's ministry:

> A voice of one calling: 'In the wilderness prepare the way for the LORD; make straight in the desert a highway for our God. Every valley shall be lifted up, every mountain and hill made low; the rough ground shall become level, the rugged places made a plain. And the glory of the LORD will be revealed, and all humanity will see it together'. (Isaiah 40:3–5)

In the Gospels the voice exclaiming these words is, of course, that of John the Baptist. John came to prepare the way for the One coming after him, which is Jesus. Yet the prophecy identifies this person firstly as the 'LORD', and then as 'God'. The divine person of the prophecy becomes the human Jesus of the Gospels. Here then is a clear indication of the essential deity of Christ. He is not just the offspring of Abraham and of David come to fulfil the ancient promises, he is God himself coming into our world, and it is this extraordinary event that the prophets also foretold.

Another such passage is found in Isaiah 8. Here we read an oracle that declares:

> It is the LORD of hosts whom you should regard as holy, he will be your fear, and he will be your dread, and he will become a sanctuary; but to both the houses of Israel, a stone that causes men to stumble, and a rock that makes them fall, and a snare and a trap for the inhabitants of Jerusalem. Many among them will stumble, they will fall and be broken; they will be snared and captured. (Isaiah 8:13–15)

As with the previous passage this prophecy is speaking directly of God, the 'LORD of hosts'. Yet in the New Testament part of this text (v. 14) is quoted and applied to Jesus. The quotation is made firstly by the apostle Paul who in Romans (9:33) takes the prophet's words 'a stone that causes men to stumble, and a rock that makes them fall' and combines them with another prophecy, one that is implicitly messianic (Isaiah 28:16), applying both to Jesus. Peter too in his first letter (2:8) describes Christ as 'a stone that causes men to stumble, and a rock that makes them fall'. The prophecy, then, identifies God himself as that stumbling stone, and yet its fulfilment is attained in the coming of Jesus Christ, which resulted in the stumbling of many among the Jews. In other words, the implication is that Jesus is the divine Person of the original prophecy.

Similar to the above texts, we find the prophecy in which God says 'to me every knee will bow' (Isaiah 45:32) to be fulfilled in the words 'at the name of Jesus every knee will bow' (Philippians 2:10). Also the prophetic oracle to the effect that 'Whoever calls upon the name of the LORD will be saved' (Joel 2:32) finds New Testament application with reference to Christ (Romans 10:13, the 'Lord' demonstrably being the 'Jesus' of v. 9).

We have seen, then, that the prophets confirm the Christian doctrine of the two natures of Christ. The same prophets predict both the advent of the human Messiah of the house of David, and also the coming of God into human history, being not two but one and the same Person.

Suggestions for Further Reading

Brown, Michael L. *Answering Jewish Objections to Jesus, Volume 3: Messianic Prophecy Objections* (Grand Rapids, Michigan: Baker, 2002).

Fairbairn, Patrick. *The Interpretation of Prophecy* (Edinburgh: Banner of Truth [reprint], 1964).

Gooding, David. *The Riches of Divine Wisdom: The New Testament's Use of the Old Testament* (Coleraine, N. Ireland: Myrtlefield Trust, 2013), Chapters 6 and 7.

Robertson, O. Palmer. *The Christ of the Prophets* (Phillipsburg, New Jersey: Presbyterian & Reformed, 2004).

7. PREFIGURATION

We now come to look at figures, or images if you prefer, of Christ in the Old Testament. Some readers will no doubt already be familiar with this way of interpreting Scripture, but for others it might be completely new. Even where the idea is known there is often a lack of definiteness in understanding how it operates. For these reasons I feel it worthwhile to start from basics and give a proper introduction to the subject that offers a definition of what we mean by prefiguration and look at the language that the Bible itself uses to describe it.

Definition and Terminology

This way of referring to Jesus has much in common with prophecy, and indeed some would classify it as a form of prophecy. It is similar in that it is based upon divine knowledge of future events, and for this reason when these future things actually happen they may justifiably be said to be a 'fulfilment' of what came earlier. However, in the case of prophecy as discussed in the preceding chapter, the earlier prediction was expressed in the form of *words*. What we are considering now is rather a kind of prophecy in the form of observable *things*. When we say 'things' this has a wide range of meaning. It might be a person, an object, an event, or some kind of ceremony, or a combination of such.

Lying at the root of all kinds of prophecy is the belief that God knows the end from the beginning. Since he knows what is to come, he is able to announce it ahead of time through the words of his spokesmen the prophets. But when we come to prefiguration we need to bring in another idea, which is that God is also sovereign in the arena of human events. What this means is that God has the ability, if he so chooses, to order certain happenings, now seen as long past from our perspective, according to the purpose that he is going to accomplish in the future. Some manner of parallel or pattern is established between the two in such a way that the earlier events present a kind of sketch, for want of a better word at this stage, of the later. The historical events and persons in themselves then become figures or pictures of Christ and the gospel.

When we use the terms 'sketch' and 'figure', it indicates that the earlier event or person is not the reality in its fulness. It is simply an outline of things to come. When that fulness comes, in the person and work of Christ, we have moved to a whole new plane of accomplishment. So it is that the earlier things most frequently consist of the merely physical, while the later are matters of a greater spiritual consequence.

To highlight the difference between prophecy and prefiguration in simple terms some have described what was dealt with in the foregoing chapter as '*verbal* prophecy', while what we are now going to discuss is termed '*picture* prophecy'. Though these are not the descriptions we ourselves are going to employ, this is a helpful way of remembering the distinction so long as we keep in mind the fact that the 'pictures' we are looking at consist of things in the real world, that is to say, actual persons and events. Additionally, some would qualify the two kinds of prophecy as 'direct' and 'indirect' respectively. In the former sort the matter predicted is expressed directly by means of words in a prophetic oracle. In the latter what the words actually describe is an event and persons involved in those events, and then these in turn become figures of other events and persons to come.

In the case of verbal prophecy, the future tense of the oracle is a common tell-tale sign that this is a prophecy foretelling events to come. In the other form involving figures, however, since most of this sort are recorded by the inspired author in the past tense (though some might be in the present), there is no clear indication in the language of the text itself that it also concerns some future person or happening. While this is so, this ought not to be taken as meaning that all prophetic oracles are expressed in the future tense. This is patently not the case. When the reader encounters a past action within an oracle, besides the possibility of it indicating a prefiguration based upon a past event, it might otherwise be an example of what is commonly known as the 'prophetic perfect'. Here a prophet might speak of something that is wholly future as though it had already taken place. This is not unusual in Hebrew prophetic style. I suppose it is based upon the fact that if God foretells the future it is as good as done. But in such instances, although the form of the verbs might be past, the intention behind them is to express something yet to come. A notable example of this is the prophecy concerning the Servant of the Lord in Isaiah 53. Here all his sufferings (vv. 1–10a) are spoken of, prophetically, as having already happened. So this is not prefiguration, but a variation upon the direct verbal prophecy discussed in the previous chapter, a variation in which the prophetic perfect appears in place of the plain future tense. This has to be distinguished from other past tenses in prophetic oracles (not narratives) which are genuine pasts, referring to actual past events from the prophet's perspective, and yet which may be taken as figures of things yet to occur. Such a case would be God's words through Hosea: 'When Israel was a child I loved him, and out of Egypt I called my Son' (11:1). This is expressed in the past tense and is referring to an event long before Hosea the prophet's own time, that of the exodus from Egypt. This in turn, as the Matthew the Gospel writer shows us, serves as a figure for Jesus, God's 'Son', going down to Egypt and being called back from there (Matthew 2:13–15), with all of what that implies for the spiritual state of Judaea at that time and the Pharaoh-like role of Herod. In view of such a twofold use of the past within prophetic texts, the reader does need to be alert so as to correctly identify each distinct use.

This might be the appropriate place to mention that I did sneak in some of these 'picture prophecies' in the list of explicit fulfilments of prophecies at the first coming of Christ given in the preceding chapter. Since the fulfilment formulae introducing them is the same as that for regular verbal prophecies, I felt that, within the context of the list of prophetic fulfilments that I was presenting, it was not proper at that stage to separate them. So there I included Hosea 11:1 and also two or three others of the same kind in which events are seen as figures of something future.

From what has been said so far about the connection between prefiguration and verbal prophecy, it should be apparent to the reader that in essence prefiguration is, just like regular prophecy, something which is *prospective*, or looking forwards. These figures exist in the Old Testament by deliberate divine design in order to serve a prospective function. They point towards the future coming person and accomplishments of Christ in the gospel. I stress this fact as some have defined this manner of interpreting the Old Testament as something that is essentially *retrospective*, or looking backwards. To be sure, there may be retrospective activity involved. Once Jesus came and fulfilled the figures, then in the light of this new revelation Christian readers can indeed look back at the Old Testament to discern what was prefigured of him there. But this 'reading backwards' only concerns later generations of believers identifying the figures that have already been put in place through the inspiring Spirit. The retrospective reading is to detect what is already there prospectively. It is not the looking back that creates the presence of figures, but they have been placed there in the older Scriptures by divine design with the intent of foreshadowing things to come. Moreover, I am convinced that Spirit-endowed prophets and the more spiritually minded among the Israelites would have had some awareness of certain of these figures and an understanding to some degree of what they signified. This would have especially been the case with respect to the symbolism of the law of Moses. It would not take a great genius to realise that the death of an animal, lacking all sense of morality and rationality, is no fitting substitute for that of a moral and rational human being. Some, at least, would have appreciated that such sacrifices were merely a temporary measure until there should come the perfect sacrificial death of one who was human.

Since the Old Testament figures are fundamentally forward-looking, they take their form from the person and work of Jesus Christ, and not vice versa. As God knew from the beginning that his Son would come into the world and what he would do and experience, the figures of the Hebrew Scriptures are modelled upon matters which from the perspective of simple human chronology are yet future. Although in terms of strict historical progression the figure precedes the coming of Christ, in terms of importance and logical ordering within the divine purpose, it is Christ that comes before all else. As the apostle Peter stated: 'He was indeed foreordained before the foundation of the world, but was manifest in these last times for your sake' (1 Peter 1:20). God's great purpose in his Son, determined from the very beginning, already leaves its mark upon the writings of the Old Testament which prepare the way for his appearance within history. So it is that the author of the letter to the Hebrews looks at the Old Testament character of the priest-king Melchizedek and declares: 'having been made like the Son of God, he remains a priest for ever' (Hebrews 7:3). Viewing Melchizedek as a figure of Christ means that the former is modelled upon the latter, the one that is earliest in time upon the one to come. Even though Jesus had not yet been born upon the earth, Melchizedek was 'made like' him, and the same holds true for all the other Old Testament figures. This priority of Christ in the matter of prefiguration cannot be overstressed.

Turning now to biblical terms for prefiguration we find that, while it is clearly a thoroughly scriptural practice, there is no fixed terminology to describe its various components. One word that occurs, which still enjoys current usage, is the term 'type' (e.g. Romans 5:14). This comes from the Greek noun *tupos*, which in its most basic sense means a blow or, more relevant for our purposes, the impression left by a blow. This latter is its meaning in the English word 'typewriter'. In this machine the hammer strikes the paper, through a ribbon of ink, and leaves the impression on the paper of the letter on the end of the hammer. In this situation the 'type' would be the mark left on the page. The hammer is the solid reality which is the cause of the type. So it is that Christ corresponds to this reality, while the pictures in the Old Testament are impressions, or 'types' of him. The sense of this word serves to further underline the important characteristic stated above—which is that the type depends upon the reality, the figure takes its form from Christ, and not the other way round.

While I prefer to speak of what a type points forward to as the 'reality' or 'fulfilment', one technical term that could be employed with this meaning is 'antitype'. This appears with this sense just once in the Bible (1 Peter 3:21). Since words beginning with the prefix 'anti-' in modern English tend to be largely negative in connotation (whereas in the original Greek it has the sense of 'corresponding to' or 'in the place of'), I will not be using this particular word.

Another term that is used in the New Testament in connection with these figures we are discussing is that of *skia*, 'shadow'. A shadow can only exist if there is first an object to cast the shadow, which corresponds to the reality described above. Again this demonstrates the essential priority of Jesus. Twice in the New Testament we find the word 'shadow' used of Old Testament figures. To the Colossians Paul writes, 'Therefore no one is to judge you with respect to food or drink or in the matter of a festival or a new moon or Sabbaths—things which are a shadow of what is to come, but the substance belongs to Christ' (2:17). By 'substance' here he means, of course, the New Testament reality. Then the author of Hebrews also tells us that 'the law has a shadow of the good things to come, not the realities themselves' (10:1). I do not believe that it is merely coincidental that in both contexts the writer is speaking of the law, that is, the law of Moses, in which the dietary regulations and prescriptions regarding festivals and Sabbaths are described. It is specifically the sacred rituals and ceremonial instructions of the Mosaic code that contain these 'shadows'. Although many modern writers tend to use 'shadow' as a virtual synonym of 'type', it would seem that the former is in fact a sub-set of the latter. Perhaps this is the case because the shadows of the law are more specifically designed to foreshow the deeds of Christ and teachings of the gospel, and have less of a meaning of their own apart from the work of Christ. This contrasts with those types consisting of persons and events which are actual characters and actions within the course of history, and not merely in ceremony, and which therefore possess a significance within their own place and time quite apart from their connection with the christological fulfilment to come.

Four other words are found in the New Testament writings to refer to Old Testament figures, albeit only once each. The first of these is 'allegory'. This may be the cause of alarm to some readers. Many modern definitions of allegory assume that it dismisses the literal fact of the event or person upon which the allegory is based. Once the inner meaning has been ascertained, it is often thought, the literal meaning can then be dispensed with. However, it is altogether apparent from the sole biblical usage of this word, that this was not the way allegory was there understood. In Galatians the apostle Paul interprets the two woman, Sarah and Hagar, as figures of the two covenants—that made at Sinai and the new covenant. Paul here uses the Greek term *allēgoroumena* (4:24), which means something like 'allegorically speaking' (NASB; cf. NRSV: 'this is an allegory'; NJB: 'there is an allegory here'). Nevertheless, it is patently obvious that the apostle considers the people involved and the things that took place at that time to have literally happened, as we see from the way he talks about Sarah elsewhere (Romans 4:19; 9:9).

The other three terms with a similar meaning are *sēmeion*, 'sign' (Matthew 12:39), *mustērion*, 'mystery' (Ephesians 5:32), and *parabolē*, 'parable' (Hebrews 11:19). The first of these is speaking of 'the sign of Jonah' the prophet, who underwent a symbolic three-day death in the belly of the whale as Christ did in the belly of the earth. The second indicates how Eve, united to Adam as his wife, is a picture of Christ and his church. The third term, referring to God's command for Abraham to offer up his son Isaac in Genesis 22, says that Abraham received his son Isaac back from the dead, not literally (as he had not actually died), but 'by way of a parable' (cf. NRSV NIV NJB: 'figuratively speaking'; NKJV: 'in a figurative sense'; NASB: 'as a type').

In modern parlance the terms 'type' and 'typology' are frequently found in the literature dealing with this approach to interpreting the Bible. But as these words may sound strange to many, they will not be the ones we use here. In certain circles the description 'spiritual interpretation' is also found, but the adjective 'spiritual' is perhaps too broad in its significance to be helpful for our purposes. Some may take this as indicating a manner of interpretation that relates to matters of the (human) spirit, which it is definitely not. So I prefer, along with many others, to use 'prefigure' as the verb to describe what we are examining in this chapter. This verb may be simply taken as meaning 'to represent ahead of time', that is, the Old Testament phenomenon of presenting figures, or pictures, of Christ long before his actual birth. As nouns I would choose 'prefiguration' for the act of prefiguring (the activity in the abstract) and 'prefigurement' as a particular individual instance of such an act. Finally, the related adjective would be 'prefigural', giving rise to the phrase 'prefigural interpretation'.

Interpretative Considerations

As regards the interpretation of these Old Testament figures there are a number of different observations, and also guidelines, to which I believe it would be helpful to bring to the reader's attention.

1. The manner of interpretation discussed here has been a major component in the effort to expound the Scriptures from the very earliest times. It was most certainly practiced by Jesus himself and the apostles, and would therefore seem to have been passed on to the church, and so authoritatively endorsed, by them. Indeed the practice may even be found within the confines of the Old Testament itself, as earlier events foreshadow later ones. This is the case, for example, with Abraham going down to Egypt as recorded in Genesis 12 (vv. 10–20) and his subsequent return to Canaan, which provides a figure of the later exodus of the Hebrew nation descended from the same patriarch. Both descents into Egypt take place during a time of severe famine, both involve difficulties with the pharaoh, resolved by the sending of divine plagues, and in both instances the Hebrews emerge bearing great possessions to return to the promised land. When the national exodus does eventually occur, this itself forms a figure of the new exodus, one on a much greater scale, as foretold by the prophet Isaiah (chapters 40–55), which is the New Testament gospel deliverance.

Clearly, then, prefiguration is a genuine feature of the inspired writings, and not merely a fanciful reading into it. It is, therefore, the cause of some concern that in the latter part of the nineteenth century the influence of the higher critical movement brought about a departure from this kind of interpretation, within Protestant theological circles at least, and advocated an approach to the Bible as though it was comprised of merely historical documents. Due to the fact that within this new movement the historical-critical approach had the tendency to fragment Scripture into independent documents, rather than see it as an essential unity with each part relating profoundly to others. Moreover, for each of these documents the contribution of the human author began to be valued above that of the divine, and hence the possibility of supernatural knowledge was diminished. These factors inevitably led to a neglect, and even perhaps a ridicule, of the figural manner of interpretation. Despite this reaction against prefiguration within the theological academy, thankfully the church, that is to say, its pastors and preachers, for the most part kept up the practice in their expositions. Significantly, today, within intellectual circles many are beginning to realise the error made by the higher critics, and very recently there have been a number of notable publications (certain of which are listed at the close of this chapter) by theologians and biblical scholars advocating a return to the well-tested and ancient Christian practice of prefigural interpretation, without at the same time having to abandon the better insights of the historical approach.

Continuing on the theme of the history of interpretation for just a moment, I feel it necessary to add a few comments about the supposed objections raised against prefiguration at other times in church history, long before the higher critical movement of the nineteenth century. It has been claimed that around the fourth and fifth centuries a reaction took place amongst a group of Christian scholars centred upon Antioch, and who are therefore named the 'Antiochene School'. The story is sometimes told that these men attempted to move away from the prefigural interpretation of the Old Testament, so common in other parts of the church, and move towards a strictly grammatical and historical approach to Scripture. Such a view, though frequently heard, is simply not in agreement with the facts. On my shelves behind me, as I write, I have a number of books by four key members of the so-called Antiochene School. One does not have to spend too much time looking through their commentaries and other writings to discover that these likewise practiced a form of interpretation similar to what is being described in this chapter. To be sure, they spoke out against the abuses of allegorisation in its extreme forms, this was one of their main emphases, yet their objections were more concerned with degree rather than with principle. In their efforts to understand and expound the Old Testament all these men saw figures of Christ present in the text in varying degrees. One of the stricter interpreters, Theodore of Mopsuestia, was only prepared to accept types and shadows which were explicitly taken as such in the New Testament writings. Theodoret of Cyrus, on the other hand, applied prefiguration much more extensively. Their chief concern with regard to this manner of interpretation, it would seem, was to preserve the literal meaning of the original text and to apply prefiguration to Christ, and not to philosophical and other concepts. For this reason they adopted their own term to describe their particular practice. They called it *theōria*. This Greek word is difficult to translate into English, but it basically means a spiritual 'contemplation' or 'discernment', by which they meant seeing a deeper meaning, that is, a primarily christological one, in the text. We note the words of Diodore of Tarsus, a leading Antiochene teacher, who stated (in the introduction to his commentary on the Psalms) that 'we shall deal with it [the text] historically and literally, yet not stand in the way of a spiritual and more elevated discernment [*theōria*]. The historical sense, in fact, is not in opposition to the more elevated sense; on the contrary, it proves to be the basis and foundation of the more elevated meanings'. So clearly, in their minds, it was not held to be an 'either/or' situation, but one of 'both/and'. For the Antiochenes it is evident that a serious treatment of the literal and historical sense did not preclude the discovery of figures. Thus it is that one recent writer concludes: 'Given their predilection for *theoria* that goes beyond the letter, it is clear that the Antiochenes cannot be regarded as the forerunners of the historical-critical exegesis that is free from fuller meanings and spiritual applications' (Stanglin, *The Letter* and *Spirit of Biblical Interpretation*, pp. 67–68; full details given at end of this chapter).

Similar comments could be made about the Reformers and their successors, during the sixteenth and following centuries. It cannot be doubted that these men paid significantly more attention to the plain literal meaning of Scripture than was normally done in the biblical exposition of the late Middle Ages. During this latter period extreme allegorisation was rife, frequently to the exclusion of the basic historical sense of the texts. The Reformers did of course react against this exegetical misconduct. This does not mean, however, that non-literal interpretation was abandoned completely. Not at all in fact. Again, it does not require too much time or effort to locate prefigural interpretations in their expositions. Not so long ago I completed preaching a sermon series on the book of Deuteronomy. One of the resources I used for preparation was Martin Luther's series of lectures on this Old Testament book (found in *Luther's Works*, Volume 9), which he worked on from 1523–1525, several years after he had launched the Reformation in Germany. It is noteworthy that here in this volume the great Luther himself employs, in a number of instances, an allegorical form of interpretation. Luther is not at all unique in this, since the same is true of the other leading Reformers.

The Swiss Reformer Heinrich Bullinger wrote a theological treatise entitled *The Decades*, which was one of the most popular works of its kind within the early Reformed Church. In his treatment of the Mosaic law Bullinger declared that its ceremonies foreshadowed 'the chief or especial mysteries of Christ and his church' (Third Decade, Sermon 5), and then proceeds to offer an outline of the way in which this was so, with respect to the sacrifices and other Levitical rituals. Of all the notable figures of this period prefiguration was perhaps approached most cautiously by John Calvin. All the same, he definitely subscribed to it in principle for he declared that 'it is beyond all doubt that that the principal and most memorable events which happened in it [Israel] are so many types to us' (*Commentaries*, on Galatians 4:22). Instances of a figural interpretation are found at intervals throughout his commentaries. What is more, later generations of Reformed theologians and expositors, the successors to men like Calvin, produced substantial works devoted to what they generally termed the 'typical' meaning of Scripture, that is to say, with respect to the 'types' that it contains. Here we have in mind publications during the seventeenth and eighteenth centuries by such men as William Guild (1620), Thomas Taylor (1635), Thomas Worden (1664), Benjamin Keach (1681), Samuel Mather (1683), as well as the slightly later Jonathan Edwards, arguably the greatest of all theologians in the post-Puritan period. The large scale of several of these writings indicates that the authors did not see their subject matter as something merely peripheral to biblical faith.

In view of the foregoing it has to be said that the emergence of a historical school of interpretation in the nineteenth century, denying as it did the presence of a deeper figural sense, was actually an innovation, something foreign to previous study of the Bible since the earliest times. It stood in sharp contrast to the way the church and its ministers had been reading Scripture for the best part of 1,800 years, in accordance with the example of Jesus himself and his apostles. To claim that there were precedents to this modern approach at earlier times in church history is, in light of the facts, merely wishful thinking.

2. From what has been said so far, the reader should be aware that the sense being described here does not in the least do away with the importance of the literal sense offered by the Hebrew text of the Old Testament. This is so important it deserves to be reiterated. As we saw with Paul's practice of allegorisation in Galatians 4, it certainly does not negate the historicity of what took place back in Genesis. The persons

here mentioned that are interpreted as figures are firstly real persons engaging in real actions. The literal sense is important because the prefigural interpretation is squarely based upon it. Every effort should therefore be made to understand the text in its original literal sense, and any implications derived from it, before moving on to the discerning of figures that might be present. More than this, it is the reality of the prior events and persons in the Old Testament that provides assurance of the actuality of the greater reality to come. As, for example, there was a literal exodus from slavery to the Egyptians that took place within the flow of historical events, there would similarly be a greater exodus, this time from bondage to sin, that would likewise occur as an actual event within time and space.

3. It needs also to be emphasised that prefiguration, properly conducted, does not result in freedom for the interpreter's imagination to run riot. While some may object that it is an arbitrary method of interpretation, this is actually far from the case. Speaking at the more general level to begin, there are three principles to which we ought to adhere, which are equally applicable to all manner of biblical exegesis (though not always followed). The first is what was just mentioned above, that is, the importance of the literal meaning. Before any figural interpretation is attempted, the reader has first to identify elements and concepts, together with their functions, as expressed in the original sense of the text. Then, if a literal element is also interpreted as a figure, there must obviously be some correspondence between the literal entity, taking into account the purpose it serves in its historical context, and the figural significance assigned to it. This need for a linkage between literal elements, concepts, and functions, and their figural counterparts in itself gives a certain measure of restraint to the interpreter's imagination. The second principle is what has become known as the 'analogy of faith' (*analogia fidei*). By 'faith' here is meant the faith commonly professed by the universal church throughout the generations, as expressed in its confessions and creedal formulae. No conclusion derived from exegesis of the biblical text can be a valid one if it contradicts the faith of the historic catholic (i.e. worldwide) and orthodox (i.e. having correct beliefs) church. Then, thirdly, it is absolutely essential to keep in mind and to apply the principle of interpreting Scripture by Scripture (*analogia Scripturae*). Since, according to the faith of the same aforementioned church, the Bible is above all else the product of a single divine mind, consistency is to be found in what it teaches.

Coming now to principles relating more specifically to the matter of biblical prefiguration, we would be greatly assisted in endeavouring to interpret one passage where the presence of figures is suspected by the use of figures in another passage where their presence is beyond doubt. It is a fact of considerable importance that there are a good many texts in the New Testament which present interpretations of Old Testament figures. The practise of prefigural interpretation on the part of Jesus and the apostolic writers can help us to establish guidelines as to how prefiguration may be correctly undertaken. An illustration of this will be given below. We may also bring in here those passages of Scripture which are, by their very nature, deliberately non-literal. Here I am thinking especially of parables, poetry, and the visions of the prophets, as described in the previous chapter. In all of these various media truths relating to the divine purpose are, or can be, expressed through symbolic means. It would seem reasonable that the interpreter should further be guided by the use of figures in such figurative passages. So, for instance, if in a non-literal context the blast of trumpets announces the end of the 'kingdom of the world' and the establishment of the 'kingdom of our Lord and of his Christ' (Revelation 11:15), then in the outworking of a prefigural interpretation of a historical passage (e.g. Joshua 6) there is some foundation for giving the blast of trumpets a similar significance. Again, if incense is likened to the prayers of the saints (i.e. the people of God) in both a poetic text (Psalm 141:2) and in a vision (Revelation 5:8), then in the symbolism of the tabernacle the offering of incense (Exodus 30:6–7) is most likely to have the same meaning. Such a method of looking elsewhere in Scripture for what a figure might signify is, of course, much preferable to going to other extra-biblical literature, and even more desirable than simply inventing it in our own minds.

It is also important to understand that prefigural interpretation is essentially a christological undertaking. Figures contained in the Old Testament writings are consistently interpreted with respect to Christ (once again reminding the reader of the *totus Christus* principle, namely that this includes his body, the church). On this basis, more fanciful interpretations can be rejected. One ancient Christian expositor, Ambrose of Milan (a fourth-century bishop), who incidentally wrote a good many things worth reading, nevertheless lost his way when he looked at the war between the four kings and the five kings in Genesis 14 and attempted to explain it as the conflict between the five senses (sight, smell, touch, hearing, taste) and the four physical elements (earth, air, water, fire) that make up the human body and the earthly creation. This he applied to the fact that, unless we put up a fight, our senses are so easily overcome by the physical attraction experienced by our flesh and by the world. As ingenious as this may be, it is not what biblical prefiguration is all about. Ambrose here was basically presenting a philosophical reading of the text, which is not its intention. Rather, Old Testament events and the characters involved in them form part of the prophetic witness to the coming Messiah, Jesus.

We note, furthermore, that it is a fundamental principle of prefiguration that it does not serve to introduce new teachings. By this I mean that no biblical doctrine is to be based upon the results of this manner of interpretation alone. That great thirteenth-century theologian, Thomas Aquinas, famously stated that 'nothing necessary to faith is contained under the spiritual sense which is not elsewhere put forward by Scripture in its literal sense' (*Summa Theologica*, 1a.1.10). So every matter derived from the interpretation of Old Testament figures needs to also be stated in plain words in another text of Scripture. This principle safeguards the application of prefiguration from leading to an erroneous conclusion. The figures of the Old Testament, correctly understood, will consistently point to a biblical truth.

From what has just been stated one may wonder why, if a prefigurement of itself does not advance any independent truth, there should be such a feature in the biblical text at all. The answer to this leads us firstly back to that matter of 'motives of credibility', as described in our treatment of prophecy in the preceding chapter. The corresponding patterns that exist between events in the Old Testament and the New provide evidence that there is one and the same divine author behind both. Like verbal prophecy prefiguration is a testimony to the supernatural ordering of events involved in the biblical story. A second function of Old Testament figures is to aid in understanding what is accomplished later through the gospel. This is done in that the figures present earthly analogies to the events accomplished at the coming of Christ. Deliverances and provisions in the purely physical realm, as depicted in many Old Testament narratives, help us in taking a step into the significance of what was achieved through the gospel with regard to the spiritual realm. Both occur within history, but the former principally have significance in connection with this life, while the latter with the life to come. So it is that the ancient Scriptures provide a rich source of illustrations for Bible teachers and preachers in order to help their congregations to comprehend the accomplishments of Christ.

4. While some evidence of correspondence in the entity or concept must exist between the figure and the reality, it should be obvious that there cannot be complete identity. If this were so, we would not be moving from figure to reality, since the two would be one and the same. What prefiguration necessarily entails, therefore, is an essential distinction between the two elements.

So, besides the correspondences that serve to connect them, the figure and its fulfilment will also display differences. One crucial matter that sets them apart is the fact that the figure is always the lesser of the two. This must be the case, as the first is simply a representation while the second is the reality that it represents. From the former to the latter a notable increase in significance, that is to say in the scope and degree of its effects, takes place. The reality is therefore always much greater than what is indicated in the figure. Biblical scholars often refer to this as 'heightening' or 'escalation'.

As well as this upwards movement from the figure to the reality, another possible difference might be the presence of actual contrasts between the two. The Old Testament contains a number of persons, for instance, who undergo an experience that prefigures the death and resurrection of Jesus. Among these I would include Isaac, Joseph, Jonah, and Daniel. Yet the fact is that in the relevant passages about them none of these men actually dies. Each looks death in the face, but they all emerge from their respective situations still very much alive. If they had indeed died and come to life again, I would think that such a stupendous event would have come too close to *the* death and resurrection of Christ, and so the heightening I have just mentioned would be somewhat diminished. Another example of a significant difference between figure and reality can be seen in the apostle Paul's Adam-Christ typology (Romans 5), where some of the differences amount to contrasts or even opposites.

5. We next consider the question of whether it is admissible to interpret every Old Testament passage in terms of figures. Clearly, the answer to that has to be 'No'. Looking at the history of this manner of interpretation it is generally agreed that certain elements of the Hebrew Scriptures are to be understood in solely a literal manner. These are, first and foremost, moral injunctions. Commandments such as 'Honour your father and your mother' and 'You shall not steal' (Exodus 20:12, 15) mean what they say and nothing more. Related to these are proverbs, which in essence also include moral instruction, like 'Do not rebuke a

scoffer or he will hate you; rebuke a wise man and he will love you'
(Proverbs 9:8).

So a figural interpretation of the Hebrew moral law and other moral
teaching is not legitimate, but when it comes to the rituals of the
ceremonial law it is an entirely different matter. Here, following the New
Testament precedent, such as Paul and the writer to the Hebrews, the
sacrifices, holy days, circumcision, and other rituals may be given a
christological, or gospel-oriented, interpretation. Christ is seen, for
example, as the Passover lamb (1 Corinthians 5:7), the Sabbath is a figure
of the everlasting rest that comes through him (Hebrews 4:8–11), and
circumcision is a work of the Spirit within the Christian believer (Romans
2:28–29).

In this matter of interpreting the ceremonial law, I consider it
appropriate to offer a word of caution. I believe, following many
interpreters over the centuries, that the sanctuary, its priesthood, and its
sacrifices, are figures of the gospel of Christ. But this does not mean that
every single detail should be made to be prefigurative in this way. So, for
example, some parts of the tabernacle are symbolic, while others are there
because they need to be. The whole sanctuary was separated from the
camp of Israel by a continuous barrier of hanging curtains made of fine
linen. This structure as a whole I take to be symbolic, since fine linen can
justifiably be taken as indicating purity and holiness. But in order for this
wall of curtains to serve their purpose they had to be attached to poles set
in sockets and supported by ropes and pegs. I have actually heard a
sermon in which the preacher said each one of these wooden poles was a
picture of the cross and the pegs driven into the ground were figures of
the nails used at the crucifixion. This, to me, is taking things much too
far. To my mind the poles, sockets, ropes, and pegs are all there to enable
the curtains to hang vertically. The white curtains are the symbolic
element, not the tackle that was necessary for hanging them. The reader
needs to develop a sensitivity so as to discern what it is that possesses
symbolic value and what is extraneous to that.

When it comes to Old Testament narrative, there will no doubt be
considerable difference of opinion as to whether there is any prefiguration
in a particular episode. Of course, when the New Testaments gives such
an interpretation there is no doubt. But when such a precedent is lacking
I would, as a general guide, include as likely candidates for prefigural
interpretation those events within the record that are directly enacted by
God, that is, the miraculous, or which are ordained by him as part of the

outworking of his redemptive plan. An example of the former would be the water from the rock which miraculously supplied the Israelites on their wilderness journey. Paul does indeed say 'that rock was Christ' (1 Corinthians 10:4). For the latter, this would be illustrated, to my mind, by that already-mentioned instance of 'allegory' employed by Paul in which the mother who is a slave, namely Hagar, and the mother who is free, Sarah, represent the old and new covenants, and their children the respective adherents to these covenants (Galatians 4:24–26). In this latter case God's hand is explicitly seen to be at work, since it was he that gave Sarah her offspring, Isaac, and who rejected Ishmael from being the heir of the Abrahamic promise.

At this point it might be helpful to introduce the principle of analogy, or association. What is meant by this is that if one particular episode of Old Testament narrative is explicitly interpreted in the New as containing prefiguration, then an analogous event, containing similar elements in a similar situation, is also most probably to be so interpreted. So, for instance, it is without doubt that certain miracles that occurred in the wilderness journey of the Israelites out of Egypt are to be understood as figures. This is plainly the case with the provision of manna (John 6, to be discussed in more detail below) and the just-mentioned provision of water from the rock (1 Corinthians 10:4), and with the raising up of the serpent on a pole (John 3:14). In view of this, the incident in which Moses makes bitter water drinkable (Exodus 15:23–25) is so closely associated with other wilderness miracles, that it is almost undoubtedly likewise intended as a figure, which is how a long tradition of early Christian interpretation understood it. The same applies to the scarlet thread of Joshua 2:18–21. This scarlet material placed in the window frame of Rahab, shut up in her house with her family as protection against the coming overthrow of Jericho, has clear associations with the original Passover. On that earlier occasion the Hebrews secured themselves in their homes with the door frames daubed in red blood in the face of the coming judgment against Egypt. In both instances it speaks of a 'sign' that marks the fact that those inside the houses will be delivered from the destruction. Again, though many modern interpreters may fail to see the connection with the gospel, early Christian expositors rightly saw the analogy, and it is a profound one, since it points to both Jew (the Hebrews in Egypt) and Gentile (Rahab and her family in Canaan) being delivered through the death of *the* Lamb, the efficacy of whose shed blood is extended to the latter as well as the former. Shortly we will examine in some depth the account of the crossing of the River Jordan. This is so closely related to the earlier crossing of the Red Sea, explicitly taken as a figure by the apostle Paul, that the event at the Jordan should likewise be taken as a figure. This principle of analogy, then, can often be put to good use in determining which passages are to be taken as containing prefigurements, and also perhaps how they are to be interpreted.

The matter of prefiguration in biblical poetry and wisdom literature is slightly more challenging. Again careful attention ought to be paid to New Testament precedents, which are not lacking. In the case of the Psalms, descriptions of God's character and the ascription of praise to him are strictly literal. Yet as so many of the Psalms concern David it is possible to interpret events within his life as figures of what would later transpire in the life of *the* Son of David, the promised Messiah. We may take as an example the words of Psalm 41:9, where David states that, 'Even my close friend in whom I trusted, who ate my bread, has lifted up his heel against me'. David here is speaking of an actual past event (it is not a prophetic perfect), which, as we learn from the historical books, was the event of David being betrayed by his trusted counsellor Ahithophel (2 Samuel 15:31). This act of betrayal of David serves as a figure for the betrayal of the greater Son of David, Jesus, by one of his intimate group of disciples, Judas. We know this is so since Jesus himself explicitly points it out as a fulfilment, citing the verse of the psalm (John 13:18). It is not without additional significance that the Old Testament Ahithophel and the New Testament Judas, as well as both betraying their Davidic masters, are the only two biblical characters who are said to have hanged themselves (2 Samuel 17:23; Matthew 27:5; both *apēgxato* in their Greek versions).

A book like the Song of Songs, which is highly poetic, may also allow a figural interpretation. Just as many psalms are associated with David, so this book is associated with Solomon, son of David. Here then there is the possibility of viewing Solomon as another messianic figure, and the woman he loves in the song, as a figure of his people, the church. Although many modern scholars would not advocate such an understanding, largely due to the prevailing influence of the modern historical-critical method, this is by far the majority interpretation given to the poem throughout the centuries.

6. Finally, mention must be made of one example that is sometimes used in the relevant literature and media to illustrate what we are talking about in this chapter. The reason I feel it necessary to include this is that it is in fact *not* what I am trying to present here. The last speech of Martin

Luther King, Jr., the famous civil rights campaigner back in the fifties and sixties, includes those memorable words: 'I have been to the mountaintop, and I have seen the promised land'. King, a Baptist minister, was making reference to a biblical text here, to the account of Moses standing on Mount Nebo, surveying the land of Canaan (Deuteronomy 34) shortly before the people of Israel crossed the Jordan to take up possession of it. There are indeed a number of connections between that ancient situation and that of King and his cause. There is a prominent leader involved in each case, one whose goal was to lead his people out of a form of slavery and oppression. And before each of them was the vision of a better land, a better world for their people. Certain modern theologians and biblical scholars look at this part of King's speech and assert 'This is typology'. In my view this claim is mistaken. King was not employing typology in the biblical sense, but rather 'allusion'. What King was doing, and there is no doubting that it was a masterful use of rhetoric, was alluding to the biblical passage to enhance what he was saying respecting the current situation. He was taking facts and circumstances from the past, bringing them into the present, and claiming some similarity, which there was to some degree. In this way his present-day hearers would then associate what was happening with the not too dissimilar events in the Bible. They would appreciate that the plight of the American black community was not unlike that of the Hebrews in Egypt, that a better country was desirable for them, and that like Moses King was doing all he could to bring them into it. This is a wonderful and highly effective use of allusion, but it is not at all the typology that occurs in the Scriptures, despite what some might claim. One essential difference lies in the fact that in the Bible the figures of the Old Testament are there by deliberate divine design with the express purpose of pointing forward to matters to come. Now it is not the case that the account of Moses viewing the land from Nebo was recorded with the particular intention of prefiguring the work of Martin Luther King. The speaker was looking back to the text, but the text was not looking forward specifically to what the speaker was saying. Another essential difference is that, as stated above, the older event, being interpreted as a figure, is the lesser of the two events. By all accounts, though the achievements of the civil rights movement were by no means inconsiderable, they bear no comparison, within the wider context of God's redemptive plan, to the exodus of the Israelites from Egypt (along with all the signs and wonders that then occurred), and to their entrance into the promised land. Lastly, we may mention the obvious omission from the figural understanding that is being asserted for the speech of any attempt to signify Christ, which is one of the principal purposes of prefiguration. For these three important reasons, then, King's speech completely fails to offer a suitable illustration of biblical typology.

The last word on this matter of interpretation has to be one that stresses the need for prayer and the guidance of the Holy Spirit. This is undoubtedly the greatest factor of all when it comes to interpreting the Word of God. No amount of institutional learning nor extra-biblical reading could ever be a substitute for the prayerful study of Scripture under the assistance of the divine Spirit who inspired it. At the end of the day prefigural interpretations are offered to the church for the spiritual edification of its members. It is the Spirit in the hearts of believers, not some academically prescribed methodology dependent upon modernist or postmodernist presuppositions, that will determine the validity of such interpretations.

An Examination of Various Figures

We shall close this chapter with a study of three specific examples of prefigural interpretation. The first of these will be an instance in which the New Testament itself views the Old Testament passage as containing a figure. Regarding the second, this is a case where there is no explicit New Testament precedent for seeing the presence of a figure, but rather there are a number of hints that implicitly point in that direction. In the third instance, we interpret an Old Testament event as a figure on the basis of its association with another event which is definitely given a figural interpretation in the New Testament.

The Manna

The relevant passages here are Exodus 16 in the Old Testament and John 6 in the New. The former tells us how the Israelites in the wilderness, just two weeks after coming out of slavery in Egypt, grumbled against Moses and Aaron about the lack of food. In response to this God miraculously provided 'bread from heaven' (v. 4), a white flaky substance that tasted like 'wafers made with honey' (v. 31). The Hebrews described this as 'manna' (which means 'What is it?'). This heaven-sent food was to sustain the people on their journeys through the wilderness for the next forty years (v. 35).

In the sixth chapter of John's Gospel we first read of Jesus feeding the five thousand (vv. 1–15). It is this miraculous provision of loaves of bread that motivated many of the Jews to look for Jesus afterwards. When they find him he tells them, 'Truly I tell you, you are looking for me, not because you saw signs, but because you ate the loaves and were filled' (v. 26). The miracle concerned the giving of literal bread. But now Jesus transposes this to a different level. He says, 'Do not labour for food that perishes, but for the food that endures to eternal life, which the Son of Man will give you' (v. 27). These words set the scene for the teaching that follows, commonly known as the 'bread of life discourse'.

It is the Jews who first bring up the subject of the manna, which is natural from the context, since what happened back in Exodus was also a feeding miracle, such as they had recently witnessed. The Jews, as if what they had just seen was not sufficient, asked Jesus, 'What sign are you going to give that we may see it and believe you? What are you going to perform?' (v. 30). Then they add, 'Our fathers ate the manna in the wilderness; as it is written, "He gave them bread from heaven to eat"' (v. 31, where the citation is from Psalm 78:24). The passage then continues:

> Jesus said to them, 'Truly, truly, I say to you, it is not Moses who has given you the bread from heaven, but it is my Father who gives you the true bread from heaven. For the bread of God is that which comes down from heaven and gives life to the world'. Then they said to him, 'Lord, give us this bread always'. Jesus said to them, 'I am the bread of life. He who comes to me will not hunger, and he who believes in me will never thirst. But I told you that you have seen me and yet do not believe. All that the Father gives me will come to me, and the one who comes to me I will certainly not cast out. For I have come down from heaven, not to do my own will, but the will of him who sent me. This is the will of him who sent me, that of all that he has given me I lose nothing, but raise it up on the last day. For this is the will of my Father, that everyone who beholds the Son and believes in him will have eternal life, and I will raise him up on the last day … Truly, I say to you, he who believes has everlasting life. I am the bread of life. Your fathers ate the manna in the wilderness, yet they died. This is the bread which comes down from heaven, so that one may eat of it and not die. I am the living bread that came down from heaven. If anyone eats of this bread, he will live forever; and the bread which I will give for the life of the world is my flesh. As the living Father sent me, and I live because of the Father, so he who eats me will also live because of me. This is the bread which came down from heaven;

not as the fathers ate and died; he who eats this bread will live forever' (vv. 32–40, 48–51, 57–58).

The Jews grumbled at Jesus because he said 'I am the bread that came down from heaven' (v. 41). They failed to understand his meaning. At the literal level Jesus spoke of bread and eating, just as had occurred in the recent miracle. But they did not perceive that by the words 'bread that came down from heaven' he was using the manna as a figure of himself.

As stressed earlier, the events of Exodus 16 are intended, in the first instance, to be taken as historical. God did literally give the Israelites manna as described. But in the John passage Jesus himself invites the Jews, and us, to understand this in a figural sense. To establish the connection between the Old Testament figure and the New Testament reality there are a number of correspondences at the literal level. Each concerns a divinely performed event, that is, one that is supernatural, in both cases what is imparted is said to come down specifically from heaven, in both what is given brings life to those that receive it, the act of receiving being one that is inward, and in both the primary recipients are the people of Israel. Yet in the move from manna to Christ there is an obvious escalation, a movement from the lesser to the greater. The manna was an impersonal substance, whereas the bread of life that Jesus speaks of is personal; it is himself, the Word made flesh. The manna was given to Israel alone, while Jesus is offered to people of all nations. The manna sustained life for just forty years, but the bread offered by Jesus gives everlasting life, as he emphatically declares several times in John 6.

However, the most important transformation in the teaching of Jesus is the fact that the physical food offered to the Israelites has now become a spiritual food, one that sustains not merely the body but the soul. And this is where the idea of eating takes on an important significance. In Exodus eating the bread is simply a physical activity. But what is crucial for us to note here is that this act involves an internalising of the life-giving substance. Bread benefits nobody unless it is consumed. So with the bread of life, it likewise has to be consumed, taken into one's inward parts. 'If anyone eats of this bread', says Jesus, referring to himself, 'he will live for ever' (vv. 51, 58). The eating that he means is spiritual not physical, but it still entails an internalising. He explains precisely what it is he means by this when he states, this time in plain words, 'whoever *believes* has everlasting life' (v. 47), as paralleled with 'whoever *eats* … has everlasting life' (v. 54), both consisting of the same Greek construction (*ho —ōn echei zōēn aiōnion*). As literal eating brings food into the stomach to sustain mortal life temporarily, so the spiritual 'eating' that Jesus intends is nothing other than 'believing', a receiving of himself into the heart by faith, which results in life immortal. But in both instances the internalisation must be done for there to be any imparting of life. The point is that Jesus, as the bread of life, only communicates that life to those that receive him in the way described, namely, by faith.

For the most part, tragically, the Jews did not partake of Jesus as the bread of life. As John writes earlier in his Gospel, 'he came to his own, but his own did not receive him' (1:11). It is sadly ironic that whereas in Exodus 16 the people of Israel 'grumbled' at the lack of food (vv. 2, 7), in John 6 they 'grumbled' at the provision of it (vv. 41, 43), and yet it was the '*true* bread'.

Joseph

The patriarch Joseph, son of Jacob, is not explicitly described in the New Testament as a figure of Christ. Yet from this we ought not to conclude that this is not the case. Just as the Gospels and other apostolic writings do not quote every messianic prophecy that appears in the older Scriptures, as noted in the previous chapter, similarly they do not present every figure of Jesus. Much is left in the Old Testament for the reader to discover for himself or herself. In the case of Joseph there exist quite a number of correspondences with the person and experiences of Christ, plus some significant verbal allusions, which taken together help to establish the patriarch Joseph as an undeniable prefigurement of Jesus.

Joseph first takes the scene as a major character in Genesis 37, and from chapter 39 to the end of the book he may fairly be said to dominate the narrative, though his father and brothers also have an important part to play. Joseph's story is basically one of contrasting experiences—rejection and acceptance, of dejection and glory, of humiliation and exaltation. At the literal level it presents a superb read, with plenty of highs and lows, an account which those unfamiliar with it are encouraged to look at before they proceed.

The best way to approach Joseph as a figure is to outline the numerous details occurring within the narrative that find a counterpart with respect to Christ. While some of them, taken in isolation, may not seem to amount to much, it is the cumulative testimony of the whole number that points to the figural nature of Joseph. The correspondences are as follows:

• Joseph is especially loved by his father. At his introduction into the

Genesis story we are told that 'Israel [= Jacob] loved Joseph more than any of his other sons' (Genesis 37:3). In the Gospels, at his presentation for baptism at the onset of his ministry, Jesus is declared by his Father to be 'my beloved Son' (Matthew 3:17; Mark 1:11; Luke 3:22), and we read several times in John that 'the Father loves the Son' (John 3:35; 5:20; cf. 10:17; 15:9; 17:24).

• Joseph is said to give an 'evil report' of his brothers to his father (Genesis 37:2). This certainly tallies with Christ's moral assessment of his kinsfolk, the Jews, calling them 'evil' (e.g. Matthew 12:34).

• Long before it happens, it is revealed by supernatural means that Joseph will one day be a significant ruler (Genesis 37:6–10). It is foretold concerning Jesus by supernatural revelation that one day he will rule over the entire creation.

• As part of this divine appointment to rulership it says that the rest of Joseph's family would bow down to him (Genesis 37:7, 9–10). With regard to Christ we are told that 'at the name of Jesus every knee shall bow' (Philippians 2:10).

• The response of his brothers to the favoured position and claims of Joseph is one of hatred (Genesis 37:4–5) and jealousy (v. 11). With respect to Jesus it is clear that his own people hated him (cf. John 15:24–25; Luke 19:14) and wanted him dead out of jealousy (Matthew 27:18).

• While the brothers responded in the way described, the response was different on the part of their father. Concerning Jacob we read that 'his father kept the matter in mind' (Genesis 37:11). Very similar words occur with respect to Mary, Christ's only true earthly parent, of whom we read 'his mother kept all these matters in her heart' (Luke 2:51). Looking at these texts in Greek we find that the main verb (*diatēreō*) and direct object (*rēma*) are the same in each case.

• Joseph's father, Jacob, 'sent him' to his brothers (Genesis 37:14). Jesus said, 'The Father sent me' (John 6:57; cf. 5:23; 6:44; 8:16; 1 John 4:14; etc.).

• When Joseph is sent to visit his brothers as they are tending the sheep, they see him coming in the distance and 'plotted to kill him' (Genesis 37:18), which is the same what the Jewish authorities planned with regard to Jesus (Matthew 26:4).

• As Joseph approaches his brothers they say to each other, 'Now come, let us kill him' (Genesis 37:20). In Christ's parable of the wicked tenants, who represent the unbelieving people of Israel, when the vineyard owner sends his 'beloved son' (Luke 20:13), representing Jesus himself, to receive what is due, they see him coming and say, 'Come, let us kill him' (Matthew 21:38). In their Greek versions both sayings use exactly the same words (*deute apokteinōmen auton*). From this it is hard to deny that in telling the parable Jesus was actually drawing a parallel between Joseph's fate at the hands of his brothers and his own at the hands of his fellow Jews. This is further enforced by the fact that the parable continues with the words 'having taken hold of him' (v. 39, *labontes auton*), again precisely the same phrase as appears in the Greek version of the Joseph account (Genesis 37:24).

• As Joseph is taken he is stripped of his special 'robe' (Genesis 37:23, where in Greek the garment is called a *chitōn*). Jesus is likewise stripped, and the one item of clothing that attracts particular attention is his 'robe' (John 19:23, also *chitōn*).

• In their desire to dispose of Joseph his brothers decide to hand him over to Midianite (or 'Ishmaelite) traders (Genesis 37:28, 36), that is to say, to Gentiles. In the Gospels, to get rid of Jesus the Jews hand him over to the Gentile Romans.

• The transaction to dispose of Joseph involves a payment of silver (Genesis 37:28), while that to do away with Jesus similarly involves the payment of silver (Matthew 26:15). In the former instance the idea to get money for Joseph is that of Judah (vv. 26–27), whereas in the latter it is that of Judas, this being the Greek form of the very same name.

• As far as the rest of Joseph's family are concerned he is as good as 'dead' (Genesis 42:38; 44:20; cf. 37:34). Jesus, of course, does literally die, though that is not the end of him.

• In the next part of the narrative about Joseph it stresses several times that 'The LORD was with him' (Genesis 39:2, 3, 21, 23), a fact that is repeated in Stephen's speech in the book of Acts—'God was with him' (7:9). That same New Testament book, just three chapters later, tells us precisely the same thing of Jesus—'God was with him' (10:38).

• The account tells us that Joseph is one who finds 'favour' and one who is 'wise' (Genesis 39:4, 21; 41:33, 39). In the New Testament Luke reiterates this fact regarding Joseph (Acts 7:10), and also attributes the same two virtues to Jesus (Luke 2:40, 52).

• Joseph is innocent and falsely accused (Genesis 39:10–20; 40:15), as is the case with Christ (Matthew 26:60; 27:12, 24; Mark 14:57; 15:3; Luke 23:2)

• Joseph finds himself with two other offenders (Genesis 40:2–4), as does Christ (Matthew 27:38; John 19:18).

• When Joseph is with these two other men, he foretells the coming deliverance of one of them (Genesis 40:13). Jesus does the same with one of the thieves on the cross (Luke 23:43). Interestingly in this context the words 'Remember me when …' occur in both narratives (Genesis 40:14; Luke 23:42, both *mnēsthēti mou hotan* in Greek). There is a good deal of irony here, however, since in the earlier case it is Joseph, the innocent man, who makes the request and is overlooked (Genesis 40:23), while in the second instance the thief, one who is guilty, makes the request to Jesus and is heard.

• Joseph is described as one in whom is 'the Spirit of God' (Genesis 41:38), which was certainly also true of Jesus (Matthew 3:16; Luke 4:1; etc.).

• Joseph is eventually delivered, by supernatural intervention, from the dungeon where he had been held. The Hebrew word that describes this place is simply a 'pit' (*bôr*), a word which elsewhere has definite connotations of death and the grave (e.g. Job 33:28; Psalms 30:3; 103:4; 143:7; Proverbs 1:12; Isaiah 14:15; Jonah 2:6; etc.). Yet he is not raised up to his former position, but to one much greater. This can be taken as a symbolic resurrection and has an obvious connection with what happened to Jesus.

• The king of Egypt then appointed Joseph as the ruler of the whole land (Genesis 41:41, 43). In the Greek translation, commonly used in New Testament times, the text of Genesis uses the term 'lord' (*kurios*) for the status given to Joseph, a title frequently applied to Jesus. In one passage Joseph ascribes this advancement to God, saying 'God has made [*epoiēsen*] me lord [*kurion*] over all Egypt' (Genesis 45:9). In his first sermon the apostle Peter says of Jesus that 'God has made [*epoiēsen*] him both Lord [*kurion*] and Christ' (Acts 2:36).

• Although Joseph rose to such a high position, the king of Egypt expressly declares that 'Only with regard to the throne will I be greater than you' (Genesis 41:40). So while being 'lord' of all the land, there is still one greater in authority over Joseph. With respect to Jesus, as he was divine he was co-equal and co-eternal with the Father. Yet since he also took upon himself our human nature and became one of us, it is proper that as man he should accord a higher status to his Father, as he says, 'The Father is greater than I' (John 14:28).

• In this exalted position Joseph is able to provide bread for all who come to him. Doing such he is said to have 'given life' (Genesis 47:25, Hebrew text, translated into Greek as 'saved'; cf. also 45:5, 7). Jesus, indeed, is the great life-giver, who gives the true bread and so saves those who come to him.

• Lastly, we may point out that the resurrection appearances of Christ to his disciples recorded at the end of Luke's Gospel present a whole series of allusions to the Genesis narrative where Joseph is eventually reunited with his family. Besides the verbal parallels which follow there is, of course, the same basic conceptual correspondence in that Joseph was thought to have been dead (Gen 42:13, 32, 36, 38; 44:20), and Jesus actually was dead. Of Joseph it says that initially 'they did not recognize him' (Genesis 42:8), and of Jesus, 'their eyes were kept from recognizing him' (Luke 24:16). But later Joseph 'made himself known to his brothers' (Genesis 45:1), as Jesus 'was made known' to the disciples (Luke 24:35). Joseph greeted his brothers with the words 'Peace be to you' (Genesis 43:23; cf. v. 27, literally 'asked their peace'), and Jesus brought the disciples the exact same greeting, 'Peace be to you' (Luke 24:36; '*with* you' is incorrect). In both situations the brothers and the disciples are fearful (Genesis 43:23; Luke 24:37). In the first case the brothers are said to be 'troubled' (Genesis 45:3), and in the second Jesus asks the disciples why they are 'troubled' (Luke 24:38), the same Greek verb occurring in both verses. And finally, in the self-declaration of Joseph's identity he tells his brothers 'It is I, Joseph' (Genesis 45:3, 4), corresponding to the words 'It is I, myself' on the lips of Jesus (Luke 24:39), both containing the *egō eimi* construction in Greek.

In view of the foregoing, both as to their quantity and the closeness of language in many instances, it is hard to doubt that the Scripture is presenting the person and experiences of Joseph as prefiguring Jesus. Even John Calvin, who as previously noted was not quick to adopt figural interpretations, remarked that 'in the person of Joseph, a lively image of Christ is presented' (*Commentaries*, on Genesis 37:6). So what was stated earlier is confirmed— that the number of Old Testament figures pointing to Jesus exceeds those that are explicitly identified as such in the New.

Prefiguration, however is not merely a matter of listing correspondences. The correspondences serve to establish that we are indeed looking at an earlier figure and its later reality. But the movement from the former to the latter, as explained above, is one that is upwards, a heightening. So Jesus is not simply another Joseph, but one greater than Joseph.

Numerous details from the Joseph story have been included above, and no doubt each deserves due attention in the light of their prefiguring role within the canon of Scripture. But in summarizing the significance of Joseph from a broader prefigural perspective, I would want to highlight three particular elements. The first of these is the rejection aspect. Joseph, favoured through divine dreams, became hated and envied by his own brothers, but Jesus, the long-foretold Messiah of divine oracles, was rejected by the whole nation of his kinsmen (cf. John 1:11, 'he came to his own, but his own did not receive him'). It was one thing for the sons of Jacob to reject the son of their father, but quite another for the sons of Israel to reject the Son of the Father. Hence the greater consequences that befell the Jews on account of the latter. The second major thing is the exaltation. After his descent into the pit, a figure of the suffering of a death-like experience, Joseph was lifted up to become lord of the whole land. In Christ's case he actually died and descended to the grave itself, a suffering of much greater significance than that of Joseph. Accordingly, his exaltation is so much the greater. He ascended to the right hand of the Father to become Lord of heaven and earth, ruling over all things (cf. Matthew 28:18; Acts 2:33; Ephesians 1:20–21; Hebrews 12:2; 1 Peter 3:22). Then thirdly, there is the aspect of deliverance. With Joseph it was indeed marvellous. During a time of severe famine people came from all over Egypt and from neighbouring lands to receive food and not perish of starvation. But with Jesus it is so much the greater. His salvation extends to all throughout the earth that will come to him. It is, moreover, a salvation not from physical death but from spiritual also, and the life he can give, unlike Joseph, is one that is everlasting.

Crossing the River Jordan

Our final examination of an Old Testament event taken as a figure is one where its figural nature is established by its close resemblance to another event which is expressly identified as such. Here we will look at the crossing of the River Jordan, especially in connection with the similar crossing of the Red Sea. We are here principally concerned with the account found in the early chapters of Joshua, especially chapters 3 and 4, and will be looking back to the earlier event recorded in Exodus 14 and 15.

Looking at things from a broad perspective we firstly note that the two events in question are both part of one and the same journey. Each takes place during the travels of the Hebrews from Egypt, where they had been slaves, to the promised land of Canaan. The first occurs at its beginning, and the other some forty years later at its end. In fact one might say that the crossing of the first body of water marks the point in the narrative at which the people are now totally free from Egyptian dominion (cf. Joshua 24:6–7), and the second marks the actual entrance into the long-promised land. Both events, therefore, are in effect demarcating.

While it is obvious that it is the same nation that undergoes each of the crossings, the forty years that separate them has seen the death of most of that generation of Hebrews who departed from Egypt. This was on account of their unbelief. When they heard the report of the spies Moses had sent into the land, they decided, with no thought for what God could do, that the task of conquering it was too great for them. They would rather turn around and head back to Egypt. All this we read in Numbers 13 and 14. As a consequence of this God did not permit that adult generation to enter the land, apart from Joshua and Caleb, two of the spies who gave a more encouraging report. That generation was condemned to wander in the desert for forty years until they had died out, and the generation of their sons and daughters would be the ones to actually pass into Canaan.

Looking at the nature of the two sea-crossings themselves, it hardly needs to be said that there is a good deal of similarity. Both involve the people of Israel coming to a significant body of water that is blocking the path of their journey. The Red Sea was of considerable width and depth, and the Jordan was in flood at the time (Joshua 3:15). There was no question of simply taking all the many thousands of people, old and young, sick and infirm, and wading or swimming across. The watery obstacle was too formidable. In each situation a miraculous event occurred which created a separation in the waters and allowed the people to cross on dry ground. Then once they had all passed over the waters returned to their original place. So we see that the two happenings bear an extremely close relationship.

In view of the related nature of the two crossings, it is not surprising that certain Bible passages bring them together. Immediately after the Israelites had completed the crossing of the Jordan, Joshua told them, 'For the LORD your God dried up the waters of the Jordan before you until you had crossed, as the LORD your God had done to the Red Sea, which he dried up before us until we had crossed' (Joshua 4:23). So the earlier event is explicitly recalled at the later. The psalmist also declares, 'When Israel came out of Egypt, the house of Jacob from a people of strange language, Judah became his [God's] sanctuary, Israel his domain. The sea looked and fled, the Jordan turned back' (Psalm 114:1–3). Hebrew poetry, as is well known, makes much use of parallelisms, and in the last sentence of the citation it is the 'sea' and 'Jordan' that are brought into a parallel relationship.

Besides the resemblance in the kind of event that transpires, there are also a number of textual linkages that connect the two episodes. In both episodes there is a reference to the waters standing up as a 'heap' (Exodus 15:8; Joshua 3:13, 16), which is quite a rare word in Hebrew (*nēd*). Both narratives use two distinct synonyms for the 'dry land', these being *yabbāšâ* (Exodus 14:22, 29; Joshua 4:22) and *ḥārābâ* (Exodus 14:21; Joshua 3:17; 4:18). The prepositional phrase 'in the midst of' (*bᵉtôk*) the water occurs repeatedly in both accounts (Exodus 14:16, 22, 27, 29; 15:19; Joshua 3:17, 4:9, 10). After the crossing we read in each instance that the 'water returned' to its place (Exodus 14:28; Joshua 4:18, *wayyāšubû* in both verses). Lastly we note that each event is followed by a reference to the peoples of other nations hearing about it and losing heart (Exodus 15:14–15; Joshua 5:1). All such details strengthen the connection between the two accounts.

These two crossings are, at the literal level, remarkable acts of God on behalf of his people Israel, to bring them out of slavery and into the land he had promised to give them. The earlier of the two seems the more spectacular, for here we see not just the safe passage of the Hebrews through the sea, but also the drowning of the Egyptian host that was pursuing them. This destruction of the enemy has no counterpart in the later crossing, at least not in any literal interpretation. In this chapter, however, our chief concern is not with the literal, but with Old Testament events and persons viewed as figures of what was to come under the new covenant order. Now the New Testament provides us with a good reason for understanding the first of these two happenings, the crossing of the Red Sea, in more than a merely literal manner. The apostle Paul, speaking of the Hebrew fathers, explains that 'they all passed through the sea, and were all baptised into Moses in the cloud and in the sea' (1 Corinthians 10:1–2). Here I do not wish to take up time and space treating the lesser details of Paul's comment. Suffice it to say, that the apostle speaks of the Red Sea crossing in terms of *baptism*. The suitability of this becomes apparent when we consider, not just the involvement of water in both the Red Sea episode and in the rite of baptism, but that baptism is itself an act symbolic of dying to an old way of life and rising to a new. This significance of baptism is clearly brought out by Paul in the first part of Romans 6. Such a sense plainly relates to what happened at the Red Sea at the literal, historical level. For there the Israelites' old way of life in subjection to the Egyptians came to an end, and they became a free people. In this figurative 'baptism' the Egyptians died, and the Israelites began a new life free from those who held them captive.

Now I believe that a consistent approach to biblical interpretation demands that we view the crossing of the Jordan in a comparable manner to what happened at the Red Sea. If the earlier event is a figure of baptism, as Paul states, then the same ought also to be true of the later. In effect, then, we are looking at two baptism-like events on the one single journey from Egypt to Canaan. Not only was the passing through the Red Sea a figurative death and rising again, but the crossing of the Jordan likewise.

As we come to try to understand these two similar events in a figural way the first question that springs to mind is obviously—why the need for two such occasions? Do they both point to one and the same truth? It is possible, but unlikely. As we shall see, there is a significant difference in the latter event which strongly suggests it has its own contribution to make. So is the reality that the two events prefigure the need for two baptisms on the part of the New Testament believer? I have heard such an interpretation. One preacher was advocating that the two episodes indicate the necessity for two baptisms in the process of Christian initiation, the first in water and the second in the Spirit. I do not wish to digress into the theological implications of such a view. Suffice it to say that the New Testament witness to a second baptism in the Spirit separate from the first is doubtful, and the existence of such is strongly contested by a large segment of the church (who would claim that when a believer is baptised in water he or she is also being baptised in the Spirit, the latter accompanying the former, as in the case of Christ's own baptism). Moreover in the details of the narrative depicting the crossing of the Jordan there is no clear element that stands out as being a figure for the

Spirit. So I would not recommend an interpretation in terms of two separate baptisms. Rather I believe that these two related Old Testament figures serve to point to two different aspects within the single act of baptism, as I shall endeavour to explain.

In taking baptism as basically a death of the old and a beginning of the new, we do in fact find that at both the Red Sea and at the Jordan there is something of great significance that is left behind in the water—it is just that in the respective narratives it is a little more evident in the first event that than the second, and also Christians tend to be more familiar with the details of the first. At the exodus people of two nations entered the place of the Red Sea, the Israelites and the Egyptians, but only one emerged on the other side. Both went in, the tyrannical master and the afflicted slave, the oppressor and the oppressed, but just one came out. For we read that 'The water returned and covered the chariots and horsemen—the entire army of Pharaoh that had followed them [the Israelites] into the sea; not one of them remained ... That day the LORD saved Israel from the hand of the Egyptians, and Israel saw the Egyptians lying dead on the seashore' (Exodus 14:28, 30). So having passed through the sea, the people of Israel looked back and saw the dead bodies of the whole Egyptian army. That power which had held the Israelites as slaves was now destroyed.

This event is a powerful picture of baptism, in its spiritual significance. Prior to coming to faith in Jesus we were under the dominion of the enemy, the devil, by whom we were held captive (2 Timothy 2:26) and oppressed (Acts 10:38). But through Christ the power of this evil one over us is destroyed (Hebrews 2:14). So it is that we are turned from the dominion of Satan to God (Acts 26:18). In the spiritual truth represented by baptism we are to understand that the power of the enemy—the one we call the devil or Satan—which had such dominion over us is now overcome. As the king of Egypt and his army lay dead on the shore of the sea so when we are baptised the power of evil over us is destroyed. In a figurative manner, at baptism we leave our old master dead behind us in the water.

Yet there is something else represented by baptism, something that is not figured in the Red Sea crossing. That the passing through the sea did not entirely bring Israel's connection with Egypt to an end soon becomes apparent as the people journey on in the wilderness. All too quickly it becomes blatantly obvious that, though they had left Egypt, the people still had quite a hankering for going back there. When faced with the hardships and challenges of what lay ahead, their thoughts went right back to where they had come from. 'Why is it you brought us up out of Egypt?' (Exodus 17:3), they questioned of Moses. They remembered with relish the various kinds of food they ate there (Numbers 11:5; cf. Exodus 16:3), and protested that 'We were better off in Egypt' (Numbers 11:18). At the report of those who had spied out the promised land, the people exclaimed, 'Would it not be better for us to go back to Egypt?' (Numbers 14:3), and even came to the point where they said, 'Let us appoint a leader and return to Egypt' (v. 4). In view of this, it may well be said that although the people had been taken out of Egypt, Egypt had not yet been taken out of the people. Clearly the episode at the Red Sea had not terminated the influence of Egypt with respect to the Israelites. After a fashion, though the might of Egypt had perished in the waters, Egypt lived on in their hearts and minds, and frequently set their intentions upon a return to that place. In short, what was represented by Egypt as a figure, namely the enthralling and tyrannical power of sin, was not something that the Red Sea 'baptism' alone had completely dealt with.

This now brings to the second baptism-like event, the passage through the Jordan. There is a very important element in this episode that is often overlooked. One contributory factor to this is the failure of the NIV (New International Version of the Bible), in common use today, to provide an adequate translation of the Hebrew at this particular point in the narrative. The matter in question is the selection and placement of a number of stones during and after the crossing of the Jordan (Joshua 4). Reading through the text of the NIV one is given the impression that there is just one group of stones, though some editions of this version do add a marginal note with the correct meaning. Here is what we read concerning the stones, closely following the Hebrew and other accurate translations (e.g. ESV NRSV NASB NKJV NJB):

> When the whole nation had finished crossing the Jordan, the LORD spoke to Joshua, saying, 'Select twelve men from the people, one man from each tribe, and command them, saying, "Take up twelve stones from the middle of the Jordan, from the place where the feet of the priests are standing, and carry them over with you and lay them down in the place where you will camp tonight"'. So Joshua called the twelve men he had appointed from the sons of Israel, one man from each tribe, and Joshua said to them, 'Go over before the ark of the LORD your God into the middle of the Jordan, and each of you take up a stone on his

shoulder, according to the number of the tribes of the sons of Israel. Let this be a sign among you, so that when your children later ask, "What do these stones mean to you?" you shall say to them, "Because the waters of the Jordan were cut off before the ark of the covenant of the LORD; when it crossed the Jordan, the waters of the Jordan were cut off". These stones shall be a memorial to the sons of Israel forever'. So the sons of Israel did as Joshua commanded, and took up twelve stones from the middle of the Jordan, just as the LORD spoke to Joshua, according to the number of the tribes of the sons of Israel, and they carried them over with them to the camp and put them down there. Then Joshua set up twelve stones in the middle of the Jordan at the place where the feet of the priests who carried the ark of the covenant were standing, and they are there to this day. (Joshua 4:1–9)

From this we see quite plainly that there were in fact two distinct sets of stones. One group were removed from the middle of the river and deposited at Israel's first encampment later that same day. The other collection of stones was placed in the river bed itself, which at that moment was free from water. Although there were two lots of stones we find that they were identical in number, namely 'twelve' (v. 3 and v. 9). This specific quantity is explained with reference to the number of tribes that constituted the people of Israel. Each group, moreover, had a connection with precisely the same place. One set of stones was taken '*from* the middle of the Jordan, from the place where the feet of the priests are standing' (v. 3). The other set was placed '*in* the middle of the Jordan, at the place where the feet of the priests who carried the ark of the covenant were standing' (v. 9), that is to say, at the very same spot from which the other stones had been removed. The essential similarity between the two sets of stones most reasonably requires that, with regard to their meaning as figures, they portray the same reality. The only difference, and it is a crucial one, is the place where each set is located.

What then is happening at the crossing of the Jordan at the figural level? Taking the similar Red Sea incident as our interpretative guide, we note that in each instance there is that which reaches the other side of the water, and there is that which remains in the middle and is covered by the returning water. The former is that which lives on and the latter that which dies. At the Red Sea it was Israel that lived on the far side of the water, and it was Egypt that died. The waters covered the Egyptian host and they perished, then the Israelites looked back and saw their dead bodies. At the

Jordan again it is Israel that came to the other side of the river, but what was it that remained in the middle? It was the pile of twelve stones that Joshua had erected at precisely the place where the people had passed across. Once the people had finished crossing they would have looked back and seen the stones covered as the waters flowed back, just as happened to the Egyptians at the earlier crossing. In effect, then, the stones were drowned, they underwent a death, a symbolic death that is.

When Israel saw the covering of the twelve stones in the water, they would also have beheld the sight of the twelve identical stones standing of the western shore. At the figural level these two piles of stones in themselves represent the same reality. Since there are twelve, and since this number is expressly mentioned to correspond with the Israelite tribes, there can be little doubt that the collection of stones serves to indicate the nation of Israel itself. The twelve-fold congregation of Israel is suitably portrayed by the twelve stones set up together (cf. Exodus 24:4). One pile is a picture of the Israel that had passed through the water and lived; the other pile is a picture of what died in the water, and that, significantly, is likewise Israel. When the people looked back and saw the returning waters covering the stones, what they were witnessing was the death of themselves. And this, it is important to note, was what was missing at the Red Sea episode.

In baptism, which is a symbolic portrayal of conversion, there has to be a death to self. The power of sin has two manifestations. There is that evil power of sin, the enemy we call Satan, symbolised by the serpent in Eden, and by Pharaoh (whose headdress incidentally bore a serpent) in his oppression of the Hebrews. The death of this aspect of sin's power is what is prefigured at the Red Sea. This, if you like, is the defeat of what we may refer to as the *external* power of sin. Yet the fact is that sin lived on in the people of Israel. As we have seen, in a sense they bore Egypt, in the sense of its influence and allure, with them to the other side. This is because sin also has its *internal* realisation, or what is described as 'the sin that dwells within' (Romans 7:17, 20). The human nature that is governed by this indwelling sin is also called the 'old man' (Romans 6:6; Ephesians 4:22; Colossians 3:9), as distinct from the 'new man' (Ephesians 4:24; Colossians 3:10), the renewed spiritual nature that is given birth when a person comes to faith, depicted symbolically through the rising up of from the water of baptism. So the twelve stones in the river represent the 'old' Israel, whereas the twelve stones on the western bank present the 'new' Israel.

We understand, then, that both aspects of sin's power, the external and the internal, undergo a manner of death in a genuine conversion. And this, I would argue, is what is depicted at the figural level by the two crossings that Israel underwent on their journey to the land. At the first it was the power of sin *over* Israel that was brought to an end, and in the second it was the power of sin *within* Israel. The in-between narratives concerning the people in the wilderness, with their frequent displays of unbelief and evil desire, show the absolute necessity of both.

As we bring things to a conclusion, we draw attention to one further element in the text of Joshua that lends support to the foregoing interpretation. It is highly significant, I believe, that the very next thing that Israel did after passing over the Jordan was to circumcise their males. This is recorded for us in Joshua 5:2–9. Like baptism, circumcision is another rite with a symbolic meaning. And circumcision, in its spiritual sense, indicates precisely what has been discussed above.

This is no doubt why the apostle Paul brings circumcision and baptism together in Colossians 2:11–12 ('in him [Christ] you were also circumcised with a circumcision made without hands, in the putting off of the body of the flesh by the circumcision of Christ; having been buried with him in baptism, in which you were also raised with him through faith in the power of God, who raised him from the dead'). The former act literally involves the cutting off of a piece of flesh, and by this it represents the cutting off of the fleshly nature, that governed by sin in the flesh. In other words, the literal act of circumcision that immediately follows the crossing of the Jordan bears exactly the same significance— the one by means of the literal enactment of the Old Testament rite of initiation, and the other through its figural portrayal of the corresponding New Testament rite. So each points to the same essential truth—true conversion to God necessarily involves a death of our old carnal nature.

In conclusion, then, through the application of prefiguration that we have discussed in this chapter we see that the Old Testament is not just a narrative about ancient patriarchs and the people of Israel, though it is indeed that. Beyond this literal sense there is much witness to the person of Christ through figures of diverse kinds.

And so those old familiar stories can be re-read in the light of Christ and the gospel, and in fact lend themselves to be re-read in this way since that was part of their original divine design. Those accounts about Ruth and Esther, about David and Goliath, about Jonah, and Daniel in the lions' den, and many others, besides being wonderful episodes in the history of God's purpose in which he displays his saving power to his chosen nation, Israel, to individuals within it, and to Gentiles also, contain figures of the greater and more lasting salvation to come through Jesus Christ, his Son.

Suggestions for Further Reading

Boersma, Hans. *Scripture as Real Presence: Sacramental Exegesis in the Early Church* (Grand Rapids, Michigan: Baker, 2017).

Danielou, Jean. *From Shadows to Reality: Studies in the Biblical Typology of the Fathers* (London: Burns & Oates, 1960).

de Lubac, Henri. *Scripture in the Tradition* (New York: Herder & Herder, 1968).

Stanglin, Keith D. *The Letter* and *Spirit of Biblical Interpretation: From the Early Church to Modern Practice* (Grand Rapids: Baker Academic, 2018).

8. PERSONATION

In this chapter we will examine a particular manner of exegesis that is not generally dealt with in modern textbooks. Although this is the case, it is in fact a form of interpretation that is frequently found in the writings of the apostles, as well as in the biblical expositions of others during the early centuries of the church. Recent scholarly publications, some listed at the end of the chapter, show a renewed interest in this way of reading the Old Testament. We will begin by a brief consideration of what this approach should be called and what it involves. Following this we will look at a number of individual texts by way of illustration. As the reader will hopefully soon get the idea of what is going on, this chapter will not be a long one.

Terminology and Explanation

I need to say upfront that readers ought not to be put off by the strange-sounding terminology that will appear in the following description. While unusual words may be used to describe it, the basic notion is in itself fairly straightforward. What underlies this particular kind of interpretation is what is meant by the Greek term *prosōpon* and its Latin equivalent *persona*. Both of these relate to the idea of 'person'. But more than this, both words also function within the context of drama, as was performed at the Greek and Roman theatre. In such a setting the terms simply correspond to that of a 'character' or 'role', that is to say, the role of a certain character played by an actor within a particular dramatic scene. So what we are looking at here is the study of roles in a given context where different persons interact with each other. From the Greek word *prosōpon* we obtain the term 'prosopology' to describe this approach. Some scholars, therefore, speak of 'prosopological' interpretation or exegesis. However, as the Latin term *persona* will doubtless appear a little more familiar to readers, I have chosen to entitle this chapter by the more English sounding 'personation', for which the simple dictionary definition would be 'acting a part' or 'portraying a character in a play'. (The Latin origin of 'personation' is also more helpful etymologically. While the Greek term *prosōpon* relates to the face, the Latin in fact relates to the voice. The noun *persona* is composed of the prefix *per-*, 'through', and the stem *son-*, the cognate of the verb *sonare*, 'to sound', from which English words such as 'sonic', 'sonar', and 'sonorous', and even the word 'sound' itself, are derived. This origin has respect to the voice of the player in the drama, while the Greek has respect to the appearance, referring to the mask that actors typically wore during stage plays). For the noun 'personation' the corresponding verb is 'personate'. These words differ in an important nuance from the more familiar terms 'impersonation' and 'impersonate', where the connotation is either to deceive or to perform an act purely for the purposes of entertainment by displaying the skill of taking on the voice and characteristics of a known person. Neither of these, of course, is the case with the biblical form of personation that we discuss in this chapter.

In the Bible personation is primarily applicable to dialogues situated in the Old Testament, although it may also occur in monologues where there might be a speaker and one or more addressees. Such speeches most commonly appear in poetic and prophetic texts, though the phenomenon is not necessarily bound to these types of literature. What the interpreter needs to do is to look at the various persons engaged in the original speech, whether as a speaker or an addressee, and then try to discern if they are performing the part, or role, of other significant persons. For the most part these latter characters who the speakers and addressees are personating consist of God the Father and Jesus the Son, and perhaps also the Holy Spirit. Sometimes the role of the community of God's people, the church, might also be expressed. In assigning such roles to the speakers of the Hebrew text, it has the effect of transforming the Old Testament dialogue or monologue to one that now relates to things to come under the New. As the following examination of specific texts will show, this manner of reading the passage might be carried out even where the text itself might not give any explicit indication that the second set of persons are in view.

Since the contents of the Old Testament speech concerns New Testament realities, what we are looking at in personation is yet a further kind of biblical prophecy. The original human speaker, perhaps David or one of the other prophets, utters the words under the inspiration of the divine Spirit. In the dialogue or monologue given by the inspired human author there is an advance presentation of words that will actually be uttered at some future point in time. Personation is in essence therefore a form of prophecy, and so, as was the case with prefiguration, a handful of examples were inserted into the list of prophecies explicitly fulfilled in the Gospels given in chapter 6. Nevertheless, it should not be overlooked that prophecy of this personating kind does have its own particular characteristics that make it distinct from other types of prophecy.

In the two preceding chapters we looked firstly at direct verbal prophecy, in which a future event is foretold through an oracle that expressly describes that event in words. We then discussed prefiguration. This was explained as an indirect form of prophecy whereby future happenings are depicted through events and persons recorded in the Old Testament that are understood to have a figural, as well as literal, significance. Personation may be seen as another kind of indirect prophecy, though differing in certain important aspects from prefiguration. This latter, as we saw earlier, involves interpreting persons, actions, institutions, and objects as sketches or images, albeit faint ones, of things to come. Personation, on the other hand, concerns the expression by an inspired prophet of the precise words of speeches before they are really uttered by the actual person or persons concerned. So the one is figure-oriented, and this deals with questions like 'What happened?', 'What does x do?', and 'How is x described?' The other is speech-oriented, or dialogical, where the important question is 'Who is speaking?' In other words, one is a foreshowing, the other a foresaying.

From what has just been stated, it should be clear that in the process of interpretation both prefiguration and personation involve a transformation or transposition. But the manner in which this is done is seen to be altogether different in each case. With the first the literal events and persons undergo a transformation whereby, while still remaining genuine historical entities involved in their own significant episodes, they become figures of events and persons of a later time and of greater signification. In the second manner of interpretation, the words that are expressed remain unchanged, but there is a transformation of the setting and persons who are uttering them. The prophet becomes a personator of one who will speak at some future time.

Along with what has just been said, a further distinction between prefiguration and personation lies in the fact that in the former the original account of persons and events is all important, as the details of this form the basis of their prefigural function. It is important, for example, to note that Melchizedek (Genesis 14) is both a king and a priest, to note the meaning of his name ('King of Righteousness') and of the place over which he reigns ('Peace'), and that he brings forth bread and wine. All of these elements within the record establish the connection with the later reality.

With respect to personation, however, the details of the original setting are not of so much concern. No correspondence of such details between the earlier utterance and its later fulfilments needs to be established. What is important is the words themselves that are spoken, which then, in precisely the same form, are transported into a new setting in which different characters now say them. This relative unimportance of the original setting for the words will be illustrated in the next section. Suffice it to say for now, that these last paragraphs have demonstrated that personation, although also a form of prophecy, is quite distinct from both direct verbal prophecy and from prefiguration.

Lastly in this introduction, we may mention that although this manner of interpreting the Old Testament is largely unfamiliar to us today, it was a common practice on the part of Jesus and the apostles, as recent studies have shown. Not only this, Christian preachers and exegetes of the early centuries of the church continued to apply the same kind of interpretation. Many examples are to be found in the works of the two major Christian writers of the second century, namely Justin Martyr and Irenaeus of Lyons. Numerous subsequent theologians and biblical expositors further employed personation. Representing both the Latin west and the Greek east and dating from around CE 200 to 650, we may here name such important figures as Tertullian, Origen, Cyprian, Eusebius of Caesarea, Athanasius, Hilary of Poitiers, Gregory of Nyssa, Augustine, Cyril of Alexandria, Theodoret of Cyrus, Cassiodorus, and Maximus the Confessor.

Examples of Personation

We will now examine a number of specific instances in which the New Testament interprets a passage from the earlier Hebrew Scriptures in terms of personation. For these illustrations I acknowledge my indebtedness to the explanations presented by others, some of whose names appear as the authors of the works listed at the end of the chapter.

Isaiah 61:1–2

We begin with what is a fairly straightforward case when it comes to interpreting an Old Testament text in terms of personation. Jesus himself directs attention to these verses when he reads the daily portion from Isaiah in the synagogue at Nazareth as his ministry is about to commence. Luke records the occasion for us:

> And he [Jesus] came to Nazareth, where he had been brought up;
> and as was his custom, he entered the synagogue on the Sabbath,

and stood up to read. And the scroll of the prophet Isaiah was handed to him. He unrolled the scroll and found the place where it was written, 'The Spirit of the Lord is upon me, because he has anointed me to bring good news to the poor. He has sent me to proclaim release to the captives and recovery of sight to the blind, to set free the oppressed, to proclaim the year of the Lord's favour'. And he rolled up the scroll, gave it back to the attendant, and sat down. The eyes of everyone in the synagogue were fixed on him. Then he began to say to them, 'Today this Scripture is fulfilled in your hearing'. (Luke 4:16–21)

Verses 18 and 19 of this text incorporate the citation from Isaiah 61:1–2, which contains speech in the first person singular ('me'). We note that these verses commence a new chapter in Isaiah. Chapter divisions and headings were features of biblical texts that were added a long time later, and so originally the division between chapter 60 and 61 would not have been so definitely demarcated. Interestingly, the previous chapter also ends with someone speaking in the first person (60:22), where the speaker is unambiguously God himself—'I, the LORD, will hasten it in its time' (speaking of the coming glory of the future Zion). Yet the plain fact is that the first two verses of chapter 61 cannot be words expressed by the same first-person speaker. The contents of 61:1–2 are uttered by someone who has been endowed with the Spirit of the Lord, has been anointed by the Lord, and who has been sent by the Lord for particular tasks. Here, therefore, the speaker cannot be not the same 'LORD' as in the last verse of chapter 60. So although there is no indication in either the punctuation or grammar (in Hebrew) that the first person of 61:1 differs from that in 60:22, it is evident that this has to be the case.

This, then, raises the question—who in fact is speaking in Isaiah 61:1–2? Well, in the first instance the words are obviously spoken by the Hebrew prophet, traditionally known as Isaiah. It is absolutely clear, however, from the above words of Jesus in Luke 4 that Isaiah is not speaking of himself. Jesus said, 'Today this Scripture is fulfilled in your hearing', which rules out the possibility of 'me' being the original prophetic spokesman who lived hundreds of years before the time of Christ. The same words of Jesus explicitly declare that the prophetic utterance of Isaiah is being fulfilled that day, or at least at that time, by which it is implied that the one intended by the first-person pronouns is none other than Christ himself. This is especially seen to be so once the nature of the events to be carried out by the speaker of the oracle is considered. The fact of the Spirit being upon him and of having been anointed, the fact that he was a preacher of good news who came to deal with the broken-hearted and to grant freedom to those held in bondage, all point to what Jesus himself came and accomplished, but do not fit so well, if at all in some elements, with the Old Testament prophet. If, therefore, the text does not apply to Isaiah but to Jesus, then we have to see personation at work. The inspired prophet has stepped into the role of a different persona, this being that of Jesus, and in that role has delivered this significant monologue, describing events that would be fulfilled in the ministry of Jesus and beyond.

So from the manner in which this text is presented, and the way in which it is interpreted by Jesus several centuries later, Isaiah the prophet is not simply speaking *about* Christ, but as, or in the persona of, Christ. It is, then, totally apparent the interpretative process that identifies the existence of personation, otherwise known as prosopological exegesis, is operative in the use of Isaiah 61 in Luke 4.

Psalm 16:8–11

The sixteenth Psalm is in important one for christological reasons as certain verses from it play a significant role in Peter's speech on the day of Pentecost, the first apostolic preaching of the gospel, as recorded in the book of Acts. The relevant part of what Peter proclaimed is as follows:

> This man [Jesus] was handed over to you by the determined purpose and foreknowledge of God; and you, with the help of lawless men, put him to death by nailing him to the cross. But God raised him up, having freed him from the pains of death, because it was impossible for him to be held in its power. For David says concerning him, 'I saw the Lord continually before me, for he is at my right hand so that I will not be shaken; therefore my heart is glad, and my tongue rejoices; moreover my flesh will also live in hope. For you will not abandon my soul to Hades, nor will you let your Holy One see corruption. You have made known to me the paths of life; you will fill me with gladness in your presence'. (Acts 2:23–28)

The citation of Psalm 16:8–11 comes in verses 25–28. The apostle's handling of the psalm proves to be highly instructive as regards the presence of prophetic personation.

We observe that the words Peter quotes from the psalm relate to two distinct persons. Firstly, there is the one referring to himself in the first person ('I', 'me', 'my'), who is the speaker. Then there is 'the Lord', also addressed as 'you', the one being spoken to. Peter attributes the words to 'David' (v. 25), and the heading of Psalm 16 (in both its Hebrew and Greek versions) also assigns the psalm to David.

So our basic question is 'Who is speaking?' Well, that has just been answered in the first instance, by ascribing the words to David, as both Peter and the heading of the psalm do. But although David is the one who utters the words, what is actually said cannot relate to himself. Peter makes this perfectly clear. The main thrust of his citation from the psalm concerns the fact that the one speaking would not be abandoned to the grave and corruption. In the words that come immediately after the psalm quotation Peter explains, 'Brothers, I may confidently say to you regarding the patriarch David that he both died and was buried, and his tomb is with us to this day' (Acts 2:29). The point Peter is making, evidently, is that since David is dead and buried until that day, and therefore is well and truly corrupted, the words of the psalm cannot be applied to David. Peter then adds, 'But he [David] was a prophet' (v. 30). In other words, in the psalm just cited David, according to the apostle, is speaking prophetically. In being a prophet, Peter continues, David 'foresaw what lay ahead, and spoke of the resurrection of the Christ, saying that he was not abandoned to Hades, nor did his flesh see corruption' (v. 31). In the apostle's understanding, therefore, the words that he quoted from Psalm 16 did not, and indeed could not, concern David himself, but Jesus the Messiah. As such this is another instance of prophetic personation. David uttered the words as a prophet and so prophetically was speaking in the person, or persona, of the Christ to come.

The matter of which David speaks prophetically as Christ in the psalm relates to a time in the life of Jesus prior to his death and resurrection. We know this from the future tense in the clauses 'you *will* not abandon my soul to Hades, nor *will* you let your Holy One see corruption'. Through the words preceding these this same person is essentially declaring his confidence in God. He had set God before his mind's eye, and so God stood by him. As a result, he would not be shaken but would have a joyful heart. Even his flesh, he says, would live in hope. So it is that, even though his bodily death drew close, this would not be permanent. Not being abandoned to Hades, nor seeing corruption, indicate the fact of Christ's bodily resurrection. Then ultimately, he says to God, 'you will fill me with gladness in your presence', which is best understood of the ascension to God's right hand a short while after Jesus rose from the tomb. (The ascension, interestingly, is what Peter goes on to talk about in Acts 2:33–34). Although the precise time these words were uttered by Christ is left undefined, it possibly being during one of his many prayer-times as his death approached, the meaning of the contents is altogether clear. Interpreted in the way proposed, as a case of prophetic personation, the passage makes good sense within the context of Peter's evangelistic speech, in which the fact of Christ's resurrection, and it being foretold in advance, are key elements.

Psalm 69:9b

We now turn to half a verse in Psalm 69, another psalm that is attributed to David. I give here the preceding lines of the psalm for context. Again the words take the form of a monologue, there being just the one speaker, but besides this speaker other persons are mentioned in different capacities.

> For I have borne reproach for your sake, and shame covers my face. I have become a stranger to my brothers, and an alien to my mother's children. For zeal for your house has consumed me, and the insults of those who insult you have fallen on me. (Psalm 69:7–9)

We see that the range of parties involved include all three grammatical persons—first, second, and third. The first is, of course, the speaker himself ('I', 'me', 'my'), the second is the person addressed ('you', 'your'), while the third refers to those others that are spoken about ('my brothers', 'my mother's children', 'those who insult you').

If David is taken as the original speaker, as the psalm heading itself claims, then it raises the question of when was it that David suffered such reproach and alienation. Certainly he experienced hostility from Saul, but here he is speaking of his own brothers, his 'mother's children'. The books of Samuel say nothing of this. Nor is there any known experience in the life of David that corresponds to the last line (v. 9b) of the citation. This suggests, then, that David is not talking about his own life.

In Romans 15 the apostle Paul offers a helping hand in understanding what is going on here. In the context of instruction regarding seeking the good of one's neighbour he writes, 'For Christ did not even please himself but, as it is written, "The insults of those who insult you have fallen on me'" (v. 3). Paul here gives an exact quotation of Psalm 69:9b, and it is evident that he applies it to Christ. So in the mind of the apostle the first-person pronouns are taken as referring to Jesus himself. He is the 'I' of the passage. This therefore means that by way of prophetic personation the inspired psalmist is expressing a speech that the Son would express to God the Father, the second-person 'you' of the text, at some future time after the psalmist had penned these words. The precise point of time at which this future speech would take place is not made clear. The verb forms in both the psalm and in Romans could justifiably be translated as 'have fallen' or 'fell'. Possibly, then, the Son addresses these words to the Father at his exaltation into heaven following his death and resurrection. This would make reasonable sense. Yet one thing is quite definite, which is that the verbs are looking back to a completed event. So it would seem that from that future perspective the Son is telling God the Father of the things he had earlier endured for the Father's sake. One of those things, according to v. 9b, was that he himself had suffered the insults that were directed at the Father. For sure, in the Gospels we read of Christ suffering insults as part and parcel of his final humiliation (e.g. Matthew 27:44; Luke 22:65). His sufferings, then, were not just due to the fact that he bore our sins, but also that he bore the reproaches of humankind against God himself, so preserving the divine honour.

It is noteworthy that the words immediately preceding Psalm 69:9b also receive a similar interpretation in the New Testament. The half-verse 'For zeal for your house has consumed me' (v. 9a) appears in John's Gospel (2:17), where again the first-person 'me' is understood to be Jesus, and the second-person 'your' is taken as God the Father (cf. v.16, 'my Father's house'). Both Paul and John, therefore, independently take this verse of the psalm and interpret it in terms of personation, thus each one corroborating the manner of interpretation presented by the other.

Isaiah 53:1

The well-known messianic prophecy of Isaiah 53 begins with the words: 'Who has believed our message? And to whom has the arm of the LORD been revealed?' Evidently these questions concern the Suffering Servant who is portrayed in the chapter. The 'message' is that about this despised and rejected one, whose appearance on earth may justly be described as a revelation of 'the arm of the LORD', in the sense of embodying the power of God acting to bring out his purpose. Prophetically, the one the passage is talking about is, of course, Jesus. The one who is being addressed by means of these questions, though left unexpressed in the traditional Hebrew text, is identified in the Greek version (the Septuagint) as the 'Lord', a reading which is endorsed in the New Testament citation that we are about to consider. But, we may wonder, who is asking the questions in this first verse? Who may we identify as the speaker? Note the use of the first person plural ('our'). This plural would seem to exclude Isaiah himself since he is but a single individual.

In order to identify the group referred to as 'our' we may look at the New Testament quotation of this verse. Isaiah 53:1 is taken up by the apostle Paul in Romans 10:16, where he reads the words, we shall discover, as an instance of personation. The accompanying verses are also cited here for context:

> But how are they to call on one in whom they have not believed? And how are they to believe in one of whom they have not heard? And how are they to hear without a preacher? And how are they to preach unless they are sent? As it is written, 'How beautiful are the feet of those who bring good news!' But they have not all accepted the good news; for Isaiah says, 'Lord, who has believed our message?' So faith comes from what is heard, and what is heard comes through the word of Christ.

Here in this part of Romans 10 the apostle is dealing with the matter of proclaiming, or preaching, the gospel. For people to believe they have to hear the gospel message, and for that to happen there needs to be those that preach it, and these have to be duly sent forth for that particular task. Paul's first Old Testament citation (in v. 15) is from Isaiah 52:7, 'How beautiful are the feet of those who bring good news!' The apostle here does not quote the original clause in full but omits the phrase 'on the mountains'. Then he makes one minor, but significant, interpretative alteration. Whereas in both its Hebrew and Greek versions the verse in Isaiah speaks of 'the one who brings good news', Paul makes this singular phrase into one that is plural, 'those who bring good news'. To do such is not playing fast and loose with the word of God, as some might suppose. Rather the apostle, inspired in the writing of Romans as he was, is unpacking the sense that may quite legitimately be conveyed by the original Hebrew phrase. This phrase may indeed be grammatically singular, but if the truth that is being stated may apply to one person who preaches good news, then the same may be applied to a second, or a third, and many others who do the same thing. In other words the Hebrew phrase does not concern one specific individual but is generic in meaning—indicating not 'the particular one who brings good news' but 'anyone who brings good news'. In some contexts there might be some ambiguity between a genuine numerical singular, speaking of a single specific person, and a generic singular. In such cases to use the grammatically plural form for the latter sense would remove any possible ambiguity. All Paul is doing by this change is making it completely clear that the phrase as used by the Hebrew prophet has a generic meaning. So 'the one who brings good news' is any one of potentially a good many others who do the same thing, or in other words, as Paul actually writes, 'those who bring good news'. So his use of the plural, while an interpretation rather than a strict translation, is nevertheless semantically justifiable.

In his citation of Isaiah 52:7, therefore, the apostle can be seen to have done two things. By removing 'on the mountains' he has made it more universal from a geographic point of view. No longer are merely the mountains of Judah in view, but the bringing of good news the prophet speaks of could now be in any place. Secondly, Paul rules out the mistaken notion that the prophet has just one single bringer of good news in mind, and makes it have regard to several of such instead. Taken contextually, there can be no doubt that Paul makes these exegetical moves to indicate that 'those who bring good news' refers in fact to the apostles, including himself. It was these men who did indeed, first and foremost, bring the good news of Jesus to Judaea and the rest of the world.

It is in this light, then, that we come to Paul's quotation of Isaiah 53:1, occurring in the very next verse of Romans 10. In view of what has just gone before, that is, how Paul has read Isaiah 52:7, there can be little doubt that he sees 53:1 as likewise having reference to the apostles, and this is so because he takes it as an instance of personation with respect to these same apostolic preachers. This manner of reading the Old Testament verse is not at all unreasonable. The prophet Isaiah, after all, is undoubtedly not speaking of himself, not just because of the plural pronoun, but because the subsequent verses of the chapter deal predictively of things that would happen long after Isaiah's own lifetime, and the statement itself in verse 1 is speaking of something that, from the time-frame of the speaker, has already occurred ('Who has believed'). Isaiah is, therefore, excluded from being the ultimate speaker of the words. Isaiah does indeed serve as the initial speaker of the words in their original Old Testament setting, yet as a prophet he does so prophetically.

Under the Spirit's inspiration he is in fact personating the apostles of Christ at some future point in time. From that future time the words in the mouths of the apostles ask questions concerning the unbelief of some who have heard their message. So once we have moved from Isaiah's time to that of the apostles the past reference of the verbs in 53:1 now makes good sense. Through the words now forecast into the future we are led to look back from the perspective of Paul and the other apostles to matters which were then past.

What Paul is saying, then, in this passage, is that it is not just a question of preachers being sent out and their message heard. The hearers also need to believe the message, that is to say, receive it with faith, for it to take effect. There were those, Paul reflects, who had not done this. There can be no doubt given the wider context in Romans chapters 9 to 11 that the apostle has primarily in mind here his own people the Jews. It is the problem of Jewish unbelief and how this squares with the ancient patriarchal promises that is Paul's primary concern here. The book of Acts presents a clear portrayal of how the Jewish nation as a whole rejected the gospel that the apostles proclaimed to them. (And note that in Romans 10:16, instead of the pronoun in 'they have not all', the NIV has 'not all the Israelites', and the NCV 'not all the Jews'). So in case there might be some who questioned the ineffectiveness of the apostolic preaching and who may have therefore tried to cast doubt upon the authenticity of their message, what Paul does is to demonstrate that the ancient Scriptures had foretold centuries in advance that there would be those who would not believe the message they proclaimed. This is in essence what Romans 10:16 is about, and the Old Testament proof that such unbelief was foretold is expressly set forth through seeing Isaiah 53:1 as a case of prophetic personation.

An interpretation in terms of the apostles, although not overtly referring to Jesus, is nevertheless christological. The apostles are the ones sent by Christ, as the ambassadors of Christ, who preached the word about Christ. The 'message' of Isaiah 53:1 and Romans 10:16 is specifically the good news about Jesus. And once more this is an appropriate place to recall the 'whole Christ' (*totus Christus*) concept. Certainly the apostles form an integral, as well as a highly significant, element within the corporate Christ.

Interestingly, less than a century after Paul penned his letter to the Romans, the important Christian scholar and writer Justin Martyr (c. CE 150) interpreted Isaiah 53:1 in a similar way to what has been described above. Justin wrote: 'Isaiah speaks as though in the person [*prosōpon*] of the apostles ... and says, "Lord, who has believed our message? And to whom has the arm of the Lord been revealed?"' (*Dialogue with Trypho*, 42.2).

Numerous other instances that occur in the New Testament could be discussed. But we also need to be aware that even the cases found in the apostolic writings where an explicit interpretation in terms of personation is given most certainly do not amount to the total number of Old Testament passages where this feature is present. Remember earlier we said that the New Testament does not deal with every Old Testament prophecy relating to Christ, nor every instance where he is prefigured. Similarly we can be sure that the New Testament does not draw attention to every case of personation in the Old Testament. Interestingly the writings of the early church fathers reveal many more places where the presence of prophetic personation in an Old Testament text makes good sense. We may take Isaiah 50:6 as an example: 'I gave my back to those who struck me, and my cheeks to those who pulled out the beard; I did not cover my face from insult and spitting'. This verse is not treated in the New Testament. Yet again Justin Martyr tells us that here 'the prophetic Spirit happens to speak from the person of Christ' (*First Apology*, 38.1). This is a reasonable conclusion, since Jesus did indeed voluntarily endure abuse of this kind (see Matthew 26:67). More of these passages in the early Christian writings are discussed in the books suggested for further reading below, and doubtless many more besides remain to be discovered.

This chapter, then, has presented nothing more than a brief introduction to this fascinating subject of prophetic personation. No doubt for those readers who are theologically well-informed it might further raise questions as to how prefiguration and personation are related. Suffice it to say that a good many Old Testament passages, especially in the psalms, but also in the prophets, notably Isaiah, that some have previously understood in terms of prefiguration (i.e. typology) will now need to be re-interpreted as instances of personation. Readers desiring to look more deeply into this and other aspects of this manner of interpretation are strongly recommended to consult the works that appear below.

Suggestions for Further Reading

Bates, Matthew W. *The Hermeneutics of the Apostolic Proclamation: The Center of Paul's Method of Scriptural Interpretation* (Waco, Texas: Baylor University Press, 2012).

Bates, Matthew W. *The Birth of the Trinity: Jesus, God, and Spirit in New Testament and Early Christian Interpretation of the Old Testament* (Oxford: Oxford University Press, 2015).

Cameron, Michael. *Christ Meets Me Everywhere: Augustine's Early Figurative Exegesis* (Oxford: Oxford University Press, 2012), Chapter 6, 'Hearing Voices'.

Carter, Craig A. *Interpreting Scripture with the Great Tradition: Recovering the Genius of Premodern Exegesis* (Grand Rapids, Michigan: Baker Academic, 2018), pp. 192–201, 'Prosopological Exegesis: A Primer'.

9. PRESENCE

Up till now all our considerations of Christ in the Old Testament have been by way of speech or figure. He has either been the topic of a promise or prophetic utterance, or has been represented in some figural manner. What we come to lastly in our treatment of the various ways in which the Hebrew Scriptures bear witness to Christ is the fact of his actual personal presence in Old Testament times. And when we speak of 'presence' we do not mean his general omnipresence, as infinite spirit, that pervades and transcends all of creation. Such does indeed pertain to Christ in his being the second Person of the Trinity, but that is not what we are talking about here. Rather we mean his special localised presence upon the earth, for a specific purpose, and in a form that was tangible, both visibly and audibly, to human beings.

Many Christians who have carefully read the Old Testament have come to understand that on certain occasions the divine Son is himself actually present in the events that took place, in the special manner just described. Since at this time there had not been the full revelation of God such as is only given once we come to the New Testament, these earlier references to the presence of Christ are quite different from those at this later period. In the new covenant age the Son was born expressly as a human being, as one of us, and he remains human to all eternity, while being at the same time wholly divine. This astounding event we call the incarnation, which literally means 'enfleshment'. Clearly this was a unique happening, one that took place at a particular date in human history during the reign of Herod the Great, king of Judaea. Before that, however, the same divine Son did make personal appearances upon the earth, and these are the subject matter of this chapter.

It is firstly important to note that when the second Person of the Trinity appeared on earth during the Old Testament era he is not explicitly called 'Christ' ('anointed one') nor is he called the 'Son' or the 'Word' (*Logos*). These terms are reserved strictly for the fuller revelation of the New Testament in which the nature of his anointing is described and the special Father-Son relationship within the Godhead is disclosed. In the earlier Scriptures he is known by other titles, and at times can be identified only implicitly through the way that he is portrayed, how he behaves, and the things that he says, and also by correspondences between parallel passages.

The aim of this chapter is to demonstrate that a common title given to the Son when he came to the earth in person during Old Testament times is 'the Angel of the LORD'. Here, of course, the capitalised 'LORD' represents the consonants of the divine name, which perhaps originally sounded something close to 'Yahweh'. In Genesis 'the Angel of the LORD' is specifically stated to have come to Hagar (Genesis 16) and to Abraham (Genesis 22). The same title is given to the one who spoke to Moses from the burning bush (Exodus 3), and who blocked the path of Balaam the false-prophet (Numbers 22). He makes several appearances in the book of Judges (chapters 2, 6, and 13), as well as later in the period of the kings (e.g. 1 Chronicles 21:12; 2 Kings 19:35). He is also mentioned a few times in the Psalms (34:7; 35:5–6) and in the writings of the prophets (notably in Zechariah). On occasions, once he has been identified as 'the Angel of the LORD' he is later in the same passage referred to as 'the Angel of God' (e.g. Judges 6:20; 13:9). This shows that 'the Angel of God' is a proper designation of the same being. A couple of times we do indeed find him to be called 'the Angel of God' at the outset (Genesis 21:17; 31:11). He is also once given the title 'the Angel of his Presence' (Isaiah 63:9).

Apart from the foregoing episodes where he is explicitly identified as this 'Angel' figure, the same heavenly being would seem to have been present on other occasions. When Abraham received the three visitors (Genesis 18), just one of them is given the name 'LORD' (vv. 10, 13, 17, and especially v. 22), while the other two are described as 'angels' (19:1, 15). It would be reasonable to conclude the first to be the same Angel of the Lord. The writer to the Hebrews is most probably alluding to this incident when he writes, 'Do not neglect to show hospitality to strangers, for by doing this some have entertained angels without knowing it' (13:2). All three of them were, then, in a sense 'angels', but just one was also the 'LORD'. When Jacob wrestled with a man at the Jabbok (Genesis 32), there is also good reason to understand his combatant to be this specific Angel (see below). On that occasion when the commander of the Lord's armies appeared to Joshua (Joshua 5), it is again highly probable that the Angel is once more in view. This can be established by a sideways look at passages in which the 'Angel of the LORD' is explicitly said to be present. At this encounter Joshua is commanded to take off his shoes (v. 15), as was Moses when he came before the Angel (Exodus 3:5). The figure seen by Joshua 'had a drawn sword in his hand' (v. 13), as did 'Angel of the LORD' when he confronted Balaam (Numbers 22:23). In the book of Daniel the 'one like a son of God' who appeared in the fiery furnace to protect the three young Hebrews would also seem to have been the same extraordinary Angel (3:25). There are other possible indications of his presence in the wilderness narrative when the Israelites were led by a particular angel (Exodus 23).

What is an 'Angel'?

When we see the word 'angel' in our English versions of the Bible we are looking at a translation of the Hebrew noun *mal'āk* in the Old Testament and of the Greek noun *angelos* in the New. It is from this latter term, of course, that the English word is derived. The basic meaning behind both words is that of 'messenger'. For this reason the word can be legitimately applied to anyone carrying out this particular role, regardless of whether they are human beings or heavenly beings. So it is that the 'messengers' sent by Saul to the house of Jesse are *mal'ākîm* (1 Samuel 16:19) in the same way that the angels sent by the Lord to Sodom were *mal'ākîm* (Genesis 19:1). In the Gospels John the Baptist is called an *angelos* (Luke 7:27) in the same way that the heaven-sent angel who came to Jesus in Gethsemane is called an *angelos* (Luke 22:43). In neither the Hebrew nor the Greek term, therefore, is there any implication as to the nature of the one referred to. The word strictly denotes the function that is performed.

Having said this, when we look at biblical passages in which the terms *mal'āk* and *angelos* occur, it is usually fairly easy to decide if the messenger in question is human or heavenly. The context and details are often sufficient to determine which is intended. In the case of a human messenger the sender is usually a king or some other person of importance. In the case of a heavenly messenger the sender is God, and the message he bears is typically one of divine revelation, that is to say, one that includes supernatural knowledge or a promise for the future, as yet unforeseeable to human eyes. Or if not the bearer of divine revelation, this heavenly being might be sent to perform some act of supernatural power. There might just be a handful of cases where ambiguity exists. Certainly every time the sender is human, the same is true of the messenger. Yet it is possible that in a few instances the messenger sent by God, when only mentioned in brief, could be a human prophet rather than an actual angelic being (cf. 2 Chronicles 36:16). In regard to the Angel of the Lord, there is no doubt that he belongs to the heavenly category of 'angel'.

Our interest here, of course, is only in angels sent from heaven. These beings are 'spirit' in nature (Hebrews 1:14; cf. v. 7), just as God himself is 'spirit' (John 4:24). Although spiritual in essence, this does not prevent them possessing, or taking on, physical properties, even if only temporarily. So what is their visual appearance? When we think of the term 'angel' doubtless the minds of many of us will conjure up winged beings clothed in white. But is that what an angel really looks like? It is important to note that in the Bible there is a significant difference in appearance between the angels that are seen in visions and dreams and those that simply appear to normal human sight. The angels that are seen in the visions of Daniel and by the apostle John in the book of Revelation are typically depicted as wearing white robes or having a shining countenance, or perhaps flying (though there is no actual mention of wings. Seraphim and cherubim possess wings, but these are nowhere classed as angels). When an angel is sent to a man or woman outside of visions and dreams, the heavenly being is most commonly described as having human appearance. The heavenly visitors that came to Abraham's tent are simply termed 'three men' (Genesis 18:2; cf. vv. 16, 22), and when two of them later entered Sodom, while called 'angels' by the narrator (Genesis 19:1, 15), the inhabitants of the city referred to them as 'men' (19:2), as does Lot (v. 8; cf. vv. 10, 12, 16). The wrestling partner of Jacob, who was no doubt a heavenly being (the prophet Hosea calls him an 'angel'; Hosea 12:4), is likewise called 'a man' (Genesis 32:24). This human appearance is also true of the one who bears the title 'Angel of the LORD'. When this particular heavenly being came to visit Manoah and his wife to tell them of Samson's birth, he is referred to, both in the narrative and speech, as 'man' (Judges 13:11; cf. vv. 3, 13). The same description 'man' applies to the commander of the Lord's army (Joshua 5:13), a being who is probably the self-same Angel of the Lord. It would seem, then, that when angels appeared on earth they generally took on human form.

The purposes for which angels are sent are manifold. They most frequently come to bring a message from God, hence their name. But they might also come to perform an act of deliverance or judgment. It is worth noting that the abstract noun related to *mal'āk* is *melâkâ*, meaning 'task' or 'work'. So angels can be doers as well as speakers, and Scripture contains many examples of this.

The Angel of the Lord as God

That the Angel of the Lord is distinct from other angels is evident alone from the title which is given him. He is referred to, even upon a first appearance, by a phrase that is grammatically definite, that is to say, '*the* Angel of the LORD' (e.g. Exodus 3:2). This suggests that he is one particularly special angel. This is further supported by the fact that the plural 'Angels of the LORD' never occurs.

As we look closely at the details of the narratives in which the Angel of the Lord appears we discover that although this being shares the designation 'angel' along with other angelic beings, he is in fact totally unique. He differs from them in an absolutely fundamental way, which is that he himself, unlike them, is nothing less than divine, which is to say, he is God! This is the unavoidable conclusion of a careful study of the passages in which the Angel of the Lord is involved. Here is what we find:

(a) We firstly observe that the narrator himself, as the inspired spokesperson of God, within a single passage refers to the self-same being as 'the Angel of the LORD' in one breath, and as 'God' in the next. We see this for example in the episode concerning Moses at the burning bush (Exodus 3). To introduce the appearance the narrator says that 'the Angel of the LORD appeared to him [Moses] in a flame of fire from the midst of a bush' (v. 2), but then just a couple of verses later writes that 'God called to him from the midst of the bush' (v. 4). Following this, we are told that 'Moses covered his face because he was afraid to look at God' (v. 6). Similarly, at the visitation to Gideon (Judges 6), the heavenly visitor is initially presented with the words, 'The Angel of the LORD came and sat down under the oak tree at Ophrah' (v. 11), and yet just three verses after this we read that when Gideon addressed him, 'The LORD turned to him and said ...' (v. 14). Besides this narrative interchange between 'the Angel of the LORD' and 'God/LORD', there is also the significant comment of the prophet Hosea. The prophet looks back at the events of Genesis 32 where the patriarch Jacob wrestles with what is there described as a 'man', as noted above, but who is obviously a heavenly being. Hosea, speaking of Jacob, at one moment says 'he strove with God' (Hosea 12:3b), and in the very next breath declares that 'he wrestled with an angel' (v. 4a). We also earlier noted that one of the three angelic beings that appeared to Abraham was described by the narrator as 'the LORD' (Genesis 18:22).

(b) The angel in question is also called 'God' or 'LORD' by those to whom he appeared. The Angel of the Lord came to Hagar in the desert to instruct her to return to her mistress Sarah and to speak of the future birth of her son (Genesis 16). At the end of his message Hagar responds by saying, 'You are the God who sees me' (v. 13). The encounter with the Angel of the Lord experienced by Manoah and his wife (Judges 13) ends with the angel ascending in a flame of fire (v. 21). The narrative then informs us that at this point 'Manoah realised that it was the Angel of the LORD' (v. 21). He immediately said to his wife, 'We are sure to die, for we have seen God!' (v. 22). The woman replied with the words: 'If the LORD had desired to kill us, he would not have accepted a burnt offering and a grain offering from our hands, nor would he have shown us all these things, nor would he have announced to us such things at this time' (v. 23). Although she uses the divine name 'LORD', it is clear from the latter part of her speech that she is referring to the angelic being who had just spoken to them. In this context we may also draw attention to the words of Jacob who, when blessing the two sons of Joseph, said, 'May the God before whom my fathers Abraham and Isaac walked, the God who has been my shepherd all my life to this day, the Angel who has redeemed me from all evil—may he bless these boys.' (Genesis 48:15–16). Though in the act of blessing he invokes 'God' and 'the Angel' he is without question only calling upon a single divine person, for the main verb (*yᵉbārēk*, 'may *he* bless') that applies to both titles is singular in form. The two titles, therefore, must indicate one and the same person. We bring in here also the prophecy of Zechariah 12:8, which states that in the last day 'the house of David will be like God, like the Angel of the LORD going before them'; the comparison is patently not with two persons, but with one, who is termed both 'God' and 'the Angel of the LORD'.

(c) Next we note the crucial fact that the Angel of the Lord speaks of himself as God in the first person ('I'). This is evident from the passage about the burning bush. While it is 'the Angel of the LORD' who appeared to Moses in the bush (Exodus 3:2), when he speaks to him he declares, 'I am the God of Abraham, the God of Isaac, and the God of Jacob' (v. 6). Back in Genesis 'the Angel of God' (for this title, see earlier in the chapter) spoke to Jacob, and said, 'I am the God of Bethel, where you anointed a pillar and where you made a vow to me' (Genesis 31:11, 13; cf. 35:1).

(d) The same Angel of the Lord speaks things that are only proper for God himself to say. He utters words that elsewhere are found only upon the lips of God. In Judges 2 'the Angel of the LORD' spoke to the Israelites at Bokim, and said, 'I brought you up out of Egypt and led you to the land that I swore to give to your fathers' (v. 1). Who was it that had earlier sworn this oath to give the land of Canaan to the Hebrew patriarchs? It was certainly God himself (e.g. Genesis 26:3; 50:24; Exodus 6:8; Deuteronomy 1:8). No mere angel is said to swear such a thing anywhere in the Old Testament. The Angel of the Lord at Bokim then further states 'I said, "I will never break my covenant with you"' (Judges 2:1). Elsewhere the one who speaks of 'my covenant' is again the Almighty himself (e.g. Genesis 17:10; Exodus 6:4; 19:5), and not an angel. To Hagar, in the passage already mentioned (Genesis 16), the angelic figure made the promise, 'I will greatly multiply your offspring so that they will be too many to count' (v. 10). It is for God to make such promises, and words almost identical to this are spoken by God to Abraham when he is tested on Mount Moriah (Genesis 22), 'I will greatly multiply your offspring as the stars of heaven and as the sand on the seashore' (v. 17). In this same episode, once Abraham had prevailed in his testing, we read that the Angel of the Lord called out to him from heaven, and said, 'Now I know that you fear God, because you have not withheld your son, your only son, from me' (v. 12). The last words 'from *me*' have definite reference to God, who commanded the offering of Isaac, and yet it is the Angel that speaks. The outcome of the test did not in any way concern Abraham not withholding his son from a mere angel. The Angel of the Lord then called to Abraham a second time, and this time swore to him an oath, in which he said, 'I swear by myself' (v. 15). Again the fact of swearing (see above), and even more so, swearing by himself, indicates his divine nature, since oaths were sworn 'in the name of the LORD' (cf. Leviticus 19:12; Isaiah 48:1; Jeremiah 12:16).

(e) The Angel would seem to have divine attributes and prerogatives. When ordinary angels come to the earth, they have no effect on the surrounding locality. This is not so with the Angel of the Lord. His presence actually imparts holiness to the place in which he appears. Once again in the passage about the burning bush we read that Moses was told, 'Do not come any closer. Take your sandals off your feet, for the place on which you are standing is holy ground' (Exodus 3:5). The same phenomenon is seen when 'the Commander of the army of the LORD' met with Joshua before the battle of Jericho (Joshua 5). There he ordered Joshua, 'Take your sandals off your feet, for the place on which you are standing is holy.' (v. 15). It is great significance that this Angel also accepts worship. For in this last passage it states that 'Joshua fell face down to the ground and worshipped' (v. 14). This being simply cannot have been, then, a regular angel. In other passages of the Bible it specifically states that angels do not accept worship. The apostle John fell at the feet of an angel in the book of Revelation, and was expressly told not to do so. John writes:

> Then I fell at his [the angel's] feet to worship him. But he said to me, 'Do not do that. I am a fellow servant of yours and your brothers who hold the testimony of Jesus. Worship God!' (Revelation 19:10)

> I, John, am the one who heard and saw these things. And when I heard and saw, I fell down to worship at the feet of the angel who showed me these things. But he said to me, 'Do not do that. I am a fellow servant of yours and of your brothers the prophets and of those who keep the words of this book. Worship God!' (Revelation 22:8)

The faith presented by both Testaments of the Bible is strictly monotheistic. There is only one true God who is to be worshipped. To do otherwise was prohibited in the very first of the Ten Commandments (Exodus 20:2). God does not share his glory with any other (Isaiah 42:8). And it should be remembered that regular angels are created beings, so to worship before such a one would be an act of idolatry. In his letter to the Colossians Paul expressly condemns the 'worship of angels' (2:18). So since Joshua accords his heavenly visitor the reverence that is due to God alone, the inference is that the Angel of the Lord is totally different from all others called 'angels' in that, unlike them as created beings, he himself is truly uncreated and divine. In keeping with this is the fact that this particular Angel accepts offerings that are made to him. Such was the case when he came to Gideon (Judges 6:17–19), and later upon his visitation to the parents of Samson (13:23).

By way of summary, then, we see that this Angel of the Lord is identified in the inspired narrative as 'God' (or 'LORD'), speaks of himself as 'God', is described by others as 'God', swears oaths and makes promises as God, and accepts worship as God. From this it is difficult, if not impossible, to escape the conclusion that he is indeed God.

At this point it might be appropriate to mention that the Hebrew phrase *mal'ak yhwh*, that is usually translated 'Angel of the LORD', does not necessarily mean 'Angel *of* the LORD' in the sense that the first belongs to the second, which is to say it expresses a relation of possession. When two words are coupled together in this kind of construction the sense could possibly be 'which is'. We see this, for example, in a phrase like 'the city of Jerusalem'. It is not the city that belongs to Jerusalem, as Jerusalem itself *is* the city. More freely translated it would mean 'the city which is Jerusalem'. The relationship expressed, therefore, by bringing these two nouns together in this way is one of identification (rather than possession)—the city which is to be identified as Jerusalem. The phrase 'the Angel of the LORD' might then conceivably be understood as 'the Angel which is the LORD', or 'the Angel which is to be identified as the LORD'. The same would apply to the lesser used phrase 'the Angel of God', which can bear the sense of 'the Angel which is God' or 'the Angel which is to be identified as God', and similarly 'the Angel of his Presence' could be taken as 'the Angel which is his Presence'. So the very title this heavenly being bears may itself be a pointer to who he is.

The Identity of the Angel of the Lord

The foregoing section has shown that the Angel we are discussing is altogether distinct from other angels. He is plainly not an ordinary angel, nor can he be a high-ranking angel, or archangel. These latter are still just created beings, and when something of their visitations is described, as in the case of Michael (Daniel 10:13, 21; Jude 9) and Gabriel (Daniel 8:16; 9:21; Luke 1:19; 26–38), none of the particular features given above regarding the Angel of the Lord are in evidence. They do not speak as God, nor do those they appear to call them God or respond by obeisance and offering. Neither does their appearance result in any hallowed ground.

When, therefore, we read of 'the Angel of the LORD' we are not, in actual fact, looking at one who is angelic in nature, that is, not a created spiritual being. Rather the term 'angel' is being used with respect to his role (or 'office', if you prefer). As noted earlier, the word 'angel' primarily refers to role, not nature. So this particular heavenly visitor is termed an 'angel', not because he shares the same nature, but because he comes bringing revelations and performing deliverances and judgements as other angels do. Like them too, when the Angel comes to earth in such a way he adopts human appearance. As regards his role, then, it is angelic, and as regards his form when he carries out this role, it is undoubtedly human. But when it comes to his essential nature, he is vastly different from those who are merely created angelic beings. And that is because in essence the Angel of the Lord is divine. He actually *is* 'the LORD'. He is not a mere representation of God, for all angels represent God, but one who himself is God. The most obvious explanation for what was discussed in the previous section is that when 'the Angel of the LORD' makes an appearance, God himself is present. It is this fact alone that renders the place of his appearance holy, and this alone that evokes the particular responses of those who see him.

This essential deity of the Angel brings us now to another question. If he is God, then how does this relate to the fact that God, according to the fulness of the biblical revelation and the confession of the church, is a Triune God? Is the Angel of the Lord a special appearance of God in a general, non-specified, sense? Or can he be identified with one particular Person of the three? Upon reflection, the latter really has to be the case, as I shall endeavour to explain.

Within the meaning of the term 'angel', that is, 'messenger', there is implicitly the idea of 'being sent'. A messenger necessarily brings a message *from another* who sends him or her. Two persons are involved, besides the recipient of the message. In certain of the passages where the Angel of the Lord is found explicit mention is made of the fact that God had 'sent' him (e.g. Judges 13:8; 1 Chronicles 21:15–16; the reader is also invited to consider the rather puzzling case of Zechariah 2:8–11, where it is hard to avoid the conclusion that 'the LORD of hosts' says that the 'the LORD of hosts' had sent him! One named 'LORD' sends another also named 'LORD'). So, then, if the Angel has been sent, there still remains a sender, who, by reason of logic, has not been sent.

The picture we seem to get therefore is that this Angel figure, although himself divine, is sent by another distinct divine being. This is confirmed by the fact that the Angel actually addresses this other being. Note the words of Zechariah 1:12: 'Then the Angel of the LORD said, "O LORD of hosts, how long will you have no mercy on Jerusalem and the cities of Judah?"' Conversely, God is seen to address the Angel: 'the LORD spoke to the Angel … the Angel of the LORD' (2 Samuel 24:16; cf. 1 Chronicles 21:27). This being so, it would not be unreasonable to conclude that the distinction between the various Persons of the Godhead is hinted at here.

The question to consider now, then, is which of the three divine Persons is present in the appearances of the Angel of the Lord? I think we can immediately exclude the Father. There is an insightful comment made by one of the early church fathers, Theodoret of Cyrus (fifth century). Speaking of Exodus 3, about the angel of the Lord in the burning bush, he states, 'The whole context shows that it was God who appeared. But it also called him "angel" [*angelos*] in order that we should understand that it was not God the Father who appeared. For is the Father anyone's messenger [*angelos*]?' (*Questions on the Octateuch*, Exodus, Qu. 5). Since the Father, according to the historical Christian faith, is the fount of the Godhead, then it would be highly inappropriate for him to be sent. As Theodoret asks—who would there be to send him? Nowhere else in Scripture do we read of the Father being sent. Rather it is the Father who sends the Son (1 John 4:14, 'the Father has sent the Son to be the Saviour of the world') and also sends the Holy Spirit (John 14:26, 'the Holy Spirit, whom the Father will send'). Besides this, the Angel of the Lord assumes a visible appearance, and yet we are told that 'No one has seen the Father' (John 6:46; cf. 14:9).

So with regard to our question, the divine Person whose presence was manifested in the Angel of the Lord has to be either the Son or the Spirit. Of these two, the evidence would definitely seem to favour the former. Firstly, there is the fact that nowhere in the Bible is the Holy Spirit said to take on human form. As is well known, at the baptism of Christ the concrete form that he does assume is that of a dove (Matthew 3:16; Mark 1:10). Jesus, however, is ordained to receive not merely a human form but human nature itself in the incarnation. Secondly, the Hebrew term *mal'āk* is expressly used with reference to Jesus, but not to the Holy Spirit. In the prophecy of Malachi 3:1 God declares, 'the Lord, whom you seek, will suddenly come to his temple, the messenger [Hebrew: *mal'āk*; Greek: *angelos*] of the covenant, in whom you delight—behold, he is coming'. The prediction concerns the coming of the Messiah, Jesus. And in this verse he is termed 'the messenger of the covenant', which is to say, 'the angel of the covenant' (NJB; cf. ASV footnote). Thirdly, the Angel of the Lord and Jesus Christ share a descriptive name in common, that of 'wonderful'. When Samson's father-to-be asked the Angel of the Lord his name, the Angel replied, 'Why do you ask my name, seeing it is wonderful?' (Judges 13:18). The same is one of the titles prophetically ascribed to the Messiah: 'he will be called Wonderful' (Isaiah 9:6). Furthermore, it is not the case that the Spirit ever speaks of the particular reason he has been sent, but we find this with respect to both the Angel and the Son. In Exodus 3:8 the former says, '*I have come down* to deliver them from the hand of the Egyptians', while in John 6:38 the latter declares, '*I have come down* from heaven, not to do my own will, but the will of him who sent me'. Besides these details, the New Testament expressly states that it is the Son in particular who is the one who reveals the Father (John 1:18).

The facts, then, do appear to allow us to identify the divine Person manifesting himself as the Angel of the Lord with the Son. In keeping with this, the very next words that Theodoret of Cyrus adds to those cited above, where he says the Angel 'was not God the Father', are 'rather, it was the Only-Begotten Son'.

One further consideration, and an important one, is that there are no manifestations of the Angel of the Lord from the time of Christ's incarnation onwards. This is what we would expect if this Angel were indeed the Son. That particular angelic role as carried out in the Old Testament was now completed, and the Son had a more significant role to play. So while in the New Testament we read of appearances of '*an* angel of the Lord' (e.g. Matthew 1:20; Luke 2:9; Acts 5:19; 8:28), who is then, quite properly, referred back to grammatically as '*the* angel of the Lord' (Matthew 1:24), or simply as '*the* angel' (Luke 2:13), the definite article here only means 'the one just mentioned', not 'the unique one'.

Readers may already be familiar with the word 'Theophany' (from the Greek for 'God-appearance'). Biblical scholars use this word to refer to manifestations of God in general, whether as some visible animate form or through natural or supernatural phenomena. Once it is accepted that 'the Angel of the LORD' in the Old Testament is a title that describes the personal presence of the second Person of the Trinity, then the theological term 'Christophany' ('Christ-appearance') may be employed to indicate these manifestations. The word is commonly found in the relevant literature.

Christian Interpreters over the Centuries

The reader should be made aware that to identify the personal presence of the divine Son within the Old Testament story is something that has been a major feature in the traditional way of reading these ancient Scriptures throughout the centuries, by Catholic and Orthodox Christians, as well as by Protestants. In fact, one could legitimately call this the majority view of the matter. There are, of course, other views. The Jews, for the most part, would see this figure as a created angel. This does not explain, however, the divine attributes and actions that he displays, nor the reverential response to him. There is also a less common Christian view, which would happily recognise the special angelic figure as divine, as being essentially 'God', but which would not want to identify him with one particular Person of the Godhead. The view put forward here, that of Christophanies, which I am convinced is faithful to the Scriptures, is the one that has predominated throughout the larger part of the history of the universal church.

The number of Christian scholars and preachers who have explained the appearances of the Angel of the Lord in christological terms is enormous. Here we just quote a selection of the more significant ones from the early centuries of the church up to very recent times.

> JUSTIN MARTYR (church father, second century): 'As Moses was tending his uncle's sheep in the land of Arabia, our Christ conversed with him in the form of fire out of a bush'. (*First Apology*, 62.3)

> IRENAEUS OF LYONS (church father, second century): 'the Son of God is implanted everywhere throughout his [Moses'] writings: at one time, indeed, speaking with Abraham, when about to eat with him; at another time with Noah, giving to him the dimensions of the ark; at another, inquiring after Adam; at another, bringing down judgment upon the Sodomites; and again, when he becomes visible, and directs Jacob on his journey, and speaks with Moses from the bush. It would be endless to recount the occasions on which the Son of God is shown forth by Moses'. (*Against Heresies*, 4.10.1)

> SYNOD OF ANTIOCH (council of church leaders, third century): 'The Son was not just a spectator nor was he merely present, but ... came down and appeared to Abraham at the oak of Mamre, as one of the three, with whom the patriarch conversed as Lord and Judge ... This is he who, fulfilling the Father's will, appears to and converses with the patriarchs ... sometimes as an "Angel", at other times as "Lord", and at other times being testified to as "God". Truly it is impious to suppose that one can call the God of all an "angel"; however, the Angel of the Father is the Son, he is Lord and God'. (*Creedal Statement*)

> EUSEBIUS OF CAESAREA (church father, fourth century): 'It has been proved that this same Being [the Angel] is both Lord and God, and Christ anointed by the Father ... So, appearing to

Abraham by the oak in human form, he reveals himself in a calm and peaceful guise, foreshowing by it his future coming to save mankind'. (*Proof of the Gospel*, 5.19)

MARTIN LUTHER (reformer, sixteenth century): 'The patriarch Jacob distinguished the Person of the Holy Trinity [Genesis 48:15] ... He calls the Lord Christ an "Angel", not as if he were an angel according to his essence and nature, for it would be manifest idolatry to pray to an angel and ask for his blessing. By his prayer Jacob, then, confesses this Angel to be true essential God'. (*Sermon on the Festival of the Holy Trinity*, 1535)

JOHN CALVIN (reformer, sixteenth century): 'Christ, who is the living image of the Father, often appeared to the fathers [i.e. patriarchs] under the form of an angel' (*Commentary*, on Genesis 18:9)

JOHN OWEN (Puritan, seventeenth century): 'He is expressly called an "Angel" [Exodus 3:2]—namely, the Angel of the covenant, the great Angel of the presence of God, in whom was the name and nature of God. And He thus appeared that the church might know and consider who it was that was to work out their spiritual and eternal salvation, whereof that deliverance which then He would effect was a type and pledge. Aben Ezra [the Jew] would have the Angel mentioned verse 2, to be another from him who is called "God," v 6: but the text will not give countenance to any such distinction, but speaks of one and the same person throughout without any alteration; and this was no other but the Son of God'. (*Commentary on Hebrews, Volume 1*, p. 224)

MATTHEW POOLE (Puritan, seventeenth century): 'Hebrew: *the Angel of the Lord*, namely, Christ ... who is called the Angel, because that redemption [i.e. the exodus] of the people [of Israel] shadowed forth our own'. (*Synopsis of Sacred Scripture*, on Exodus 3:2)

JONATHAN EDWARDS (preacher and theologian, eighteenth century): 'This redemption was by Jesus Christ, as is evident from this, that it was wrought by him that appeared to Moses in the bush; for that was the person that sent Moses to redeem the people. But that was Christ, as is evident, because he is called "the angel of the LORD" [Exodus 3:2]'. (*A History of the Work of Redemption*)

CHARLES WESLEY (Methodist hymn-writer, eighteenth century): 'The great redeeming Angel, Thee, O Jesus, I confess'. (*Collection of Hymns*, no. 894)

CARL FRIEDRICH KEIL (Old Testament scholar, nineteenth century): 'The Angel of Jehovah was therefore none other than the *Logos*, who not only "was with God," but "was God," and who in Jesus Christ "was made flesh"'. (*Commentary on the Pentateuch, Vol. 1*, p. 191)

WALTER KAISER (Old Testament scholar, present-day): 'It is clear from this abundance of evidence that the angel of the Lord in the Old Testament was a preincarnate form of our Lord Jesus Christ, who would later permanently take on flesh when he came as a babe in Bethlehem'. (*Hard Sayings of the Bible*, on Judges 6:22–23)

VERN POYTHRESS (Old Testament scholar, present-day): 'the "angel" [of Exodus 23:20]—the messenger—is himself divine. This messenger is then similar to the instances in Genesis where "the angel of the Lord" has divine attributes. We are dealing with a preincarnate appearance of Christ, anticipating his incarnation'. (*Theophany: A Biblical Theology of God's Appearing*, pp. 278–279)

The last citation comes from a publication as recent as 2018. The traditional view regarding this angel, then, can be seen to be far from dying out.

Understanding the Christophanies

As we reflect upon the Old Testament appearances of Christ as the Angel of the Lord, there are two matters of crucial importance that we need to emphasize. Both might be obvious to many, but they are of such theological significance I feel it is necessary to spell them out. The first of these is that, although he is described as 'the Angel of the LORD', Christ *is not an angel*. There were several heretical groups (e.g. the Paulicians) during the early centuries of the church who claimed that the Son of God was in fact an angel in his true nature. The biblical facts simply do not fit such a view, and so it was that these heretics were opposed by orthodox believers. A heavenly angel, while being a spirit like God, is most certainly to be separated from God in at least two fundamental ways, namely, with respect to creatureliness and divinity. An angel is created, God is not. God is divine, an angel is not. Thus, not just one, but two great chasms exist between angelic beings and the Persons of the Godhead. The Angel of the Lord belongs on the divine, uncreated side of the divide. The writer to the Hebrews reminds us that the Son (whom I have identified as 'the Angel of the LORD') is the object of worship, not just of human beings, but of other angels also—'Let all God's angels worship him' (Hebrews 1:6). So we ought not get confused by the title given him. It is one thing to call him by the title of 'angel' in virtue of his role in the Old Testament stage of revelation, and quite another to actually take his essential nature as being angelic.

The second important matter is that when the Son shows up on earth as the Angel of the Lord in the Old Testament *he is not becoming incarnate* in the New Testament sense. The incarnation was a unique event at a fixed point in human history, in which the Son *became* a human being like us. His divine nature took to itself, or 'assumed', as theologians like to say, human nature. This he did by being born into this world in the usual human manner, having first been supernaturally conceived within the womb of the virgin Mary. For him becoming human was necessary in order to save humankind from their sins, since to do so would involve death, and deity cannot die. Having taken our nature upon himself, the Son is now both human and divine—one Person in two natures, as the creeds proclaim—and this remains so to all eternity. In other words, the one-off event of the incarnation is permanent in its duration. Such is in reality something far removed from the Old Testament Christophanies. In these earlier visitations of the divine Son to earth he merely adopted human form for a short season. It was not a permanent assumption of that nature, but the form was discarded once his task upon earth was completed. At these times he was not the 'God-Man' we read of in the Gospels, but was God, in human form, on an angelic mission. So when he ascended once again into the heavens, he resumed his spiritual existence as pure deity. Once he had become incarnate ('enfleshed'), however, and had fulfilled his ministry upon the earth, then his ascension to the right hand of the Father actually took his humanity with him, to which he is inseparably united. This is an important and sometimes overlooked element of the gospel message, that there is now a human being in heaven able to intercede for us and represent us effectively to God the Father.

A Christophany, then, is essentially a pre-incarnate appearance of the Son of God upon the earth. Like other angelic figures, he was sent to bring special revelations, to deliver, and on occasions to judge or pronounce judgment. Yet over and above these things, his appearances uniquely served as precursors to his actual incarnation. His temporary adoption of the form of human nature was an anticipation of his permanent assumption of the essence of human nature. Right from the fall of humankind and their expulsion from Eden in the beginning it had been the divine intention to be reunited with his creatures, for him to be present among them once again. This purpose was a gradual development over many centuries. The Christophanies occurred in the preparatory stage of that larger purpose. For God to take the form of man temporarily was an initial step towards God becoming man eternally—his temporary presence in the old creation paving the way for his everlasting presence in the new. The divine Son, then, was not just spoken of in the Hebrew Scriptures, but was present in person. We understand that Christophanies, therefore, play a significant part of the Old Testament's witness to the coming full revelation of God in the humanity of his Son.

Suggestions for Further Reading

Borland, James A. *Christ in the Old Testament: Old Testament Appearances of Christ in Human Form* (Fearn, Ross-shire, Scotland: Christian Focus Publications, 2010).

Pentuic, Eugene, J. *Jesus the Messiah in the Hebrew Bible* (New York: Paulist Press, 2006), pp. 56–77.

Smith, John P. *The Scripture Testimony to the Messiah, Volume 1* (London: Jackson & Walford, 1837), pp. 445–459.

Walsh, William P. *The Angel of the Lord, Or, Manifestations of Christ in the Old Testament* (London: Seeley, Jackson, & Halliday, 1876).

CONCLUSION

In the preceding chapters we have seen how the Old Testament is incomplete in itself. It is not an independent volume, but requires a completion. It speaks of a fall, but contains no ultimate redemption. The resolution only comes in the events recorded for us in the New Testament. The Old necessarily progresses towards the New, the preparation towards the full accomplishment. Following the *protevangelium* revealed in Eden, the ancient Scriptures present numerous pointers to the coming Saviour. Through direct promises and prophecies, through less direct prefigurements and personations, the advent of God the Son incarnate is fore-announced. More than this, he actually shows up in person through those temporary visitations called Christophanies, tokens of his coming permanent incarnation. By all of these different means the Hebrew writings give their testimony to the One to come—as the New Testament declares, 'at various times and in various ways God spoke long ago to the fathers by the prophets' (Hebrews 1:1).

The main aim of this book has been to offer an outline for the benefit of the modern reader of those various ways in which God spoke in the Old Testament about the coming of his Son. My principal guide in this has been the interpretations given by Jesus himself, and by the apostles he appointed, of those ancient Scriptures. I firmly believe that such are given precisely for that reason—to open up the way for us to understand how those writings speak of Christ. This is one of the very first things that Jesus passed on to his apostles following his resurrection (Luke 24:27, 45). Instructed in this manner, the apostles then announced the gospel message through proclamations such as those found in the book of Acts, fully utilising the methods which they had evidently learned from Jesus. And these same methods appear in their letters, in which they admonish and instruct the Christian churches. Their interpretations are neither naïve, nor misleading. Nor are they simply to be ignored. This, somewhat tragically, would be to neglect the God-given means of enabling us to correctly interpret the Old Testament.

Certainly the generations of Christian pastors and teachers that took up the role of leading the church following the age of the apostles carried on in precisely the same manner of interpretation. Two treatments of the Old Testament in the light of Christ have come down to us from the second century: *The Dialogue with Trypho the Jew*, written by Justin Martyr (c. AD 150), and *The Demonstration of the Apostolic Preaching*, by Irenaeus of Lyons (c. AD 180). In both of these the authors seek to unpack the Old Testament with respect to Jesus, and all the various approaches to reading those Scriptures that I have endeavoured to explain in this volume are to be met in these two books. One can hardly turn a page without encountering the Christ-focussed exposition of an Old Testament promise or prophecy, or an instance of prefiguration, personation, or Christophany.

So the situation remained within the church throughout the succeeding centuries. There were different emphases in different places at different times, and some emphases went too far. We may mention the decline of the Christophanic interpretation of the Angel of the Lord in the Western Church during the Middle Ages. But the Eastern Church all the while retained the view put forward here. And with the coming of the Reformation, even in the West, the Christophanic view was to a large degree revived. The Middle Ages also saw the minimising of the literal sense of Scripture in favour of an excessive use of allegory. Besides neglecting the basic historical meaning, the manner of allegorising employed was often non-Christological, and was rather applied to philosophy or matters of the mind and soul. This was one of the problems that the Reformation sought to rectify, stressing once again the importance of the literal meaning, and yet at the same time continuing to apply a more balanced figural reading of the text in terms of Christ. Such deviations and their subsequent correction ought not to detract from the basic solidarity of the overall approach to the Christian reading of the Old Testament.

So it continued throughout the seventeenth and eighteenth centuries, and on into the nineteenth, with many biblical scholars, including those holding high academic positions, devoting works to Christological interpretations of the Old Testament. During this time it was not uncommon for someone holding a professorship in divinity, or the like, at a European or North American institution to publish serious works on the subject of biblical typology or the Christophanies, or to include such as a serious component within their investigations of the Old Testament. The highpoint of all this Christ-centred exposition was perhaps the two-volume work entitled *Biblical Typology* published by Patrick Fairbairn (later Professor of Theology at the Free Church Theological College, Aberdeen) in 1845. It was described at the time as 'one of the most important theological works of its day'. But then things began to change dramatically with the rise of an exclusive historical-critical approach to the Bible. This primarily impacted the church in the West, and perhaps Protestantism far more than Catholicism. The Orthodox Church of the East, for the most part, continued to read Scripture in the traditional manner. Such a new approach, developed for the study of history and historical documents in general, rather than for inspired Scripture, soon saw the downplaying of the kind of approaches to Old Testament interpretation advocated in this book. It was a largely rationalistic method which emphasised the human author of a biblical book over the divine, and hence looked more to the disunity, rather than the unity, of the various documents. In such an approach in which supernatural revelation and knowledge was mostly overlooked, prophecy and prefiguration were quickly discarded.

Thankfully the historical-critical movement of the nineteenth century is now showing signs of beginning to lose its dominance in biblical studies in the West. Perhaps it is be viewed, like medieval allegorising, as pushing matters to an extreme, though in the opposite direction. To say that attention should be paid to questions of a historical and grammatical nature in examining the biblical text is, of course, a good thing. This is the basic starting point for all sound exegesis. But to claim that such a method alone will result in the full meaning of Scripture is going much too far, especially if the possibility of supernatural knowledge is excluded. So while there is much that is good that has been accomplished by the historical-critical movement, it has sadly had, on the whole, a negative impact upon Christianity in the West, and may indeed be one of the major contributing factors to the decline of the faith in this part of the world.

Over against the approach that has dominated the last century and a half of biblical study, there is currently a strong movement within academic circles in the West to bring back the best of the traditional manner of interpretation. Mention has been made in the lists of books suggested for further reading of scholars such as Hans Boersma and Craig Carter, whose works, along with those of others, are warmly recommended to the reader.

At the heart of the matter of interpreting the Bible lies the question of how we view the biblical writings and how we regard the person of Jesus Christ. If we merely see the books of the Bible as the compositions of men on religious themes, and if we take Jesus to be nothing more than a godly man, then we will arrive at very different conclusions than if we embrace the Bible as divinely inspired Scripture, for the people of God of all ages, and Jesus as the pre-existent divine Son. This latter, of course, is what the mainstream church down through the centuries has confessed to be the truth. But the matter goes significantly further—how do we relate Jesus and the Bible? This is an important question because our answer to it affects our whole approach to the interpretation of the Old Testament.

For many Christians in the West when they hear the phrase 'the Word of God' their minds will immediately go to the Bible. For our Eastern Orthodox brothers and sisters, however, the Word of God is primarily a description of Jesus. This second view is undoubtedly that of Scripture itself. In the opening to John's Gospel the apostle speaks of the 'Word' (Greek: *Logos*; Latin: *Verbum*), and it soon becomes apparent that this 'Word' is in fact a person, and, more than that, a divine Person: 'In the beginning was the Word, and the Word was with God, and the Word was God. He was in the beginning with God' (John 1:1–2). As the passage continues it becomes clear that John is speaking of Jesus, in whom 'the Word became flesh' (v. 14). Corresponding to this, at the beginning of his first letter, John there calls him 'the Word of life' (1 John 1:1). Later still in the New Testament, in the great vision of the book of Revelation, Jesus is given the name 'the Word of God' (Revelation 19:13). Ultimately, then, the Word of God is not a book, but a living being. In agreement with this, the writer to the Hebrews tells us that 'the Word of God is living and active' (4:12). So God's 'Word' is an appropriate descriptive title of the Son, the second Person of the Holy Trinity.

That the Son should also be called the 'Word' suggests his particular role within the Godhead. A word is, in essence, an utterance by which a person's thoughts and intentions are made known. The title therefore, as applied to the divine Son, indicates one who is a means of revelation. The Son reveals the Father, or, in other words, the Word expresses the mind of God. More than this revelatory role, however, there is a further dimension to idea of the divine Word. For God, who is sovereign in power and authority, the utterance of his Word is also a performative act. Unlike us humans, our words merely express ideas and wishes. These then have to be implemented in order for their contents to become reality, and in this we often fail. With God, however, the mere expression of his Word also sees its enactment. His Word is attended with omnipotence. Directly it is uttered, its accomplishment is sure to follow. This we unambiguously see in the account of creation (Genesis 1). God simply utters the words, and whatever he speaks of comes into being (e.g. 1:3, 9, 11). As the psalmist declares, 'By the word of the LORD were the heavens made, and all their host by the breath of his mouth' (Psalm 33:6; cf. 148:5). The New Testament tells us that this Word that brought creation into being was Christ himself (and the Genesis account, though presenting a less distinct revelation of the relations within the Godhead, may itself hint at his involvement in the use of the plural pronouns 'we' and 'our' in 1:26). What was enacted by God's Word in the Old Testament creation narrative is applied to the Son in the New. The apostle John, with regard to Jesus, the Word that was in the beginning with God, writes, 'All things came into being through him' (John 1:3). In concord with this, Paul informs us that 'by him [the Son] all things in heaven and on earth were created, things visible and invisible … all things were created by him and for him. He is before all things, and in him all things hold together' (Colossians 1:16–17). The writer to the Hebrews states the same essential truth when he speaks of the Son 'through whom he [God] made the world' (Hebrews 1:2), and further adds that it is the Son who 'sustains all things' (v. 3). So he not only acted to bring creation into being, but continues to act in order to maintain its ongoing existence. Therefore, we see that Jesus, as the divine Word, has both a revelatory and a performatory role. He not only makes known the mind of God, but he is the agent who brought all of creation into being and who still keeps it so.

What this means, then, is that when we talk about the Bible as God's Word, we need to do so with the foregoing in mind. His Word is first and foremost a Person, and only secondarily something found on the written page. Jesus is pre-eminently and essentially that Word, while the written Word (*Verbum scriptum*), though of vital importance, must ultimately be viewed as something derivative, that has a subordinate subsistence within that greater Word and owes its existence to him. This is shown, in one respect at least, by the fact that the purpose of the written Word is to bear witness to the personal divine Word. The two Testaments that comprise that written Word do this in different ways—the Old looking forward to the Christ to come, and the New looking back to the Christ who has come. The testimony of the one is prospective and of the other retrospective. Yet both testify to the same Christ, the essential object of saving faith.

So it is, then, that in this whole subject that we have been discussing in this book, the starting point from which we need to approach the matter is not that of 'Jesus in the Old Testament', but rather that of 'the Old Testament in Jesus'. This latter more accurately reflects the actual relationship that adheres between Christ and the Bible. And from this basic perspective we can see that because the Old Testament is in him, as the lesser is in the greater, then we may expect to encounter him in it. The Old Testament, no less than the New, is essentially christological.

For this reason, many of the criticisms raised in certain academic quarters against reading Jesus into the Old Testament can be dismissed. Some speak of specifically Christ-centred interpretations of the Hebrew Scriptures, such as prophecy, prefiguration, and personation, as a 'reading into' the text (or *eisēgēsis*, rather than *exēgēsis*, a 'bringing in' rather than a 'bringing out'). While in some extreme cases such criticisms might be valid, the general idea, according to the historic Christian faith, is that Jesus is deliberately intended, by divine design, to be found in these sacred writings. Indeed, it cannot be otherwise, for they owe their existence to him, have their significance only in him, and cannot be understood apart from him. Therefore, the contrary of what many critics maintain is true. It is the failure to see Christ in the Old Testament that is to misinterpret them. Such would be to miss utterly its main intent.

In the preceding chapter we spoke of the 'presence' of Christ in a particular sense, that is, with reference to his appearance as the Angel of the Lord on various occasions in the Old Testament. As we bring things to a conclusion, there is now one other important sense of his presence in Scripture that it is crucial for us to appreciate. In both Old Testament and New there exists the all-pervading, spiritual presence of the divine Son that can be encountered through a proper reading of those Scriptures. As *the* Word, each of us individually can meet him through the written Word. Such an encounter requires that we read with openness, with humility, and with much prayer. In order for this to be so, it also requires with respect to the older Scriptures that we should read them with a regard for the various kinds of interpretation that have been set down for us by Jesus and the apostles. A personal encounter with the divine Word on the part of the reader or hearer is essential for those Scriptures to serve their ultimate purpose. This is the ultimate goal of the Old Testament's witness to Jesus.

Scripture Index